The Bird That Ne

I dedicate this book to my family and to you
and yours whoever you may be.

THE BIRD THAT NEVER FLEW

THE UNCOMPROMISING AUTOBIOGRAPHY OF
ONE OF THE MOST PUNISHED PRISONERS IN THE
HISTORY OF THE BRITISH PENAL SYSTEM

JOHNNY STEELE

MAINSTREAM
PUBLISHING

EDINBURGH AND LONDON

First published in Great Britain in 1992 by
Sinclair-Stevenson Limited

This edition published in 2002 by
MAINSTREAM PUBLISHING (EDINBURGH) LTD
7 Albany Street
Edinburgh EH1 3UG

ISBN 1 84018 649 6

A catalogue record for this book is available from the British Library

Typeset in Ehrhardt

Printed in Great Britain by
Cox & Wyman Ltd

Part One

1

Johnny Boy

As a kid I learned a little rhyme which belongs to Glasgow's coat of arms. We would chant it while out playing and even in the classroom:

> The bird that never flew,
> The tree that never grew,
> The bell that never rang,
> The fish that never swam.

I was born on 27 March 1956 at my grandmother's home in Carntyne in Glasgow's East End. Glasgow, as far as Glaswegians are concerned, is the flower of Scotland. Our motto – 'Let Glasgow Flourish' – seems to say it all, but there are parts of Glasgow that will never flourish. When I was born Glasgow was full of slums, but there was wealth in every street – the neighbours flourished while Glasgow decayed.

In the street where I was born there was nothing but houses: tenement buildings three storeys high. We lived on the second floor: we had two bedrooms, a living-room, a kitchenette known as the 'scullery', and a bathroom. At the bottom of the street, about 20 yards from my close, stood the massive steel gates of the main entrance of the greyhound racing track. Our playground was the streets and the back courts and sometimes the racing track – which was forbidden and, as far as we kids were concerned, all the better as a result.

The streets and back courts were filthy with broken bottles, cans, burst drains and bits of old furniture. Each back court had a rubbish tip known as a midden, which we kids sometimes used as gang huts. All the neighbours in our close were regarded as uncles, aunts and cousins.

I reckon we kids were spoiled, and better off than most in the neighbourhood. I was happy when I was very young, and it seems as if everybody was happy then. More often than not we had a lot of people staying in our house, which was one of the most notorious houses in the city, since almost all my relations were thieves, mostly safe-blowers, and most of them had been to gaol.

My mother had long black hair, and I can remember everyone saying how pretty and young looking she was. She had five brothers: Uncle Alec was the oldest and he lived with my Aunt Chrissie and their children, Betty, Alec and Christine, in another part of the city. My Uncle Tam, who used to stay with us at Carntyne, had a reputation as a safe-blower and the tips of some of his fingers were missing. My mother's brother John lived next door with his family; he also had a reputation for blowing safes. Though all Ma's brothers were good looking, Uncle Billy was said to be the most handsome; small and wiry, he too was a safe-blower. He lived elsewhere in the city with his family, but would often come to visit. His son Peter and I would go wandering (or 'gallivanting', as Ma put it), trying to catch pigeons. Ma's youngest brother Arthur, or Atty, was a soldier and, unlike the others, he wasn't a thief. When he came home he would sleep in the same room as me and my older brother, Jim, and tell us stories. In all, my uncles were well known and very well liked.

My dad, Andy Steele, was a country boy, born in Blantyre, the birthplace of David Livingstone. I don't remember seeing much of Dad's mother, or even of his sisters and brother. They kept very much to themselves and worked hard. When my dad was in borstal he met and became pally with two of Ma's brothers. They decided they would get together when they were released and crack open safes, which they did. Then my dad fell in love with Ma and they got married. My dad had a considerable reputation as a safe-blower, robber and gangster. Jim and I – and often a couple of uncles as well – slept in the same bedroom, which faced the street. The other room was occupied by my mother, my younger sister Lana, and my grandmother. I can't remember my dad being there at this time – whenever I asked about him I was told he was in the army.

The only soldier I can remember was my Uncle Atty; he would come home in tartan uniform and everybody was proud of him.

Although she was blind, my grandmother, Elizabeth Padden, was one of the finest people I have ever known. She was very much a mother to everyone – so much so that she was universally known as 'Maw'. As a kid I used to ask 'Maw' why she couldn't see: she told me she had fallen out of a train when she was a little girl, but I found out in later life that she went blind after the birth of her first child. If you had met her you would have sworn that she could see. She would walk about the house, make dinner when Ma was out and do the washing, never letting her handicap get the better of her.

Maw and her family had moved to Carntyne from the Gorbals, on the South Side of Glasgow. My grandad, an Irishman named Harry, died when he was quite young. The Gorbals was full of slums and condemned buildings. Rats would come into their house during the night and frighten Maw and my Ma, till her sons got up and killed them. Maw told me stories about the Gorbals; how all the neighbours knew each other and were always ready to help each other whenever anyone was in need – and they were all in need of something. When people cannot get what they need, many of them turned to crime, and that's what my uncles did. They started off very young, going through approved schools, remand homes, borstal and, finally, prison.

In Carntyne I was too young to know all this. I would play in the back court with Jim and our pals, climbing the dykes or playing hide and seek. We did everything and anything to amuse ourselves. We used to bang on doors and then run away, with our neighbours shouting and threatening to tell our parents – or else they'd laugh and tell us to 'chap' on so-and-so's door and annoy them.

My particular pal at that time was Danny McGlachlan, who lived a couple of closes down from us. We'd go hunting for rabbits in the dog tracks, or collect the empty beer bottles that were lying around. We'd take them to the pub, saying our fathers had sent us with them, and make twopence a bottle. Danny was like me in many ways: we were the same size and build – both of us were skinny, with light fair hair. Everybody called him Dannyboy and I was called Johnnyboy. We would go and rake the middens with all the other guys in our area. We went to what we called the toffs' houses. It was rumoured that they even threw out money as well as toys of every sort. Whenever they saw us marching along their street singing and shouting they used to shout to us not to go near their middens or they would set their dogs on us, but that didn't deter us. It was like a gold rush, with all of us leaping over fences and through closes and into these 'lucky middens', as they were known. I guess many kids in Glasgow had done this. Dannyboy and I would share whatever we got.

We invented a new game called 'daredevils'. We would climb up drainpipes and onto the roofs, or else we would climb up high bridges, far above the road, and crawl along the steel beams. Passers-by would stare at us in disbelief. If you fell off and didn't kill yourself by the fall, the chances were you'd get run over by a vehicle, so all the traffic would stop and the drivers come out, some cursing us and others telling us not to move till the fire brigade came. We'd be off and away before they knew what was happening.

Jim and I and often an uncle or two all slept in the same bed, and occasionally one of us wet the bed and soaked everybody else to the skin. As the youngest I got the blame, and my Ma would laugh and say: 'I know my poor wee Johnnyboy gets the blame for everything.' When it was just me and Jim in the bed he used to wake up during the night, feel that his shirt was soaking and run in and tell my Ma that I had wet the bed and that he was soaking wet. Then I would get up and tell my Ma that it was him who wet the bed. The two of us would stand at the foot of my Ma's bed arguing who it was, and she would say: 'Keep quiet or the neighbours will hear you.' Then she'd get up and change our sheets, saying: 'It's just as well there's a rubber covering over the mattress.' Lana thought it was all very funny and would start giggling at the sight of me and Jim standing there arguing over who it was that had wet the bed.

In the summer our neighbours would carry chairs and sofas down into the little patches on the street that were meant to be their gardens, though there were never any fences round them and nothing ever grew in them.

The neighbours sat in these patches for hours talking to each other, and they would often comment on how I was my dad's living image, or that I was just like my mother. Sometimes they got out a half bottle and passed it round and when it took effect they would start to sing. Other neighbours would be looking out of their windows, and they too would manage to get a song in. They would ask us kids to sing for them and give us whatever small change they had, and we'd all scramble to the sweet shop.

Poor guys would come round the back courts singing; some of them were crippled and one was blind. They would stand beneath the windows carrying an old hat, and the idea was to throw the money into it. Some people used to throw down a red-hot penny, and the poor guy would scream as he picked it up. When the blind man came round, my Maw would produce a pound and something in a little bottle; I don't know whether it was whisky or cough mixture.

As kids we were warned never to go near strangers, as they could murder us or beat us up. Ma, Maw and my uncles told me I would love it at Elbow Lane Primary School at Parkhead, but that first day, sitting in a class full of strangers, was really frightening, even though Ma was there with me to start with. As soon as she left I panicked and ran after her, crying to be taken home.

Ma took me and Jim to chapel each Sunday, after making sure we were spick and span, and she always gave us money to put in the poor plate. I was taught my prayers at home and at school. I learned about God and how He came to be, and how He made the whole Creation, and how Jesus died on the Cross. Like school, chapel and prayers were a frightening experience, sinister and intimidating. The silent chapel had an eerie atmosphere and the priest, with his long robes and booming voice, seemed a menacing figure, telling us that hell was for bad people and that to get to heaven we had to be good. The only thing I liked about chapel was singing hymns, when everyone seemed happier.

It was great when our aunts came to stay with us, especially my Auntie Ruby. She was my Ma's cousin – Maw's sister's daughter − and she was very attractive, with blonde hair. I loved it when she brought her son Brian with her. Brian, whom we called Broono, was my favourite cousin.

As soon as Aunt Ruby saw me her purse was out and she would give me some money. She would bounce me on her knee and stroke my hair, asking me if I would like to come and stay with her, knowing fine that I would be so excited that I could hardly get the words out.

I can remember Auntie Ruby asking my Ma, 'When does Andy get out?' and I knew she was talking about my dad. On the night he came home we had a full house and there was a party. Everyone was drinking except my Ma, who never drank. Jim and Lana and I got out of bed and went into the living-room where everybody was singing and dancing. My dad had us all on his knees, cuddling and kissing us and emptying his silver onto our laps. He told us how he had missed us and that we were certainly growing up. Everyone told him that I was his living image, and this is my earliest recollection of my dad.

His commandments were:

> Never talk to strangers.
> Never wander away from home.
> Always be in on time for supper.
> Never be out late when it's dark.
> Never climb buildings.
> Never throw stones at windows or vehicles.
> Never get into cars with strange men.
> If anybody hits you, hit them back; if they're too big to fight with, hit them with the first heavy object available, and aim for the head.
> Never talk to the police, and should they stop you for anything, tell him immediately.
> Never steal or take anything that doesn't belong to you and, most important, always *be good*.

He told me all this much more often than he told Jim. He was asking us to change our ways, and to us it seemed wrong because it restricted our fun. But most fathers were very strict with their sons.

If he saw me climbing he would go crazy and say that I was ruining my shoes, and that would be me in for a couple of days: if my pals came to the house asking if I could come out to play, he would slam the door in their faces. I felt quite confused. He gave Lana and Jim everything; it seemed that I would get nothing until I learned to obey.

Ma would tell me to try to avoid him and not go climbing when he was about, as it would only mean him putting me to bed again. But he always found some excuse to put me to bed.

He came into my bedroom and said, 'You'd better behave yourself, boy, because if you don't you'll rot in that bed of yours.' I couldn't understand it because I hadn't done anything. He said, 'Are you listening to what I'm saying to you?' I wouldn't look at him but I looked at the floor and said, 'Aye.' He shouted, 'Aye what?' I looked at the window, trying to think what to do or say, and again he shouted, 'You fucking look at me when I'm talking to you!' When I did look at him he grabbed me and pulled me about like a rag doll and said, 'Don't you ever fucking look at me like that!' My Maw told him he was sick. I was sent to bed again.

One evening he told me to go to the chip shop. He gave me ten minutes. I could never have got there and back in that time, so when I saw a corporation truck turning the corner I jumped on its back. It started gathering speed and we sped past the chippy. I banged on the side of the van, hoping they would hear me, but they didn't stop until we got into the city centre, miles away from home. I didn't know what to do or how I was going to explain to my dad why I was so late.

I got home to Carntyne eventually on foot and went to the chippy and got my order. I met one of the neighbours who told me my dad was out looking for me. When I knocked on the door my Ma answered, and she sighed when she saw me. She told me they thought something had happened to me, and asked me what had kept me. I told her that some big boys had chased me and tried to steal my money. When my dad came in he was about to go for me, but Ma told him what had happened. He went mad. He went into his room and put on his hat – and he had something in the waistband of his trousers. He wasn't angry any more – at least not at me. He asked me

13

if I could recognise them again, and I told him that I could. He told me to go downstairs and wait in the car for him. On the way out I heard my Ma say something like, 'Don't, Andy, you'll end up in gaol.'

Once in the car he said, 'If the police ask you any questions at any time, tell them nothing.' He kept saying this as we drove to the chippy. He saw a bunch of guys standing at the corner and slowed down, asking me if I could recognise them. I told him no. We drove around for a while, and I kept saying I couldn't see them. We went back home. My Ma and Maw were relieved to know that nothing had happened.

In school my teacher took to shouting at me to pay attention when she was speaking to me and when I wouldn't look at her she jabbed her pointing stick in my chest. She would prod me quite often with this stick of hers. My dad got to hear about it and he asked me if it was true. I told him it was. He took me to school and he walked into the class with me and his two Alsatian dogs. He told the teacher that if she ever put a hand on me again he would put her into hospital. The teacher must have taken him seriously because she never laid a hand on me after that – but she hated me, and showed it. When she spoke to the class she would never look at me. It was as if I wasn't there any more. I got so fed up that I started playing truant. We called this 'dogging' school. Me and my pals would go into the shops in the city centre and look at all the sweets on the shelves. We'd go in a group but pretend that we didn't know each other. One of us would walk straight up and say, 'How much are those sweets?' pointing a finger at a jar of sweets on the top shelf. When the owner looked behind him to see which sweets he was referring to, someone else would reach over the display counter and lift a bar of chocolate. By the time the owner looked round we'd all pretend to be looking at the prices of things. Once we got outside the shop we'd all laugh at how easy it was. This was a new experience. I knew to be caught would mean getting sent to a home but I didn't care.

My Ma became suspicious and asked if I was 'dogging' school. I didn't like to hurt her by telling her the truth, so I told her lies. She found out in the end but she didn't tell my dad, as she knew he would beat me. But one day, when I came home from school, I noticed something was wrong. Everyone was too quiet. My dad said, 'What did you get taught at school today?' Maw was sitting on one of the armchairs, her head hanging down; my Ma was raking the coal fire, as though she didn't want to see me getting hit. My dad was standing in front of me waiting for an answer: I noticed that his bottom teeth were showing. I kept looking from Ma to Maw, but he told me to never mind looking at them as they weren't going to answer his question. I told him I was being taught maths at school.

'You're a fucking liar!' he shouted. 'You weren't at school!'

He kept me in my bed for weeks, telling Jim and Lana not to go near my room as I was an animal and was on punishment. Even though he terrified them they managed to sneak in and give me sweets and biscuits. I looked out of my window and talked to Dannyboy and my pals.

I developed a squint in one eye – my Maw and aunts said it was caused by shock. I stopped eating and would only take nibbles here and there. My Ma and Maw, and even my aunts and uncles, tried to bribe me to eat. But I couldn't; all I wanted was to get away from my dad.

I believed in God, and it was an awful shock to me when I made my first communion to be told I would be given part of the body of Christ to eat. When the priest put the Holy Communion into my mouth I was terrified. It stuck to the roof of my mouth; I tried to budge it with my tongue, but it would not move. I panicked and spat it out into my hand and hid it under my seat. I never told my family about this.

Ma arranged for me to go and stay with Aunt Ruby for a week or two. She would have taken me home to stay with her for good, but even she was terrified of my dad. He was all against me going to stay with her for even a day, saying that I had a house of my own. My Ma said that a wee holiday would do me the world of good. In the end he agreed, and everybody was happy. Ma washed and pressed my clothes and gave me a couple of pounds for my pocket money.

When we arrived by taxi the close was in darkness and Auntie Ruby was scared in case there were rats. So I went in first with a big stick and banged the walls so that they would scatter and run into their holes. When we reached her door we heard screaming. She quickly put the key in the door and as we entered I saw that Broono was standing in the sink and my Uncle Hugh was pouring bottles of cold water over him. Uncle Hugh didn't even look round to see who had come in. He was threatening Broono, saying, 'Don't you ever go on a roof again.' Each time he poured the cold water over Broono's head, Broono would raise his shoulders and shiver, as though he were having a fit. My aunt looked at me and shook her head in a sad sort of way. Broono was almost blue with the cold when she lifted him out of the sink and dried him, arguing with Uncle Hugh.

'I've brought Johnnyboy to stay with us for a couple of weeks,' she told Broono, and I could see his face light up. But before we could say anything his dad had told him to get to bed, and he went off without a word. I hardly looked at Uncle Hugh, but I told my aunt that I was tired and asked her if I could go to bed. She knew I couldn't wait till I was in beside Broono. She told me to wait till I was fed, but I told her I wasn't hungry. She gave me a wink and said I could go off and that she would feed Broono and me in our bed.

It was great for Broono and me to tell each other all the different tricks we were up to. We would sit up all night talking about how we would beat up our dads when we were grown up and send them to their beds, or run away together to London. Broono showed me his bruises and I showed him mine. What we were doing was natural – climbing and jumping in puddles. What else could we do? When I asked my Auntie Ruby if Broono could come out and play she told me to ask his dad. He said, 'You can go out, Johnnyboy, but that bastard stays in his bed.'

2

Flying Without Wings

I started running away from home when I was very young.
The first time I did this was about one o'clock in the
morning. I looked out of the window and saw that it was foggy.
I only knew it would be better out there than in here with my
dad, in that bed of mine.

Since my dad had come home, Maw and Lana were sleeping
in the living-room. I stood by the door looking at their faces lit
up by the moonlight. It hurt me to see Maw sleeping so
peacefully because I knew that when they discovered I was
gone that peaceful look would turn to worry. I was about to go
into the scullery and climb down the drainpipe when Maw
called my name in a sort of whisper. I tiptoed over to her.

'Tell me where you're going, son, and don't have me and
your Ma worried about you,' Maw said. 'I know you're running
away, son,' she said, 'but where do you intend to go? Out there
at night on your own would be too dangerous for a wee boy
like you. Your Ma will be worried sick and would die if
anything ever happened to you – and so would I. I know your
dad is giving you a hard time, son, but you'll only make things
worse by running.'

I told her that I was going to run away and pleaded with her
not to tell. She said she wouldn't. The poor old soul was crying
her eyes out and her whole body was trembling. She said, 'If
you're going to run away, go to your Auntie Annie's in
Bridgeton. You'll be safe there, son, and at least we'll know
where you are. But God knows, Johnnyboy, it will only be a
matter of time before he gets to you, and I dread to think of
the beatings he'll give you.'

Maw gave me a pound and asked me to wait till morning
before I left. I was off at the crack of dawn – down the drainpipe

outside the scullery window, across the back yard and through a close into the main road. It was dark and I had to walk carefully so as not to lose my footing. I had one hand on the wall for balance and was making my way towards the steps in the street when I felt something like a bundle of rags beneath my feet. As I put my weight on it I knew something was wrong and then someone grabbed my leg. I thought it must be my dad. I was so terrified I couldn't scream or run – I had lost all my strength. He started to pull himself up by the long woollen scarf that Maw had given me, dragging me down at the same time. I thought I was going to be murdered, until I got a glimpse of his face, covered in black hair, and old and horrible looking. I panicked and struggled – I didn't want to die at the hands of a tramp. The next thing I knew I was running back towards my close. In fact I was in such a panic that I ran straight past it. I didn't know if he was following me or not – I just kept running. I passed men and women going to work. One or two shouted at me as I sped past them: 'Hey, son, what's the matter?' I wouldn't even look round, never mind answer.

I was a few streets away before I stopped running. The houses were different from ours; they were big sandstone buildings, mostly condemned, and lots of the windows had corrugated iron on them. The streets were ill-lit and haunted looking. This part of Carntyne was 'original', and these houses had been built long before ours. Rats were scurrying about the street as if they owned them. Nearby was the cleansing department, where the rubbish from the middens went, and it was moving with rats, some as big as cats. The houses had outside toilets and at night people took candles as there were no lights in them. Some of my pals who lived there told me that they never used the outside toilets at night – they would pee in the sink, and if they needed to shit they did it in an old newspaper and threw it out of their window. Huge puddles caused by burst drains filled most back courts; they stank of urine and the smell was awful until you got used to it. I thought about Maw and Ma and the rest of the family lying in their beds nice and warm. I wanted to go back, but I couldn't.

At ten o'clock as I was passing the chippy I met one of my pals who told me that everyone was out looking for me. I asked him not to tell anyone he had seen me. The women who worked in the chippy knew me, so I gave my pal sixpence and he bought me a poke of chips. I ate half of them and put the rest up my jumper. I left my pal and made my way towards the dog track. There was enough room for someone my size to crawl in under the back gate.

Once beyond the gate I was inside the corrugated-iron corridor over a hundred yards long. It was pitch black and I stood there for about an hour without moving, listening and wondering if I should go somewhere else. I'd never really been scared of the dark, but I didn't know what darkness was till I found myself standing there.

I moved a couple of feet at a time, then stopped and listened, and when I didn't hear anything I moved a couple of feet again until I got myself to the empty car park, where hundreds of rabbits were running in every direction. It was much lighter out here with no roof over my head. At the far end of the car park were the massive steel gates and about 20 yards beyond the gates was our house. I was freezing cold, it was raining, and my teeth were chattering. I took the chips out of my jumper but they were cold and I threw them away. I pulled my jumper down over my knees and rocked to and fro on the grass, trying to keep myself warm.

There was a lot of shouting in the street just beyond the gates. I stopped rocking and stood up, trying to make out what was being said. 'Haw, Johnnyboy!' the neighbours and my family were shouting. 'Haw, Johnnyboy!' It sounded like an echo. Some added that it was all right for me to come out and that I wouldn't have a finger laid on me. I was biting my nails and staring at the gates, wondering what to do, when I heard a noise from behind me. I froze like a stone. I could hear footsteps. My senses told me to run, but fear kept me there. I couldn't turn round to see who it was. The only things I could move were my eyes, which were going from side to side, trying to look behind my head. Then I saw a man out of the corner of my eye. He walked on past me towards the big steel gates, never looking back. I was still standing there when the two big gates slid open and everyone came through with torches shouting, 'Haw, Johnnyboy!'

19

I made my way up the railway embankment and sat there. I saw some men carrying bags of coal on their backs and I hid until they went by. All was quiet; there was no more shouting. I wondered where they were. I wondered whether Broono would look after me and hide me in his gang hut, and wished he was there to keep me company. I thought every noise was a murderer on the prowl; every weird shadow I saw resembled something ugly, moving towards me; every drop of rain that ran down the back of my neck was like a bucket of water, and every time the cold wind blew against me it was as if it was trying to blow me back home.

There were tramps sleeping on newspapers, others sitting together talking. As I moved down the embankment towards the road I heard footsteps on the other side of the road. It was so misty I couldn't see, but I recognised the noise of high-heeled shoes, and I ran across the road in the direction I imagined the woman to be. The money in my pocket was jingling, making a lot of noise. When I reached the other side I stopped and listened, looking all about me. Then I heard her shouting. I started walking forwards, calling out that I was lost and scared, until I saw her. She was a young woman, staring at me and looking about to see if I was alone. When she asked me my name I said, 'Johnnyboy'. She came towards me and put her arms round me, shaking and clinging to me as if I was her guardian angel. She told me everyone was out searching for me, including the police. She came from Carntyne and wanted to take me home: I agreed, though for every little step I took forwards I wanted to take ten backwards. She asked me where I had been and as I told her she kept interrupting with 'Oh, my God!' and 'Holy Mother of God!' She said she would take me home and ask my dad not to hit me.

Outside our close was a Black Maria with two policemen in it, and they stared at us as we rounded the corner. I was terrified and tried to run. I thought they were going to take me away to jail as they got out of their car and came towards us. The woman was holding on to me with both hands so that I couldn't get away, and the police radioed to say that they had found me. One policeman took me upstairs while the other stayed with the woman. The policeman who took me upstairs told me I was going to get the hiding of my life from my dad, and that I deserved it.

The door opened and I saw my Uncle Billy standing there; behind him I could see only Maw, crying and asking if I was all right. Uncle Billy was glad to see me, and I was glad to see him. He beckoned me and the policeman in, and Maw held on to me and hugged me. When she realised my clothes were damp she told me to strip off there and then. Uncle Billy went out of the room and I could hear taps running; the thought of a nice warm bath made me feel better. Maw asked the policeman to go so that they could get me fed and bathed and into bed, but he said that he had to find out where I'd been. In the end he agreed to come back in the morning.

Maw had wrapped her long woollen cardigan round me and sat me near the fire to keep warm. 'God must have answered my prayers,' she said. She told me that I wouldn't be beaten, that they'd just be glad to know I was alive and well. Uncle Billy came back as I was telling her where I'd been and what I'd been doing, and shouted at me that I had almost worried my Ma to death and that I could think myself lucky that he wasn't taking the skin off my arse.

He looked at my hair and hands and feet and said I was filthy. Then he removed Maw's cardigan and picked me up like a rag doll – he had never even shouted at me before, never mind grabbed me violently. I was on the verge of crying and probably would have had he not thrown me into a cold bath. A strange noise came from my throat. Maw shouted at Billy to leave the wean alone, and he said he wasn't putting a hand on me. Maw was shouting at me but I couldn't answer – the noises were still coming from the back of my throat. My body jerked in the water as I tried to get out, but Billy held me in. Maw fell over something in the living-room as she tried to find out what Billy was doing to me. I could hear her calling for help and cursing Billy. Once I stopped twitching Billy let go of me and left the bathroom, telling me to get scrubbed from head to foot. I sat there just staring and feeling numb. I couldn't grasp what was happening, I only knew it was something terrible and that I couldn't get away.

The outside door opened and I heard my Ma's voice saying

something about giving me a good scrubbing with disinfectant. I could just make out her face and her long black hair hanging down. Her eyes looked strange, and her head was shaking from side to side. Her hand came into the water and she let out a scream as she dragged me from the bath. She wouldn't let me go when the others came in, and she carried on screaming the building down. Someone was shouting for a doctor, others were telling her to wrap me in blankets and keep my limbs moving, and my legs and arms were being rubbed hard by lots of hands.

Ma kept lifting up my head and looking at my eyes. I could hear her calling my name. I heard Ma say to someone that when Andy Steele got to know about this there would be murder.

There was fighting that night amongst Ma's brothers because of what Billy had done to me. As for my dad, I didn't see him that night, nor for a long time after it.

3

Growing Wild

My dad had gone back to the army. The house was full once more, with Uncle Billy sleeping in my bed with me and Jim, and sometimes Uncle Atty as well whenever he was home on leave. Uncle Billy and his wife had split up and his children had been put away in an orphans' home. His youngest son was adopted by my Uncle Tam.

I was happy at that time, not only when I was having fun, but when I was going to the shops and helping Ma to do the cleaning and the washing; even when I went to bed, since I knew that I would be out of it as soon as my eyes opened. Ma would come into my bedroom in the morning and lift me out, tickling me and making me laugh. She'd carry me into the living-room, where the coal fire was burning away. I'd stand in front of it while she put my clothes on, then she would turn me round to inspect me, and if there was a little bit of fluff on my trousers she would pick it off. She'd say, 'Who do you love the best in the world, son?' and I'd say, 'You, Ma!' Then Maw would say in a sad voice, 'Oh, what about me, son?' I would look at Ma and then at Maw, trying to figure out whom I loved the best. I'd say, 'I love the two of you the best in the world,' and Ma would hug me and Maw would kiss me too. Then Ma would hold me by the hands and Maw would have my feet and they would swing me from side to side, and I'd be laughing and shouting, 'Swing me higher, up to the ceiling!'

In Carntyne there were a lot of very poor people, and quite a few would be evicted for not paying rent or bills. Sheriff's officers, who worked for the authorities, would charge into where these people lived and take the furniture. If they thought they couldn't sell it they would throw it into the garden or the back court: sometimes they even broke it up in the house and

23

threw it out of the window. The family being evicted felt so humiliated that you'd see them in the street weeping and holding their children, staring up at their windows. It was horrible to watch. Most of the neighbours would be looking out of their windows or standing in the street, shouting at the sheriff's officers.

I remember visiting my dad when he was in the 'army', sometimes hundreds of miles away. Me, Lana, Ma and Jim were taken through a huge gate by men with hats on and uniforms. Ma told us that our dad would be glad to see us again and that he'd have sweets for us. We were led away by the men with hats and taken to a room. There were rows of windows with wire mesh on them, and people on either side talking to each other through the mesh. We followed Ma into a little box about the size of a telephone booth, and there was my dad on the other side of it looking at us. Ma had us stand on a little ledge and he tried to kiss us but couldn't because of the glass, and when he put his face to the window we would try to touch it. Dad asked us how we were keeping and if we missed him, and we all said yes. He and Ma whispered to each other and we'd sit there watching them.

For some reason me, Lana, Jim and Ma left our house and went to live in another house in Carntyne, a dozen or so streets away. I think there had been a fight between Ma's brothers. Maw and some of my uncles stayed behind in the old house and I went to visit them almost every day. My Uncle Bobby Campbell, who we went to live with, stayed in Rigby Street with Aunt Nelly and my cousins, who were all older than me and Jim. Uncle Bobby was kind to us, and he would let me and Jim stay out quite late. One day his son, Tommy, who was called 'T.C.', chased me with his friends through the streets and closes. They shouted at me to stop, but I kept running and jumping over walls and squeezing through railings. I could hear them all laughing and shouting at one another. I thought they were chasing me because I had slipped out of the house and had been out for ages, so I just kept running. T.C. finally caught me. He was a good few years older than me. I was struggling and kicking, trying to get away, but he held me tight and told me to calm down and not to be afraid as no one was going to hit me. He told me my Ma had a nice surprise for me, but I didn't believe him and said he was just saying it to get me to come in. When we reached their door, I could tell that something was going on. T.C. took me in and told my Ma that he had had to chase me all over Carntyne. Ma said it was just as well that he had caught me or I wouldn't get to see the big surprise she had for me. I was really excited. I didn't know what to expect. Ma pulled me over, and there beside her was a tiny baby. She told me it was my wee brother and that his name was Joseph. Everyone began to laugh at the expression on my face. Someone gave me money – I think it was half a crown – and told me to give it to the baby; a gift to a newborn baby is traditional throughout Scotland and is meant to bring it good fortune. Ma let me hold my baby brother for a couple of minutes. I asked her if I could go and tell all my pals. She let me out but made me promise to be in early as I was to have a bath before going to school.

I don't know how long I stayed with the Campbells, but eventually we moved back to our old house. When Christmas Eve came me and Jim were up most of the night talking and listening for Santa Claus coming down the chimney. Next morning our toys and games would be at the foot of the bed all wrapped up in colourful paper. We tore the parcels open, amazed at what we had: cowboy suits, guns, rifles, football strips, little motor cars, clothes and lots of sweets – everything you could dream of.

Jim and I dressed up as cowboys and Lana put on her nurse's uniform and bandaged us up when we pretended to be wounded. The neighbours came in to celebrate, drinking and singing. Maw got drunk very easily and she'd always, 'Where's my wee Johnnyboy?' I'd touch her hand and be lifted onto her knee and she'd start singing and telling me how happy it made her to know that I was happy. I'd be passed from knee to knee and everyone would say how I looked much healthier and less nervous.

My dad came back home from the army and, like the first time, he gave us kids everything. His friends came to the house and he carried me among them saying, 'This is Johnnyboy – he's my favourite.' He gave me money and said he'd take us to the pictures or the zoo.

But before long I noticed the atmosphere creeping back. My dad and his friends would gather in one of the rooms to talk. My uncles would stay away, or not come as often as before. When I asked my dad if I could go out to play, he snapped, 'Yes, but don't you be wandering or climbing, do you hear?'

I could feel the fear coming back. I wanted to get away from him. Sitting in my room I could hear Ma crying and saying that she couldn't take any more of his picking on me for the least little thing. Everything I did seemed wrong to my dad, and yet everybody else was doing the same things.

My teacher kept coming to my desk and moving my pencil from my left to my right hand. But it didn't feel right, and it always ended up in my left hand. She'd be back again, and once more the pencil was moved from my left hand to my right. I was the only one in the class who wrote with his left hand, she said. I knew she didn't like me, and often found some excuse to nag or hit me, but now it was because I was writing with a hand I wasn't supposed to write with. She took to calling from her desk when she got fed up with coming up to me: 'Get that pencil in your other hand, Steele.'

I began to hate school and being the odd man out in class. Writing with what to me was my 'right' hand was looked upon as a handicap. Whenever Ma and Maw asked me how I was getting on at school I was afraid to tell them I was left-handed; I merely said I didn't like it, and would ask them to keep me off and let me do all the housework for them. But no way would they keep me off – they told me I needed to go to school for my learning. I noted that Jim and Lana and my Ma all wrote with their right hand. I just sat in class, not day-dreaming, as the teacher thought, but worrying. It was a bad experience for me and my only way of showing it was by dogging school, which got me into even more trouble. My school reports were terrible, as my writing and dogging school didn't help my learning. As a result I was way behind the rest of the class.

One day Uncle Atty came home, but without his uniform on. He was at home with Maw and me when there was knocking on the door. It was dark, so when I answered the door I took Major the dog with me. Three men were standing there in white hospital coats. They asked me who was in the house and I told them. They pushed past me and looked in each room till they found Maw and Atty in the living-room. Major was barking and growling at the three strangers. Atty stood up and the three men jumped on him, kicking and punching and dragging him out of the door. Maw kept moving her head about, listening to the thudding sounds coming from Atty's body; she threw ornaments in what she thought was the direction of the fight, calling them bastards and animals for kicking her son. In her panic she walked about with her arms outstretched, knocking down lamps and ornaments, feeling for Atty and the strangers, but she was nowhere near them. I could see the fear in her face when she bumped into walls and stood there helplessly, calling the three strangers every name imaginable. They eventually got Uncle Atty out of the house, and I picked up the lamps and ornaments and put them back.

It was only later that I realised that Uncle Atty was in a mental hospital. I have been told that while he was in the army a gun backfired on him, which was why he needed psychiatric care. He was sometimes given shock treatment. His attitude to us never changed: when he came home from the hospital on weekend visits he would spend all his money on us kids and was forever buying us sponge cakes and bottles of ginger.

Ma had another baby – a little girl named Brenda, who was born on 9 March 1963. I gave her some money, placing it in her tiny hand and wishing her luck and a happy life. So there were now five of us – and still I was the only one who was getting into trouble. My dad was over the moon when Brenda was born.

Soon I was stealing, pickpocketing and breaking into shops with some of my pals. I was nine years old when I made my first court appearance. I'd already been in front of a children's panel, where social workers decided what was to be done with children in trouble. They sat round a large table and from time to time they'd look at me; some of them would smile, while others looked over the top of their glasses in a way that scared me. I was so frightened that I found it hard to answer their questions and looked at the ground while Ma nudged me under the table with her foot.

This time I was charged with theft. Ma inspected me before we went into court. She took off her head-scarf and spat on it and rubbed my face and combed my hair until she was sure I was spick and span. She told me not to worry too much, as she would ask the judge to give me a warning and tell him I was a good boy, if I promised that I would behave myself and that I'd never do it again. I kept praying that I wouldn't be sent to a home.

Courts can terrify kids – they certainly did me. They have a strange atmosphere and everything is quiet: it was great to hear someone coughing or rustling a piece of paper. I kept feeling I was going to faint. Men in black gowns were sitting round a table, reading. Occasionally they'd whisper and look over to me and I'd quickly look away. Every so often a door opened and someone walked into the court and whispered something to someone. When the judge came in we were told to stand, and when he was seated we were allowed to sit.

I was given two years' probation. When we left the court I was so excited that I skipped all the way home. Maw told me God must have answered her prayers, but everyone said that the next time I got into trouble I'd be put away. Uncle John told me that he had been put in a home when he was a little boy, and that the monks who worked there beat him up for the least little thing. What he told me was enough to make me never want to get into trouble again.

Ma got a letter from the Education Board saying that I was to be transferred to a special school that catered for backward children and cripples. To me this made no difference as it was still school, but it made a difference to my dad. He told me I was an embarrassment to him and that the dog was more welcome in his house than I was. I started to cry, but was told to 'button it'. He pulled my clothes off, threw me onto the bed and closed the curtains, shutting out the daylight and leaving me alone in the dark. I could hear him playing with Lana, calling her his little darling. There were times I lay in my bed after my dad had given me a beating and I would think of him and me being happy some day and playing football together and him loving me and me loving him – I would picture this and I'd get a strange feeling that would have me crying with joy.

4

Gar-T

When I was nine we moved house to a place called Garthamlock, on the outskirts of Glasgow – a housing estate completed in the early 1960s. The buildings were three storeys high and each house had a veranda. We had three bedrooms, a bathroom, a scullery, a living-room and a very long hall. The first thing I noticed was the number of our close, which was 999. Ma said she thought it would bring us bad luck.

I found new pals there almost immediately, and we went bird-hunting and looking for foxes. Garthamlock was great; it was something new, and I hardly gave a thought to Carntyne. There were a lot of fields nearby, and some farms. I'd never seen a farm before, except when I went to visit my dad in prison, and I'd watch the cattle and play in the haystacks. I even got a job helping the farmer.

The Brown family lived on the floor below. They had three sons and a daughter, Katrina, my first girlfriend. Next door was the Smith family. There were four girls, and one was as wild as a boy. Jean would play football with us and come climbing, and she could fight like a boy. Then there were the Fergusons, the Smalls and the Gallachers, and I liked them all.

The quarry near our house had cliffs as high as 70 feet, which we kids often went climbing over. Some of the older guys would leap off the cliff face into the murky water below, while us younger ones hooted with laughter. To us they seemed like heroes. One of them, John Henry, was about 14 years old, but he had a beard and looked twice his age. Everyone liked John – especially our mas, who could depend on him to find us young ones and bring us home for our dinner. He knew all our haunts and dens, and he'd search and give chase. He couldn't catch us all; we'd scatter in every direction, but John would have others hiding in the long grass and they'd pursue half a dozen fleeing youngsters. They'd tickle us till our sides almost burst with laughter and throw us up in the air as though we were balls.

I used to wear glasses. I hated them and would throw them away, but I always got a new pair. I was made to wear them in the house, but as soon as I went out I put them in my pocket. I had what the doctors called a 'lazy' eye. When I was nine I went to hospital to have it straightened. Miss Wright came to visit me in hospital and the other kids were amazed to learn that she was my probation officer; they'd never heard of such a thing. Ma liked her very much and she would tell me to be thankful that I had Miss Wright as my probation officer. She was forever buying me presents and asking me to behave myself and stick in at school.

In the summer I went camping with my pals. We used to sleep in the back court in a tent – the back courts there were safer and cleaner than those in Carntyne, and the gardens were all looked after – and the Stevensons took us camping once to Loch Ness and showed me how to use a fishing rod. I'd never been so happy in my life. Jackie and George Stevenson and I would roam everywhere and have great fun. We'd write each other notes to give to our girlfriends and build pigeon huts or rabbit pens – everything but steal.

One day I was playing with my girlfriend Katrina, and she bet I couldn't climb a huge thin tree in our neighbour's garden. I grabbed the opportunity to show her that I was as good a climber as any, so up I went, and Katrina followed up behind me. We were having a good laugh, but before long the owner of the tree appeared below as in a fit of rage. Terrified and crying, we both came down, snapping twigs in the process, which seemed to madden him even more. When my feet touched the ground he pounced on me, putting my arm up my back so that I screamed with pain, and marched me up the path. As we entered the close my Uncle Billy appeared, raging at the man for hurting me. Billy attacked him and they went crashing into the hallway. The neighbour needed stitches as a result of a wound that he received in the fight.

Each week I went to visit Uncle Atty in the Gartloch Mental Hospital nearby. I loved him very much and I begged Ma to let him live with us. I was too young to understand that hospital was the only place for Atty.

One summer day I set off with Broono to visit Uncle Atty. Atty took us for a walk through the woods and showed us where the birds' nests were. When we got back to the hospital grounds he told us to wait while he went to get us our bus fare home. As soon as he had disappeared, Broono, who was a scrap collector, climbed onto a building and threw down some copper tubing, which he said he'd sell to the scrap man. He hid the copper from Atty. Atty said he couldn't get us our bus fare, but that we could borrow his pal's bike, and we promised to bring it back in good condition.

We rode home together, with Broono on the bar, hugging his copper tubing with one arm and holding on fast with the other. Suddenly, a car came up behind us pumping its horn and almost ran us over. We knew it was trouble and Broono jumped clear and bolted across the fields, still clutching his copper tubing. The bike toppled and I fell with it, hurting myself. A man grabbed me and pulled me into the car.

'You stole my bike!' he shouted at me, poking at me with his finger, and he drove me back to the hospital.

There he put me in a locked ward with some mental patients to wait for the police. Some of the patients began to touch me on the arms and face as if to make sure I was real. I'd been in wards before but I'd never experienced anything like this. The patients were all shapes and some had crazy, staring eyes: they were dangerous to themselves, if not to others, which was why they were in the locked ward. One was laughing out the side of his mouth, which was distorted. No sooner had the nurse chased them away than they came back. The windows and doors were locked and barred – maybe they were going to keep me here forever?

Eventually the police arrived. They towered above me with their little black books out, taking my name and address and questioning me about the theft of a nurse's bike! A nurse told me if I didn't admit to the theft, and tell the police who the other boy was, I'd be kept in the hospital. When I told the truth they said, 'Try again, sonny.' So I told a lie and they never questioned it.

As we went up the close, they made me point out my cousin to them. Poor Broono turned chalk white when the two big policemen caught hold of him and took him up to our house. Broono was in a state of shock – he would get a terrible beating from his dad when he went home. I wanted to tell him that Uncle Atty must have stolen the bike and given it to us. When the police left, I told my Ma the truth, but we didn't tell the court as we wanted to protect Uncle Atty. In court Broono and I pleaded guilty to the theft of a bike we never stole. I was given a six-month deferred sentence. Uncle Atty was never told of the incident, and I was warned never to take anything from him again unless I was sure it was his.

I still had to go to a special school. I hated it and wanted to go to the same school as my pals. Every morning a grey van would pick me up. It was known throughout the city and it was embarrassing to be seen in it. The pupils at that school were like outcasts, and were treated as such. Looking out of the van windows, I felt like a prisoner. I couldn't help but skip school because of the hate I had for it. There were kids there with callipers and wheelchairs, and others who acted as if they were really crazy and could hardly speak. My pal James Morrison had been sent there because he was thought to be backward in his education. The kids in callipers and wheelchairs, and those with Down's syndrome, got a hard time from the other kids, and James and I would defend them and get into fights for them. I was given a truant card that had to be signed every day by the teacher to let my parents know I was at school. Often I got someone else to sign it, copying the teacher's signature.

One day Danny Brown and I ran away when we learned that the school board inspector had told our parents we hadn't been at school all week. We hitched lifts and skipped onto the back of lorries when they stopped at traffic lights, not knowing where they were going, and stole from fruit shops when we were hungry. We knew the police would be looking for us, so every time we saw a police car we ran in panic, leaping hedges if they were small enough and even hiding under parked cars. We ended up in a place called Bo'ness, 20-odd miles outside Glasgow.

People gave us strange looks – we were filthy after sleeping in a field in cardboard boxes. A police car pulled up and called me over. I turned and ran, almost knocking down an old man who hit me with his walking-stick in return. The police said we looked like two miners, and they seemed quite amused about it.

In the police station we told them why we had run away. They said they had run away from home when they were our age and that they regretted it. They didn't lock us up in a cell but let us sit about the bar, and one of them played cards with Danny. I couldn't play so one of the police showed me the cells. One was full of lost-and-found items, dozens of bikes all crammed in. That night Ma came to take us home, and it was lectures all the way.

One day Dad said to me, 'Right, you're going to the shops to buy a couple of newspapers.' I was about to open the door when his hand fell on my shoulder and he pressed my face to the glass of the window frame. 'It's fucking raining,' he shouted. 'Are you mad, wanting me to go out there without a fucking coat on?' Before I could answer, he picked me up by my jumper and threw me onto my bed. He said that if I wanted to get out of bed I would have to apologise to him.

I could hear Ma calling him an animal; Lana was frightened and crying. Jim was sitting with his lips glued together, and Maw was walking into walls in her panic and rage. She said, pointing at a wall and thinking my dad was in that direction, 'You're making Johnnyboy's life a misery; all you do is pick on him and send him to his bed.' To which he replied, 'You've no say here – I married your daughter, not your family.' He came quietly to my room and said, 'See what you've caused? You're not wanted here, I don't want you!'

I wouldn't say sorry so I lay in bed for over a week.

5

Crime, Punishment and Pals

One night, when I must have been 12, I was approached by John Henry and another of the older boys, John Stuart, who palled around with my brother Jim. They asked me to go in through a small window for them and open the front door of a house and let them in. I was frightened at first, because we weren't sure if someone was in the house, but they needed me because I was so small and skinny and they promised me money and cigarettes. They lifted me up to the window ledge and helped me through.

Once inside I was terrified. I could hear the two Johns hissing through the window for me to hurry: I'd nothing to fear, they said, for if anyone was in there, they'd kick the door in and beat them up. I opened the room door slowly and it creaked and groaned. The silence in the house was terrible and I was haunted by the fear of someone grabbing me. I wished I'd never come in here. They were knocking on the window for me to hurry and open the door. Once I was in the hall and couldn't hear them at the window it was even worse. A car tooted outside, and I fell over something.

'Hurry up, Johnnyboy!' I heard John Stuart saying through a window. I got up and moved towards the front door. My fingers trembled for the lock and at first failed to find it; then the two Johns came in and ransacked the house, while I stood by and watched.

As soon as they had finished they took me with them to a fence who bought almost anything from crooks. When the fence came to the door I was standing there almost covered by a huge imitation fur coat. He was a small man with a foreign name – it was rumoured he was a Jew whose whole family had been slaughtered by the German SS.

'I give you five shillings,' he said as he gave the coat a thorough going-over. I told him I was to accept no less than £100. He laughed and closed the door in my face, repeating, 'Five shillings.' I told the two Johns, who eventually went to the door themselves, arguing over a price and even threatening to beat the fence up for trying to cheat them. But five shillings it was. I was given a shilling, with which I bought two cigarettes.

One of the Garthamlock beat cops was nicknamed 'Nero' by the older boys in the area – he was forever chasing us kids and he would often arrest us for breaches of the peace or loitering. He came to the house and arrested me for the break-in. He said all the Steeles were thieves, and that I was a thief and would be locked away in due course.

Nero disliked me and harassed me for things I knew nothing about. He asked me to plead guilty to things I'd never done, saying it would go better for me in court if he could tell the judge that I had been co-operative. When I refused he'd slap and kick me. On this occasion he took me to his office – John Henry was already there – and said I'd best plead guilty as they knew everything, even about the old fence. I denied knowing what he was talking about, and Nero cuffed me around the ears and warned me not to lie.

John Stuart was eventually caught as well. An identification parade was set up and the fence was there to pick us out. We were charged with house-breaking, and I was remanded by the court for approved school, social and background reports. Ma was in court and waved to me before I was taken away to the dungeons below. Once in my cell I cried my eyes out.

Later that afternoon the remands were taken from the court to Larchgrove remand home for boys. They took us there in a big black bus known as the meat wagon. It was full of kids, the oldest of whom was fifteen and the youngest eight. I'd taken my first ride in the meat wagon when I was ten. I'd heard a lot about Larchgrove. Some of the older boys were talking about it and how they had been there plenty of times and weren't scared to go back. I was amazed at these kids and was dying to ask them about the place, but I was scared to talk with the two turnkeys sitting next to me. The meat wagon had three wooden benches in it, two up the side and one along the top, and we were all squashed in together. I fell off my seat when the meat wagon turned a corner and everybody laughed at me, even the two turnkeys.

There weren't any windows in the meat wagon, so we couldn't see where we were. Eventually we stopped and the turnkeys opened the door. I noticed that the meat wagon had reversed up against two other open doors, and that men in grey jackets were waiting for us to come out. They marched us into a square and made us strip off all our clothes and put on institutional clothing instead. I was given a pair of brown cord shorts that came down to my knees, a khaki shirt that was too big, a pair of grey socks and sandals. We were told not to talk. A kid standing next to me was crying and kept saying that he wanted to go home. I was about to start crying myself until I saw him being slapped about by one of the turnkeys, who shouted at him that he wasn't the hard case he thought he was. He said, 'I've got to laugh when I see you horrible lot coming in here for the first time and listen to you crying for your mas.'

One of the older guys who was standing next to me whispered to me that I ought to ask the turnkey for my 'coco' ticket. I didn't know what a coco ticket was, but I did what he said. The turnkey slapped me about the head and told me not to be smart, and everyone laughed.

We were marched away up a flight of stairs into a room with two long wooden tables and told to sit on wooden benches and wait for our tea. I could hear other boys coming up the stairs, and saw them pass our dining-room going to their own. They were all dressed like we were and they looked in as they passed to see if they knew any of the new arrivals. When tea was served I didn't eat anything but watched the other boys scoffing their food down. When they realised I didn't want mine they all fought over it. We were allowed to talk here, and we all asked each other what we were in for: it was usually shoplifting or stealing cars or house-breaking, pickpocketing or running away from home. We all whispered when it came to asking if anyone had any cigarettes.

After tea we were taken to our dormitories till six o'clock, when the turnkeys came back. Then we were taken into a gymnasium. Over a hundred boys were sitting about talking about everything and anything, boasting about how many times they'd been there or how much money they'd stolen. We were made to sit in rows and the turnkeys came round and started splattering white cream on our hair. It was nicknamed 'jungle juice', and we were told to rub it into our scalps. Then we were taken off for showers, and back to our dorms and bed. I couldn't believe it when a turnkey walked up to me and said, 'Put your bed down there beside the door.' Under his arm was a canvas affair about five feet long, with a metal frame and four very small legs. All the other beds looked like hospital beds and were made of steel. I thought the turnkey was joking, but he dropped the bed at my feet and walked away. We talked till lights out; a red light was left on all night so that the night-watchman could see us and keep a count.

When I thought everybody was asleep I put my head under the blankets and cried my eyes out. I asked myself why I was getting into trouble, but I didn't know why. When I stopped crying I lay in my bed thinking about Ma and Maw and the family, and all the good times we had – never once did I think of the bad times.

I heard the night-watchman come in and look about. As soon as he had left I got up and looked out to see where he had gone. I could see him walking down a long corridor waving his flashlight. He turned a corner and disappeared. I took a good look round the dorm and noticed that all the windows were made of cast iron and were so small that I couldn't get out of them even if I removed a pane of glass.

After breakfast we were marched back to the gymnasium. New arrivals were taken down a long, highly polished corridor and into the sick bay, where an Irish matron examined us, checking for lice and rashes and asking lots of questions. Other people then asked us our names, addresses, dates of birth, how many were in our families; after which we were taken to our classes.

All I wanted to do was escape and go home. Almost every week boys would try to escape. Some would, without warning, pick up their wooden desks, throw them through the window, and try to follow after them. I was in a classroom once when someone tried to throw his chair through the window and it bounced back, hitting the boy on the head. He got dragged away to the solitary cell. He was my brother Jim.

At recreation we were allowed five little stones to play with. We had to find them ourselves. We would put them in the palms of our hands and throw them up and try to catch them on the back of our hands, and then throw them back on to our palms. We played this game night and day, every day!

One evening I was sitting in the gymnasium talking to a boy about running away when a turnkey called my name and told me I had a visitor. I thought I was going to cry with sheer joy, I was so happy. I ran back and told the boy I'd been talking to that I had a visitor – it made me feel more important than saying that my family had come to see me. When boys' names were called for their visitors everyone would be silent: there was no laughing or talking – each one of us hoped his name would be called.

And there Ma was, all dressed up to see me. I saw her taking sweets from her bag and placing them next to her. As I walked into the visiting room one of the turnkeys shouted, 'Visitor for John Steele!'

Another new pal in my dorm was called Gak. He was very tall for his age, with red hair and freckles on his face, and anyone he didn't like he called a 'sneak'. He got blamed for things by the turnkeys because of his size – he'd often trip over his own feet, he was that clumsy, but in a funny sort of way. He had been here before, and at night, when I was lying in bed feeling sorry for myself, Gak would prance about the dorm and say, 'Don't let any of these sneaks get you down, boys. They don't worry me – nobody can ever worry you as long as you know he's nothing but a dirty sneak – and one thing the whole world hates is a sneak!' He'd go round all the beds asking us what we hated most in the world and we'd all say, 'A dirty sneak!'

'I'll bet anyone of yous a smoke that there's an old sneak sitting outside the dorm drinking whisky,' he'd say, his voice growing louder so that the night-watchman could hear. As soon as the night-watchman opened the door Gak would jump into bed and pretend to be asleep.

There was an old turnkey who was nicknamed the Flipping Tit. He went about with an elastic band with a bit of leather on one end of it: he'd hold the bit of leather, stretch the elastic back and hit boys on the back of the ears with it and say to them, 'You flippin' tit' or 'Bird brain'. That was all he did – walk about with this elastic band of his, hitting boys with it. Everyone said he was crazy. The first time I got hit with his elastic band was when I was having a shower one morning. He came up behind me and hit me across the bare backside, saying, 'Get a move on, you flippin' tit,' and something about my wetting the bed. It stung where he hit, and he turned the water off and told me to get dried even though I was still covered in soap. As we walked past him to our dorms, he said, 'Bird brains.'

One night I told my pals that I was going to run away. A small window pane in the shower room had been broken and was covered over with a bit of cardboard. I went under the shower and covered myself in soap, and while I was doing this my pal Homer threw my clothes out the window so that I wouldn't waste any time if I did manage to get out. As soon as one of the boys had managed to persuade the turnkey out of the shower room I ran out of the shower, naked and covered from head to foot in soap. I jumped up on the window ledge, which was a good bit above my head, pulled the cardboard off and gave it to Homer. I put my legs out first while the others supported my body with their hands so that I wouldn't fall down as I wriggled and twisted, moving myself out very slowly. I was in agony, but I kept on wriggling till I got my backside out and then my back – I didn't know I was out till I hit the ground and heard Homer and the others shouting, 'Run, Johnnyboy.' Someone put the bit of cardboard back as I was pulling my clothes on.

At the other end of the garden was a 16-foot fence with spikes on the top of it. I crept down below the dorm windows and headed for the fence, and I managed to climb over it without much difficulty. It wasn't till I was running across the road that I realised I had no shoes on.

My home was a mile or two away. I ran across the Edinburgh road, through the Olivetti factory and the Queenslie housing estate till I came to the canal, which was only a couple of feet deep and eight or ten feet wide. It was muddy and full of rats and bits of prams and old chairs.

It was pitch black and I couldn't see any makeshift bridges across the canal. My feet were bleeding, and I was scared to wade in the water in case I poisoned my blood with the filth. I tore my shirt in two and wrapped the bits around my feet, making a crude pair of shoes, then I limped all the way to the real bridge next to the quarry. I was freezing and I had to stop every so often to massage my feet. Once past the bridge I had a couple of hundred yards on waste ground before I could see my house. I lay in the grass for a while, waiting to see if the police would go to my house.

I could see Lana's bedroom light on and someone moving about. When she opened the window her face dropped as she saw it was me. We talked in whispers and I asked her if she would get me some clothes. She threw them down to me along with some money and asked me where I was going.

I went to Ferrans' house, a couple of streets away, and tapped on Marie and Christine's bedroom window. When I said I was on the run, they told me to climb in and to be quiet about it so that their ma and dad wouldn't hear me. It's not that they would have thrown me out, but they would have tried to persuade me to go back or brought my Ma round to get me, knowing that she would be worried about me.

Marie and Christine were the same age as me and, unknown to their parents, they sheltered me all through my teens when I was on the run from homes and gaol. They made me something to eat and sat there wide eyed as I told them about the remand home. Marie, who was the smartest of the three of us, said, 'I know they're cruel in there, but wouldn't it be better to give yourself up and get out as soon as possible and settle down?' She said that even though I was on the run I wasn't free either.

Christine said, 'Marie, stop trying to tell Johnnyboy to go back to that place. How would you like it if it were you?' The truth is that they were both right in what they were saying, but all I knew was that I was on the run again, and it didn't worry me. What did worry me was when I wasn't on the run. We talked for hours: I slept under one of their single beds, and we went on talking till we fell asleep.

Eventually I went home to Ma. They all stared at me as if they'd seen a ghost when I walked into the house. Ma was a nervous wreck not knowing where I was. She made me my supper and I told them about the turnkeys in Larchgrove hitting me for nothing. Ma was worried sick in case the police came and gaoled her for hiding me in the house. She begged me to go back and said she would make sure they didn't hit me again. She said I couldn't run away all my life; I'd have to face the music sometime. Mr and Mrs Brown, our neighbours who lived down the stairs, tried to convince me to go back for my own good.

When we got outside the remand home I made a bolt for it – the look of the place was enough to put the fear of death into me. I ran as fast as my legs could carry me, but Mr Brown's son grabbed my jacket and stopped me. I begged him to let me go. Ma pressed the bell; I heard her say that they weren't to hit me, and they told Ma they didn't do that there. I was taken up and down various corridors, and after I had changed my clothes, they opened a big heavy door with a huge key. The turnkeys shouted at me, pulling me about and calling me names, and threw me into a small cell with a bit of wood on the floor as a bed. That was all there was. The window was low, with tiny little frames of glass in it, and so thick that it was impossible to see through it. One of the panes of glass was missing. There was a lot of writing on the walls that must have been done by kids who had been here before me. The turnkey who had been lured into the dorm the night I ran away came up to me and held the huge cell key under my nose, digging it in and making me stand on my toes. He cursed me and said that nobody ran away from him and got away with it. He hit me with his knee between my legs, and when I bent down he hit me on the head with the key. I could no longer feel the pain between my legs, but my head was aching and I could hear a noise like a siren. I felt more blows on my body, but made no attempt to ward them off. I held my head, wondering what the noise was that seemed to come from inside it. I was terrified in case it didn't go away.

When the noise stopped, I realised I was on my own in the cell. I sat on the floor and felt the lump on my head, and I started crying. I heard someone knock on the door and ask if I was all right. Before I could answer, some comics and sweets were slid under the door. It was one of my pals.

Next morning I was taken down to the head turnkey's office. He was a bald-headed man, sitting behind a desk and holding a leather strap. He looked me up and down and said something about my being taught a lesson for running away from his home and causing him problems. He removed his jacket and told me to bend over. As he hit me with his belt I tried to put my hands on my backside to cushion the blows, and eventually he got a turnkey to hold me while he belted me. My body jerked with each blow of the belt. I was put back in the cell again and the turnkey slammed the door.

I couldn't sit down, so I lay on my belly. When I heard people talking in the corridors I felt a bit better, knowing that someone was near. To pass the time I looked at the names on the walls and on the back of the door and on the wooden bed. I kept some bread to feed the birds, and I stood and watched them for hours. I left most of my food and the turnkeys said that was why I was so skinny. They'd let me out for a wash and to go to the toilet, but a turnkey was always with me. I'd always take as long as I could; I'd wash my hands and face three or four times and sit in the toilet for ages, till the turnkey told me to get out. Occasionally there would be a good turnkey who wouldn't shout and closed the cell door quietly. I loved it when the door opened; it didn't matter who was there or why, just as long as it opened.

I was taken to the Glasgow Sheriff's Court. This was unusual, as I was a juvenile and should have appeared in the juvenile court. Rather than sentence me in public, the judge had me taken into a little room, into which only lawyers, the fiscal, the baillies and the turnkeys were allowed. This was because my co-accused were older than me. I was on social inquiry and background reports, which meant I could get anything from a warning to being sent to an approved school. My Ma was standing behind me, and I could feel her hand on my shoulder.

The old man in his fancy attire told me I would be sent to an approved school for one to three years.

I felt my legs shaking under me, then a turnkey's hand gripped my shoulder and pulled me away. He took me through the courtroom and down to the cells. These cells are very small, with a small, stinking urinal bowl attached to the wall. I told John Stuart and John Henry that I was to be sent away to an approved school. They passed me some cigarettes down the cells by swinging a jacket from cell to cell, till it finally reached me. On the cell doors there was a latch big enough for an arm to get through. John Henry was to be sent to borstal, John Stuart to a senior approved school. Most on my landing had been sentenced and were waiting to be moved out to various establishments. They joked about their misfortunes. There was a lot of shouting, and cell doors were opening and slamming every few minutes. Eventually my cell door opened: 'Steele?' 'That's me, sir,' I said and held out my hands for the handcuffs.

Larchgrove was as busy as ever. Some boys were cleaning the corridors, the smell of polish and brass was strong, and somewhere a turnkey was shouting orders in an exaggerated tone. In the head turnkey's office I was told that I was going away to another home where it was hoped that I'd be taught a lesson I'd never forget. On the desk in front of me – the same desk that I had been bent over to have my backside beaten – a warder was writing furiously, occasionally stopping to ask me questions. The little room was gleaming clean.

A turnkey entered, throwing me a glance that stung – it was the one who had beaten me up after my Ma took me back to Larchgrove when I ran away. He slammed something down on the desk and exchanged a few words with the head turnkey. On his way out he said, 'Good riddance, Steele.'

The silence was broken by two strange-looking monks entering the office. Both were tall and their long black cloaks gave them a creepy look. The head turnkey promptly got up from his desk and shook their hands. It was obvious they all had met before. After a few minutes they turned their attention to me, and the two monks looked me over thoroughly.

On my way out some boys said goodbye as they were

scrubbing floors and, as ever, a turnkey nearby shouted for silence and more work.

The two monks took a firm hold of me as we walked out of the main door and into a black motor car. They put me in the back seat on my own and warned me not to try to run away as the back doors only opened from the outside. Then they lit up cigarettes and chatted to each other.

I really felt uncomfortable sitting in the back seat of the car with the two De La Salle brothers dressed in their long black robes. As they chatted to each other I was busy thinking about escaping from this school the first chance that I got.

As we made our way towards Tranent, near Edinburgh, we passed fields and countryside I'd only seen in postcards, books and films. I could see haystacks in the distance like blocks of flats and the air smelled fresh and clean. This is what I'd longed for; wide open spaces, streams, forests and hills where I could roam without having to glance over my shoulder to see if I was being followed. I thought about my family and was saddened to be taken away from them and was fully sorry for what I had done. I guess anyone looking on would have reckoned I was some sort of typical Glasgow thug, but the truth was I was just a mammy's boy.

I could see St Joseph's in the distance, a large dark brown building with many rooms. A hundred or more kids were playing in the fields and yard as we drove up to an office.

Almost all the kids had gathered to see the newcomer. Someone was calling my name, then another and I realised it was some of my friends from Larchgrove.

I was taken away for a shower and made to scrub myself under the watchful eye of one of the brothers, then I was taken to one of the dorms and my bed was pointed out to me. It had a big metal frame with a waterproof covering and instead of pyjamas I was given a Wullie Winkie-type nightgown. All the wet-the-beds had to don this gown, known as the 'sark of shame'.

I was then marched through some corridors and taken to see my housemaster, a kind-looking man, tall with an extraordinarily large red nose. His nickname was Mr Strawb. He made me feel welcome and told me he would do all he could to help me have a pleasant stay and should I wish to talk about anything I was just to come into his office.

The school was made up of all kinds: thieves, gang members, pickpockets and orphans. Like everywhere else, there were always kids there ready to bully others if they could get away with it. Some of those in authority were aware of this and did nothing about it because to them it was a sort of entertainment.

On my first day there I was fighting with a guy who called Ma a name. This was a ploy by many bullies to see how far they could push you. I attacked the guy, but I was the one who was punished for it and made to stand in a small circle in the exercise yard for the remainder of the day whilst the brothers looked on as if daring me to step outside the 10-inch circle. As I stood there I was scanning the fields and a very large coal bing in front of me. I could see the small village of Prestonpans not too far away and knew I had to get there to get back home.

That night I lay in bed and the night-watchman, who was a De La Salle brother, came round the rooms checking the numbers and on the wet-the-beds. He was putting his hands under the blankets to feel if we had peed ourselves, but his hands were wandering, and so we would try to be on the alert for him on his rounds. There was no one to tell about this and we thought if we had raised the matter with anyone in authority we would come out the worst.

I spoke to my friends about the route away from St Joseph's and was given many directions. I was made to wear shorts that came to my knees because I was known as an 'escapee'. These shorts were like knickerbockers, and embarrassing.

There were kids in the school who were known as the 'hounds' and they were given the order to chase anybody escaping; these guys were trustees and had served a good part of their sentence.

No sooner there I was gone in a Glasgow direction, scurrying across fields, running this way and that; I heard whistles blowing and a voice call, 'Stop, Steele!'.

I glanced over my shoulder and could see the hounds in pursuit, all excited and calling out like wild tribesmen chasing a wilderbeast. I noticed they had caught another kid and were dragging him back. One of the hounds caught up with me in the bush. His name was Ginzo and I'd known him from Larchgrove. Instead of taking me back, he gave me directions and wished me luck.

My legs were stinging having being torn in the nettle bushes, but I ran for all I was worth. It was great being on the run again. I felt alive and happy in a strange sort of way and now it was my turn to act like a tribesman as I ran over hundreds of acres of land on the road to God knows where.

But like all runaways, I was caught and brought back to St Joseph's. Two policemen had caught me in a busy part of Edinburgh as I ran through the streets in and out of the crowds.

The punishment was severe. I was told to wear black pants and then beaten with a leather belt across the arse. I tried to run, to escape the brutality, but to no avail; others held me down whilst the brothers beat me. I was told to pray for my sins and wrongdoings and told it was all my own fault.

I showed my friends the welts on my legs and backside and they told me they had heard me scream at each stroke.

I didn't want to be here and so took to escaping at every opportunity.

Most times I would have to steal money to get my fare home as Glasgow was a good distance away. I broke into shops and schools and would pickpocket.

Soon the De La Salle brothers were warning me that I would be sent away to another school if I didn't behave myself and stop running away and causing problems for them. But it wasn't in me to stay in that place, it was easier to run than stay.

A new brother came to St Joseph's and because of the size of his feet he was quickly named Bootsy. One day I walked past his office and noticed his door was wide open and there on his table lay a tobacco tin and lighter. I went to get my pals and informed them about my find. While my mates Tony and Gak kept a lookout I went into his room and grabbed the tobacco tin.

But it wasn't to be that easy.

As I touched the tin I felt something strange and painful surging through my arm. I had no idea what was happening to me but it turned out I had been electrocuted. Bootsy had wired up his tobacco tin to the electrical current to set up would-be thieves.

I was badly shaken by this ordeal. I also wasn't the only one who fell into this trap. It didn't put me off nicking things, though. I, along with my pals, ran away one night in our Wullie Winkie nightgowns and made our way into Tranent where we stole clothes from washing lines in some of the gardens. To us this was fun and made us laugh as we went gallivanting into the night knowing fine that somewhere someone would be hunting us. We lay in a haystack in a field and marvelled at the stars above that seemed so big and bright and mysterious. It was a peaceful feeling, and something up there had my undivided attention.

I thought about my family, Ma and Maw especially. I knew they'd be worried when the police went to their door informing them that I had once again escaped.

We broke into a shop, then a gypsy caravan site, stealing all we could. The gypsy site sent shivers down our spines as we had heard all sorts of stories about these people and to be caught stealing from them would result in severe repercussions. But we were freezing that night as frost lay on the ground and the temperature dropped. One of my pals wanted to hand himself in to the nearest police station. In the end we all made our way back to St. Joseph's in the wee small hours.

It was eerie to be there in the darkness and under these circumstances. I broke into the cookhouse and stole food, which made us all feel better, and then we broke into the offices to steal some cash. Next we forced our way into the tailor's shop and clothed ourselves like tailor's dummies, then the school shoe shop. I knew when they discovered what we'd done they would show no mercy.

With our bellies full and sensibly dressed we made off across the fields in a much better spirit than when we had arrived. On the way home on the train we broke into the buffet for no reason other than we were thieves, and even though we had the money we skipped on the train never intending to pay a penny.

In Glasgow I took my friends home to Garthamlock where we met my old friends who were still into fighting with other gangs in various neighbourhoods. My friends Marie and her sisters looked after me and put me up under one of their beds for the night. They told me they were worried about me and wished that I would get home free soon.

Naturally, I was caught and taken back to St Joseph's where I was punished by the usual means. At a meeting, the brothers informed everyone that I was an embarrassment to the school and giving it a bad name by running away and breaking into places. I could hardly believe what I had heard. Me? Giving an approved school a bad name!

They said they were getting rid of me and the sooner the better but Mr Strawb spoke up for me and told them I deserved another chance.

When Ma came to visit me Mr Strawb told her he was concerned for me and wanted to know how he could help me settle in. Ma told him I used to be a pigeon fancier as a kid. I was stunned to see this old man leap to his feet and come over to me telling me he would build me a pigeon hut and buy me pigeons. He was all excited and happy for me.

Poor Ma asked me to try harder to behave myself whilst here because she thought everyone was as kind as Mr Strawb. My dad, though, and two of his friends came to speak to the brothers about the treatment I was given, telling them they didn't want me being brutalised. Ma was there and was worried that someone would get hurt and told my dad to calm down.

There was a bit of an atmosphere in the school that day and I knew that my dad had threatened revenge should I be beaten or humiliated again but the brothers accused me of being in the wrong. Before my dad left he gave me his friend's phone number in Edinburgh and told me to phone him should anyone beat me up again and they'd come for me and take me away from the school.

I had the pigeon hut built and, as promised by Mr Strawb, I was given a dozen pigeons. I felt happy and privileged to have this hobby at the school, but there were others in authority who reckoned I was being rewarded for my crimes and wanted the pigeons to be given to someone who deserved them.

I became a target for my enemies in authority, but as ever Mr Strawb came to my defence and defied anyone to punish me further. He was always so smartly turned out in his three-piece Harris tweed suits, shirt and tie and handkerchief to match. He was a gentleman with so much humanity for so many. I felt ashamed because he had so often asked me to come and talk to him before I ever escaped, and at every hand's turn I felt I had betrayed him.

The women who worked in the cookhouse were kindly folk, their food hot and tasty. In the dining hall there were five or six rows of tables and when it suited the brothers they would decide which 'row' would be first to be fed. And that was whoever was sitting in what they believed was the smartest position. Some of the kids would be sitting arms folded, shoulders back and eyes straight.

'This row!' a brother would roar, and in one swift movement 20 or more kids would rush to the hotplate for their food. Some would have a hop, skip and a jump walk, others would half run. It was like a game to the brothers, the words 'This row!' causing panic amongst the ranks. Others would be arguing with each other if they were last to be picked or refused extra food because of the antics of others.

It didn't matter to me as far as the food was concerned, I wasn't here for the food, all that really mattered was my family. I missed them so much. But to this day I still hear the words 'This row!' in my mind, closely followed by 'Stop Steele!'

I guess I ran away more times than the average kid and perhaps caused more trouble and embarrassment than most without realising. However, contrary to what those in authority thought, that was never my intention. To me my only crime was escaping from hardship and a system that was geared to torment me and keep me away from my loved ones. That is what hurt me, and yet I was in no position to express myself for I was just a kid (albeit a delinquent) trying to fit into an adult world. In many ways my actions should have expressed my feelings.

'Why is it always you, Steele?' a brother shouted at me.

I couldn't reply, for to answer back would result in further punishment and humiliation.

Finally, my escapes led to my pigeon hut being taken away by those who thought I didn't deserve it.

In the summertime we were all taken berry picking in Montrose, further up the east coast of Scotland. Six weeks we were to stay picking berries, living in a mission hut. This was great; the atmosphere was heavenly partly because we were surrounded by civilians. We went berry picking each day and some guys would urinate in the berry bucket to add weight to it and thus earn more money. Others would steal berries from some kids. This was called 'Niggering' and you would often hear the mournful wail, 'I've been Niggered!'. The brothers would take umbrage at this and would annihilate anyone caught stealing another boy's berries.

Of course, I was caught indulging in such practices. The brother who caught me went crazy. 'Thief!' he screamed as he held onto me like a prized possession. 'This man is a thief!'

After that it would be 'Stop Steele!' because I was off like a hare across the country.

One day at a school meeting the head brother said that certain individuals were causing great problems by running away and stealing and breaking into premises in the area. So in future, he said, should anyone want to run away they were just to come to him and ask for their train fare and he would gladly give it and by doing so would save us from stealing. And give us half an hour's start before phoning the police.

All the while he was talking his eyes were focused on me.

A few evenings later I went up to his office and nervously asked for my train fare home. From outside his office door I could hear my pals laughing at my audacity.

The head brother flew into a rage and beat me severely with a thick leather strap. So I ran anyway, train fare or no train fare.

After my 15th escape they decided to get rid of me. One day I was called to the hall where everyone was present and informed I was being transferred to another school because I was unruly, a troublemaker and an embarrassment.

I was also told that my dad had been sent away to gaol for safe-blowing. He and the other guy who had threatened the brothers at St Joseph's had both been given six years. My dad had sworn that the police – the serious crime squad – had planted explosives in a heating cupboard in our house and had manufactured evidence to help convict him.

My dad would often write to me and ask me to settle down, get a job and be good as crime didn't pay.

The same two brothers who took me from Larchgrove to St Joseph's took me to another approved school in Helensburgh, on the west coast of Scotland. 'You'll never learn, Steele!' is what they told me as we drove across the country to my new school.

I tried to remember the route back to Glasgow as we made our way to St Andrew's for I had no intentions of staying. My only thought was to get home somehow.

St Andrew's seemed somewhat different from St Joseph's. The guys there were older, the atmosphere seemed different somehow. This place seemed like a holiday camp in comparison to St Joseph's.

I was the youngest kid there at this senior approved school and already had a reputation for escaping and causing trouble. Here we were allowed to smoke and wear our own clothes. Ginzo was there. He had re-offended and was sent by the courts to St Andrews. He said he wasn't surprised to find me there having heard of all the trouble I had been in.

Most of the kids at St Andrew's worked, whilst others and I were sent to school. I hated school, but work somehow appealed to me because I felt it would make me seem more grown up.

But it was still in me to run away and within a few days of my arrival I was up the hills above Helensburgh heading for God knows where. Later I found out that we were up in the Arrochar hills; for days I wandered unaware that both the police and Military Police were searching for me and the guy I ran off with.

I stole a policeman's car and crashed it. This drove us further and further into the hills. It was bitterly cold but we kept searching for a way home. Finally, it got so cold that I stopped a police patrol jeep and asked to be taken back to St Andrew's. The copper told me there were many people looking for me and my pal and that there was great concern for our health and safety.

Despite that concern for my health and safety, I was once again beaten by the housemaster. All the time he told me how worried they'd been, that they'd thought me dead or murdered in the hills. All the kids at the school heard about me stealing the policeman's car and thought it funny, but the authorities did not.

Where my life was taking me I had no idea and sometimes I couldn't care. So long as I was running I was happy.

Sometimes I questioned myself as to who I was and how I came to be and how I'd end up. Punishment seemed to be part of my life. It seemed the more I complained, the worse it got. But I could not accept being locked up. I even ran away from this school to help my pals escape from another.

Soon I was causing as much embarrassment to the authorities at St Andrew's as I had at St Joseph's. I got the impression that I wasn't wanted and was told that I would be sent elsewhere if I didn't respond. But still I ran. I didn't care about the punishment. All that really mattered was my own freedom.

Life there was so much different from St Joseph's but despite all the goodness I still couldn't settle in, and me being the age I was I still had to attend school, only occasionally being allowed to work with the older boys in the work sheds.

I ran away again and unknown to me Ma was coming up the path to visit me as I ran along the railway line heading for home. When poor Ma reached the school no one could find me.

I had run away with another kid from Garthamlock who had been sent away for not going to school as often as he should have and when we got home we went on a stealing spree. Eventually, we were caught breaking into an off-licence. We were charged and I was sent to a place called Longriggend to await my trial.

I'd heard much about this place, and even though it was a remand gaol for unconvicted young offenders the warders there were often cruel and ran the place like a military camp.

When I saw the huge steel fence with roll upon roll of wire I had a bad feeling about it. As soon as we were taken to a reception area the brutality started. They seemed to thrive on tormenting kids who'd never been there before.

I was taken to see a doctor for an examination. I was put on a chair whilst a warder shaved my hair off. I was shattered at this and felt ashamed and humiliated. I was given an army-type uniform to wear but being 15 and skinny it was far too big for me.

I heard some of the warders talk about my dad and one of them asked me what relation I was to him. This would not be the last time my dad's reputation would precede me.

We were taken to our cells and I was made to hang my clothes outside my cell door as a security precaution. One of the warders told me I wasn't to look out the window, or talk to anyone, or to smoke.

'And don't press that bell unless you're fucking dying,' he growled.

When the door slammed behind me I was almost crying. I looked around the room. There was a small chamber pot in the corner, a hard wooden chair, a bed and a rule book. I found it hard to believe that I would have to piss and shit into the pot, for there were no toilets in the cells.

Beyond the locked door, I could hear warders shouting and cursing and giving out orders. I went to the cell window to look through the bars and could see kids being put through their exercise training. Someone spotted me and I was told to get away from my window and made to sit on the chair during the day. But it was hard not to look out. It was easier to look out than in.

The warders had this thing about Glaswegians. They said we all thought we were tough cases running around with knives and open razors and slashing people.

We weren't allowed any photos of our families or radios, but we were allowed to smoke. In the evening we were allowed to watch TV but the warders decided what programmes. No one was allowed to talk at the recreation period or at TV. Some would whisper and then it would be, 'Shut the fuck up, cunt!'

'Face the front, cunt!'

'Are you stupid, cunt!'

In the dining hall the warders would steal our food. One in particular would hide pies under his hat thus amusing his colleagues. Another would come round our cells stealing sweets.

We were forced to go to church and chapel each Sunday but beatings were a regular occurrence. Some boys couldn't take the regime and committed suicide. Some of them were pals of mine.

Us school boys, as we were known, were kept together in one of the halls and when we got a chance to communicate the main subject was crime: who done what and how. It was a breeding ground for young offenders and also bred hatred for the authorities. Often kids would talk about 'revenge' on the warders when they were released.

I refused to use the chamber pot as I had learned to do what most kids did and that was to shit in a newspaper and throw it out the window, but to be caught would mean a beating from the warders.

Ma and my girlfriend, Jeanette, came to see me. I felt ashamed sitting there with my head shaved into the skin and I just wanted to get up and run back to my cell. Two weeks I had been there and every now and then I thought about trying to escape and even suicide. It was horrible being there.

I swore I would never return.

On Christmas Eve a warder came for me and told me that I was to be escorted back to St Andrew's. I had made a few friends in Longriggend and we promised to meet up when released and go stealing. I felt sorry for them to be left here whilst I was going back.

Once back at St Andrew's, the headmaster sent for me and asked me to try and get my life straightened out before things got any worse. He wondered if I would like to join the Merchant Navy and see the world. The idea appealed to me and I listened to what he had to say. He said I was to leave it in his capable hands.

I managed to get a home leave and went back to the scheme. Nothing much had changed. Street gangs were everywhere and fighting was an almost everyday thing, with running battles in the fields around Garthamlock. The police seldom intervened except to pick up the pieces and a few stragglers.

An elite group of coppers nicknamed 'The Untouchables' would roam the streets in a Commer van and snatch kids off the streets, charging them with loitering or being a known thief. They would just attack us for no reason. The authorities were taking a heavy approach in trying to put an end to the gangs in and around Glasgow. There was a curfew and those known to the police had to be in their houses by nine o'clock in the evening. My older brother Jim was also on the run by now and was earning himself a reputation amongst the gangs.

At one point, the cop we called Nero gave chase to Jim whilst on the run. The copper came to an emergency halt when Jim turned on him and chased him with a meat cleaver.

My wee brother Joe had started to get into trouble too and my sister Lana was also sent away to a convent for being unruly and hardly going to school.

With my dad in gaol and all of us in trouble, Ma was surely demented. Some of our neighbours told us that Ma was ready for a nervous breakdown and didn't know how she put up with us. But there was worse to come.

On my return to St Andrew's I was called to the headmaster's office and was devastated to learn that I was to go back to the special school when I was finally released. By law I had to attend it till I was 16 years of age, and so therefore my dream of joining the Merchant Navy had come to an end.

I responded as I'd always done. Again I was off. Again I was caught and sent to Longriggend. Again I was beaten by the warders.

Then, one fine morning I was released from St Andrew's. I was fifteen and a half. The whole school had gathered in the assembly hall and when my name was called I stood up to be informed that I was a free man.

The headmaster wished me luck and as I was walking down the aisle everyone started applauding and whistling. It was a great feeling but there was a sadness within me to know that I would be leaving some pals behind.

Some years later there was a big inquiry into the conditions and treatment of kids in Larchgrove Remand Centre, and a few of the turnkeys were exposed for ill-treating the kids. They were sacked from their jobs. No one was charged because not enough witnesses came forward, but I know the brutality went on, as do countless others. In the mid-'70s Nero himself was charged and convicted, along with other police, for organised crime and house-breaking. He was sentenced to six years. All the Garthamlock kids were cheering when they heard this news.

6

Borstal Boy

It was no surprise to many that I ended up inside again, and this time I was sent to borstal. This was in March 1972, and I was 16 years old. The charge was house-breaking.

When the van stopped outside the hall at Polmont, my heart was beating fast. The warders were there to greet us. They weren't wearing uniforms, just plain trousers and jackets, but they still had those long chains hanging from their pockets on which they carried their keys. I think they had keys on their chains that were of no use to them, simply in order to rattle them.

'Quick march! Move!' – and they started shoving and pushing us into the reception area. This was to frighten us – and it worked. They punched and kicked and mocked us, and those who had long hair were called poofs and girls. It all happened so fast: 'Stand up straight! Get over here! What are you in for? Do you think you're a hard man? Get those shoulders back! Arms straight! Quick march! Left, right, left, right!' We didn't know what was going on – one warder told us to do one thing and another ordered us to do the opposite. One of the kids had long frizzy sideburns, and he was pulled by them along the floor, screaming in agony.

We were taken to the Allocation Centre, where everyone spends a few months when they first enter borstal. As soon as we entered I could see guys in immaculate gaol uniforms marching here and there in military fashion, the warders screaming, 'Left, right! Left, right!' We were pounced upon immediately by warders, who yelled at us to march. We didn't have a clue – at least I didn't – and I was slapped about the head for being out of step. When I turned to see who was hitting me I was slapped and punched from behind by another warder who shouted at me to face the front and keep my shoulders back. All the humiliation and brutality were deliberate.

On the galleries above us I could see prisoners marching back and forth, and some marching down stairs with their arms pressed to their sides. The place was spotless – it even smelled clean. In the mornings all were up sharp, with each bed made up into a bed block: the warders carried small sticks during inspection, and the bed block had to be the exact length of the stick or else . . . The cell floor must be highly polished, with not a speck of dust to be seen; anyone whose cell was not up to standard would be deprived of recreation. Inspections were carried out every day, and at night we were forced to stand in our pyjamas at the foot of our iron beds to await another inspection.

We were allowed no more than two minutes in the toilet, after which the warders would start shouting into the small cubicles with their half doors, 'Nip it and get out of there now!' I've seen kids being dragged off the toilet seat. Sometimes we weren't given a chance to clean ourselves – our pants would end up dirty, and we could only change them once a week. The warders found that funny. I was standing next to a guy on parade and he whispered that he was badly in need of the toilet. The warder caught him whispering and started shouting: then he punched the guy on the belly, knocking the wind from him and causing him to mess his pants.

We had to jump to attention whenever the governor came in and shout out our names and numbers. Then he walked about checking for dust. Many times I was deprived of recreation because my cell wasn't up to standard, and instead I was given a bucket and brush and made to scrub out the toilets. Some of those who carried out inspection were none too clean looking themselves, but what could one say.

The bottom floor was reserved for epileptics and other medical cases, and some of the suicide risks. I was on parade one day when a guy had a fit, wriggling violently on the floor in front of us all. The warders screamed at us to stand to attention and face the front. They took their time in getting the poor guy up off the floor, after which some medical warders took him to his cell.

Sitting alone in my cell one day, on the wooden chair they provided, I felt overcome by panic, by a sort of claustrophobia in which the cell seemed the size of a phone booth. I dashed over to the window and was glad to see everything the right size in the world beyond. The next thing I remember is being beaten up by the warders, who said I had attempted to escape by picking my lock with a plastic comb – and it's true. I did. I didn't know where I was going, except that somehow I was getting out of that cell. While I was down on my knees, slipping the comb in and sliding out the lock, I thought I heard footsteps on the landing outside. I paused for a moment, and then the door came crashing in on my face and nose, stunning me. I came out of my daze when I felt the warders' boots digging into me.

'Up!' They made me stand to attention while they interrogated me and slapped me about. I couldn't tell them about the panic attack – I was afraid, not so much of them but of the panicking itself: I didn't know what had happened to me.

'You were trying to escape!' they kept repeating. Even though I hated the bastards I was glad they were there, for I preferred their company to being alone at that particular time.

I was marched down a long corridor known as the 'mile'. They kept screaming, 'Left, right! Left, right!' – and to confuse me one warder told me to swing my arms shoulder high while the other said I was to swing them waist high. The corridor smelt strongly of disinfectant and was grey looking and cold. There were doors on either side, but I could only guess at what lay behind them. We stopped at one and I was marched into North Wing. People were moving about, some of them from the various schools I had been to. They called to me, but the warders told me not to answer. Other warders were waiting to take me down to the dungeons. They too began screaming out orders; the bastards from behind were kicking and those in front were pulling, trying to make me fall. Once we were underground they strip-searched me and put me through the usual humiliating procedure of bending over, as if they got some sort of satisfaction from it.

I was found guilty of attempting to open my cell door and damaging government property – the comb – and I was ordered to be kept in the cells for a week: four days in the dungeons and three in the cells above. So back I went to the dungeons. I wasn't allowed any tobacco at all, and I was given one book to read, at night only. I was told not to write anything about my punishment in any of my letters.

While I was in the dungeons I was taken out every day to scrub the 'mile' corridor with a brush the size of a nail-brush. I was glad to be out of the cells and back amongst my pals.

I think there were some 400 guys in Polmont borstal, between the ages of 16 and 21, and I was one of the youngest there. Each of its five wings had a governor. But the worst wing was the Allocation Centre: this was where all the hard punishment took place. If some guy wasn't standing up straight on parade, it could cost him a punch in the gut and abuse from one of the sadistic warders. There was a room known as the 'sweat box', used for marching lessons. It was very hot in there, and the dust was always so thick that we all coughed and spluttered while marching on the spot, and this had the warders calling us all sorts of names, from old women to morons. Some guys were pushed beyond the limit. One warder always carried a bed-block stick under his armpit, like a sergeant-major. He was notorious for hitting guys with it and he seemed to enjoy his reputation. He would boast to the newer guys that he was the 'stick man'.

'Have you never heard of me?' he would growl, sticking out his barrel chest, his face all screwed up to look mean. If anyone ever attacked one of the warders, they'd get a terrible beating. Everyone was aware of this, and that's exactly what the warders wanted, as it put fear into a lot of guys.

There was one warder in the Allocation Centre who was as strict and regimental and smartly dressed as they come – but he was also very fair, and whenever he was on duty the warders' attitudes changed and their bullying wasn't so obvious. If he thought a warder was out of order he'd put him in his place. They hated it, but he was the principal warder and their superior. If there was extra food on the hotplate, instead of throwing it away, he would give it to those who wanted it. The warders weren't happy at this but they didn't show their true feelings. The senior warder came to work in a different suit every day, with shirt, tie and handkerchief to match, and he was known as 'the Baron'.

I hadn't been long in borstal when my brother Jim hit the headlines. He and two other guys had got away scot-free after being charged with robbery and discharging a sawn-off shotgun over the head of a hotel owner: they had been kept on remand a day too long under Scottish law. I read about Jim in the newspapers at recreation time, and was really glad to learn he had been freed. I remember the day when he was arrested: Ma went berserk and threatened to kill herself, saying she couldn't take any more – and now I could picture her face at the news of Jim's release. One of those set free with Jim was a guy called Shadow, who had married Tommy Campbell's sister and was close to our family. Everyone was talking about the trial, and most of the guys were laughing because the police and court officials had been humiliated.

There were always fights in the Allocation Centre, and occasionally I kept watch for some guys who were having it out in the toilet or a cell. Nearly all the guys in there were members of a gang, and some of them continued their gang wars inside. Some guy would get a slight stab wound and never report it, as it would mean an inquiry.

One day Ma came up with some of the family, including my Uncle Atty. Then some weeks later I was sent to the East Wing. The night before I was to move I hardly slept a wink, I was so glad to get away from the Allocation Centre. I was more bitter than I could remember, and felt a real hatred for the warders – not forgetting the matron who we always had to thank for our food, even when she wasn't there! Maybe that was the whole idea of the short sharp lesson – to make one hate.

As it turned out, East Wing was more modern than any other place I'd been in, but the regime was as old as ever. I was taken to a cell in 'B' section. It contained a small sink, a small locker, a chair and a bed. The same rules applied here as in the Allocation Centre: cells to be spotlessly clean at all times and the floor kept highly polished.

When I was taken along to see the governor of East Wing the first thing he said to me was, 'I know your father.' I can remember him saying to me – as many others had – that I'd end up in prison all my days: I wonder now why so many of them drummed that into my head, and whether it wasn't wishful thinking.

Before long I became involved in a fight with a guy from Dundee. He fancied himself as Jack the Lad and must have thought me an idiot, so he had a go at bullying me, so I challenged him to fight. He looked astonished and then tried to laugh it off. By then all the guys had gathered to watch, as they usually do. It was agreed that there'd be no knives used or any other weapons, and that the fight would take place in my cell. As I walked into my cell the guy leapt on my back and tried to strangle me, shouting that he was going to kill me. I staggered across the floor and I almost slid, but I managed to keep my footing. However hard I tried to shake him off my back, I couldn't. I tried biting him but I couldn't get my teeth near him, and I ran at the wall, using him as a ram. I caught a glimpse of faces peering in at us, and it maddened me to think that they were going to watch me lose the fight. I took a crazy turn and threw him over my shoulder onto my bed and started butting him with my head; when I saw the fear in his shifty eyes it gave me more strength, and I kicked and punched him till he said he had had enough.

He never bothered me after that, nor did I bother him. Everyone was talking about it, and some of the Glasgow guys said that if the 'outsiders' tried to give us Glaswegians trouble then we should do battle with them, but nothing came of it except paranoia and verbal abuse behind backs.

One day I was walking along the corridor with about a dozen other guys when the pass-men came by with our dinner. There were a couple of trays of duff for our pudding, so we stole a slice each. Matron was watching without our knowing. I was the only one there from Glasgow and she came straight up to me and said she was having me put on governor's report for stealing a slice of cake. I was locked in my cell till I could see the governor in the morning, after which I was sent to the dungeons for three days – all because of a slice of cake.

After I'd been in the wing for about a week I was allocated to a work party. This involved working with textiles, and I was asked if I could use a sewing-machine! I couldn't, and I didn't even know that guys used sewing-machines. I felt humiliated sitting at a sewing-machine, and I guess the others had too when they first arrived.

One day the governor asked me if I had ever done any bricklaying, and I told him I had been on the bricklaying party at St Andrew's. He asked me if I would like to help to build a new gaol for women, known as Cornton Vale. I told him I wouldn't like to help build any gaol and would rather tear them down. He wasn't amused and told me I had a bad attitude.

I got a letter from Ma in which she told me that my aunt Ruby had been murdered by my uncle. I cried all night for her. She was the first person to die who had meant something to me, and I thought of all the good times I had had with her and how she had sheltered me when I was on the run. I thought about Broono and my other cousins, and wondered what would happen to them. I asked for leave to go to the funeral but was refused. I was told it had to be someone in my own family. A few nights later I opened my eyes and saw my aunt standing near my bed. I got the fright of my life and hid under the blankets, too scared to press the bell. This was the first time in my life I had seen a ghost, but when I finally looked out from my blankets there was nothing there. I was sorry I had hidden, and prayed that the ghost would come back again. But she never did and I never told anyone about it in case they thought I was crazy. A few months after my aunt's death her husband Hugh was serving life for her murder.

I was allowed home in April 1973, after serving 11 months. I said goodbye to my pals, some of whom I promised to keep in touch with when I got out. The warders drove us to the station and left us to catch the train into Glasgow. It was a great feeling to be free again. It was like finishing a life sentence. I said to myself the hard life was all over: regardless of what the bastards thought, I'd never be back in again.

7

My Wee Job

Ma and Maw were as excited as I was when I got home.
Ma made a huge dinner for me while I sat and told Maw
all about my borstal training. Maw felt my arms and shoulders
and said that I was a thoroughbred and couldn't be fattened.
Ma made me promise to get a job and settle down and was
forever preaching to me that I didn't want to spend my life in
and out of gaols. She was right – I didn't.

I took Maw out for walks at night. We'd have a good talk
and a good laugh, and if we passed anyone we knew we'd
stop to say hello. There's something about the wee small
hours that attracts me, and Maw was the same. I loved the
peace and tranquillity. I remember asking Maw if there was
any gipsy blood in me, but she just laughed and said I was a
true blue-eyed Scot. It was great to be with my family again.
If my dad had been home we'd have all been together for the
first time in a long time. Jim had married while I was in
borstal, and it seemed that he would settle down to a quiet
life with his wife and kid. He had moved away from
Garthamlock, so at least he had a good start. Everyone knew
that the police would hound him after he had got out of the
Stepps Hotel robbery. My dad wrote to his MP and the
Chief Constable about his fears for me and Jim being
harassed by the police – I think he even wrote to the Prime
Minister.

Jobs were plentiful then, but I hated work – I'd had enough
of it in the textile party at borstal. Ma kept pleading with me
to get a job, so I made an effort and looked up the adverts in
the papers. I spoke to a man at the unemployment centre and
was offered a job at the zoo! I thought he was kidding at first,
and when I laughed he seemed upset. It might please him to

know that I ended up in a zoo later – in a human zoo known as the 'Cages' or Porterfield Prison.

In the end I found a job as a store boy at a grocery store – an aunt who had worked in one of the many Henry Healy shops saw her boss about me. She said I'd better not embarrass her by stealing anything from the shop. Ma and Maw were really chuffed; Ma wrote and told my dad in Perth Prison that I had myself a wee job, and I received a nice letter from him. All my aunts were talking about it, as were the neighbours, and Ma boasted to one and all saying, 'That's my Johnnyboy got himself a good job.' I went to see one of the Henry Healy managers, but two days later I gave up. I just couldn't do it. I think it was because I was too shy, though the people who worked there were good, decent people.

My job was to carry boxes in from the vans to and from the fridge and freezer. The shop was in the city centre, a few yards from the bus terminus, so I could see all the Garthamlock people coming and going from their work and they could see me in my white coat. I wasn't allowed to serve the customers, but on my first day there a wee woman came in while the others were upstairs having their tea break, and she approached me to serve her. I was going to shout one of the lassies down, but I didn't bother, and I asked her what she wanted. Whatever it was she wanted I couldn't find it, so I grabbed the first thing I could see, which was a huge lump of meat. I gave it to her for nothing and asked her to leave in case they discovered it. She had a job getting it into her shopping bag. I was trying to listen out for the lassies coming down from upstairs, and instead of getting out of the shop and away with the meat that she had got for nothing she asked me for some more. She pointed to this and that, so I grabbed handfuls of what she wanted and gave them to her. She thanked me and as she left she said in a whisper, 'God bless you, son.'

When I came home from my first day's work Ma had a huge meal laid on for me. All I got out of her was, 'How do you like your new job, son?' I couldn't tell her the truth because I didn't want to hurt her. She was so happy and I lied to protect her. That night I was out stealing and breaking into shops. It was easier than working. Ma had the alarm clock set to get me up for my work in the morning and had my breakfast ready, and she gave me some cigarettes to take to work. I didn't have the courage to tell her I wouldn't be working much longer. I can remember clearly the look on her face when one of my aunts told her that I was no longer working and had only lasted two days. She looked humiliated and shattered. I wouldn't be surprised if she'd had a cry that night.

Ma told me to be in early at nights, saying she didn't want me wandering around the streets to get lifted by the police, but once she was asleep I slipped away and went out stealing. Whenever I saw a police car coming towards me I sprinted through a close and away – especially late at night, because if it suited them they could lift me for being a known thief.

There were wild parties at the weekends on the estate, and more often than not they ended in a fight. Some of my pals' mothers thought their sons were angels, never knowing that they had done more stabbings and slashings than Genghis Khan. Big Gerry from Garthamlock had a ma who thought him an angel. At home he'd speak politely and have me doing the same, and I had to pretend I was working whenever she asked, and deny I was ever in trouble with the law. Most of us told our mas lies to protect them and stop them worrying.

I never spent many Christmases with my family because I was either on the run or locked up, but I have fond memories of the ones that I did spend. Dad was usually in gaol, but his friends delivered presents from him. Ma always did her best to give us a good time, and Maw had a good excuse for getting drunk.

'It's Christmas,' she'd say to Ma, 'and this may be my last one.'

Although Ma detested drink, she felt obliged to let Maw have hers, and Maw would sing her party piece and favourite song, 'No Regrets'. She was always happy when she was drunk, and she'd tell us how much she loved us all and that we were the best weans in the world. She'd grab hold of us and start dancing in an old-fashioned way, staggering and knocking things over. She never seemed to tire and was the life and soul of her own little party. When Maw had a wee drink in her she would ask me if I would remember her and miss her when she was gone, and she'd grip my hand hard. Of course I'd remember and miss her and I told her so. She'd ask me if she had been good to me through the years, and she'd go on about her wee Atty and tell me that she was scared to die because she wouldn't know what would become of Atty and her sons and grandsons. 'Oh, if only yous would settle down then I could die in peace,' she told me.

To hear Maw talk like this really frightened me. At night I would pray for Maw, asking God not to take her away from us. Sometimes life can be so beautiful amidst all the hardship and suffering – and it's this that makes it all worth living for. It was great to watch Maw open up her presents and to see her two useless eyes give a sparkle. Inside I'd cry, but no one looking on would notice. I'm sure my reason for seeming hard-hearted when it came to showing my innermost feelings was a defence. If my folks had really known what my love for them meant to me I reckon it would have hurt them more. Maybe they didn't think I was giving them all the love they deserved and so continued loving me in the hopes that one day I would return it. If only they knew . . .

At about this time my pal Eddie Dobie and I thought we would rob a farmer who delivered eggs to the estate. We knew he kept his money tucked into his wellington boots. He looked like a big country yokel so we imagined he would be an easy target. Eddie decided that he would steal some chloroform from his science class and knock Wullie unconscious so that we could get his wellington boots off. He got the chloroform and hid it. I'd never done anything like this before, and it seemed more of a good laugh than a robbery.

One night Wullie came to Garthamlock to collect his egg money and we were ready to pounce. We watched Wullie's big, clumsy shape move up and down the streets, collecting from the messengers who worked for him; we followed him for a while, giving him plenty of time to collect most of his money. Some of the Garthamlock Young Team were out looking for their pals, but we stayed in the shadows so they wouldn't see us. If they had known what we were doing they might have wanted to join us, and we wanted all the money to ourselves.

Once the street was empty we made our move towards Wullie's little van. He looked as clumsy as ever in his huge welly boots and dungarees. We walked up behind Wullie, and before I knew it Eddie was up on the farmer's back and I was trying to wrench his welly boots off his legs, and even though Eddie had the rag over the farmer's mouth he kept shouting, 'This is a robbery.' Wullie was swinging Eddie about like a rag doll. The rag fell to the ground, but Eddie wouldn't let go. He started punching Wullie about the head, but Wullie threw him over his shoulder with the swift movement of a judo expert. I couldn't move for laughing, and even Eddie was in fits of laughter. After that I decided that I would stick to simple stealing. My fear of gaol was long gone, the old desire to steal was strong and I couldn't help myself.

8

The Big House

One day there was a running battle in the field behind
Garthamlock with the gang from a housing estate called
Cardowan. I heard that my young brother Joseph was there
so I went to get him, fearing that he could be seriously
injured as he was only nine. In the middle of the fields was a
small burn that ran between Garthamlock and Cardowan. We
were on one side and the Cardowan gang on the other, and
each was wary of entering enemy territory. By the time I got
there the Cardowan team were beating up one of the
Garthamlock boys and there was panic amongst our own boys
as they were outnumbered. There was only one thing to do,
and that was to charge at them as fast as we could. My pal
Peter Henderson and I charged at the other team and others
followed, brandishing steak knives, hatchets and broken sticks
and screaming abuse and threats. They let the guy they were
beating up go and we gave chase, right into their own estate.
There were too many of them for us to handle, so we headed
back across the fields over the burn and on to safe territory –
but then we saw the police coming towards us in their jeeps
and panda cars. We were caught between the police and the
gang beyond the burn. People were dropping knives and
scattering in every direction. Peter and I stuck together and
dived into the burn, which came up to my knees. I was
soaking and filthy, and I could hear the gang from Cardowan
shouting to the police that some of us were hiding in the
burn.

I scurried through the burn as quietly as I could, but the
police heard me. There was no way out except to surrender.
As I made my way up the side of the burn, I put my hand
out for the policeman to help me out, but he kicked me back

in and I went under the water. When they finally got me out I was so filthy and wet that none of them wanted me in their car. Eventually they drove us to the police station, where we were charged with mobbing and rioting and breach of the peace and locked up in a cell. There I stripped off all my clothing and wrapped the one woolly blanket around me while I scrubbed my clothes in the water from the toilet pan. We were refused visits from our families and denied tobacco and a change of clothes. Peter was a first offender and I laughed when I heard him shout to the turnkey that he wanted his 'rights' and a solicitor too. They just told him to fuck off.

Next morning we were taken to Glasgow Sheriff's Court and appointed a lawyer through the Legal Aid system. We were both refused bail and remanded in Longriggend for a social inquiry and background report. Peter was shattered – he'd never been in gaol before and he didn't really know what lay ahead. In the gaol bus he complained that the handcuffs were too tight, but the warders paid no attention to him even though his wrists were beginning to swell. I wasn't too happy because I had only meant to do a good deed and get our Joseph away from trouble, and I ended up in trouble myself.

I told Peter all about Longriggend on the way there, but he thought I was kidding him. He soon changed his mind. We were marched into reception and made to line up outside the 'dog boxes'.

'Listen for your names and answer "sir"!' one of the warders growled to us, but when it was Peter's turn to answer his name he failed to say 'sir' and was slapped about the face until he did so. He hesitated, unsure whether or not to attack the bullying warder, and on seeing him hesitate other warders ran over and started threatening him and daring him to make a wrong move.

I met a couple of guys in there with whom I became quite friendly. One was called Mulsy and he was in for gang fighting and attempted murder. At a carnival somewhere on the south side of Glasgow he hit another gang member on the head with a hatchet. It went in so deep that it was said that Mulsy had to put his foot on the guy's head to pull it back out again. He was quite a good kid in his own way, but one bad deed had branded him as a sort of madman. He was sentenced to eight years. My other new pal, 'Fingers', was a good kid. Fingers was so affected by Longriggend that he eventually hanged himself. The warders laughed and joked when they described their grisly findings to some of the prisoners. It was sickening. The bastards who governed this place had much to answer for – they made up rules to suit themselves, depriving prisoners of what few rights they had. Who would believe that untried prisoners weren't allowed radios or photographs – or weren't even allowed to talk at their recreation? Some guys said that when they got out they'd come back and give the warders a hard time, or even take their revenge on the warders' families.

Peter told me that he couldn't handle the place and thought of committing suicide. I don't think that he was alone in thinking that way, though most guys tried to pretend that being locked up had no effect on them.

Peter and I appeared at Glasgow Sheriff Court and were found guilty of breach of the peace. The mobbing and rioting charges were dropped. The judge sent me to a young offenders' institution for three months, but Peter was fined and allowed home. I was sick, even though I'd got only three months. As Ma said, it was a waste of life.

The young offenders' hall is one of the five huge buildings in Barlinnie and it is known as E Hall. It is the same size and shape as the other halls, but the regime is much stricter. It reminded me of the American-type gaols with huge galleries. All the guys on the four galleries looked down at us new admissions on the ground floor and called our names. My own name was called and I looked up to see John Henry and another guy from Garthamlock known as Forry. Both were in for serious assault.

In E Hall we all had to wear blue shirts, whereas the other cons in the gaol wore red-striped shirts. The attitude of the warders was much the same as that at Longriggend, so I knew what to expect. I was put into a cell on the third gallery with two other guys. John and Forry gave me some tobacco and soap and toothpaste to help me out till I got my wages.

After slop-out next morning we were taken to the dining

hall for our breakfast: a bowl of pig-meal, a thin round sausage, two slices of bread and a small piece of margarine. We were given our food in plastic or steel bowls. I then had to see the doctor and go through the usual humiliating routine; after which I was passed fit for slave labour and taken to what was known as the 'scrap party'. Our job was to strip old copper piping from its oily wrappings. It was filthy work, yet we were given only one shower and one change of clothes a week, and we were lucky if our weekly wage earned us an ounce of tobacco. Each day after work I would strip off all my clothes and stand in a basin of water and scrub myself with a nail-brush to get the oil off my skin. For our daily exercise we were marched around a small yard – if it was raining or too cold then we took our exercise inside.

Most of the guys in young offenders went around in little gangs just like they did outside, and if a guy had an argument with someone from another gang the chances were that there'd be a battle and weapons would be produced – and it was just too bad if someone got hurt. Grassing wasn't tolerated – those who did it were shunned and put into protection for their own safety. Rape cases and child molesters were also protected, and they weren't allowed into the workshops with the others. They were given work to do in their cells, and when it came to exercise time they were separated again.

There were tobacco barons among the young offenders and throughout the prison system: if a guy wanted to borrow half an ounce of tobacco he would have to pay back double the amount borrowed. Some got themselves into debt and couldn't pay up, and they were beaten up or went into protection; there were always fights over non-payment of debts. I didn't smoke much then so I never went near the tobacco barons.

We were told that we couldn't write anything about our lives in gaol, whether in letters or in book form. I guess the reason for this is that the authorities have much to hide. Every weekend someone seemed to crack up and slash his wrists or smash his cell window and his locker. These incidents seemed to put a bit of life into the gaol: guys would howl out of their windows and under the doors, and their shouts would echo round the huge halls. We'd listen to the warders scurrying into the hall to get to the guy in distress, and we knew what was coming to him when they got to him. As soon as we heard the thuds and screams, we'd kick or bang on our doors with our mugs and shout for them to leave the guy alone.

Craigend was a new housing estate next to Garthamlock. Many of the Barlinnie warders moved there with their families, and soon the Garthamlock Young Team were fighting with them and smashing their windows. The warders came out in their uniforms, pretending to be police, but they were recognised for what they were. They knew the kids who had hassled them and waited till they came into the young offenders, when they took them into the notorious cell 43, where all the beatings-up took place.

We were allowed two visits every three months, so Ma always made an appearance and was forever begging me to get a job and settle down when I got out this time. I never did tell my Ma about me getting a beating as it would only have caused her more worry. Ma had a pal called Mary Carroll and they looked very much alike. Everybody thought that they were sisters, and they were always together. Mary was a good laugh and she wore very stylish clothes, which made her very attractive. She was brought up with Ma in the Gorbals and at one time in her teens she courted my Uncle Tam. Whenever Ma went visiting me, my dad or my brothers, Mary always drove her there. I called her 'Auntie' and she treated me like her own son, always eager to do things for me and running to gaols and police stations for me along with Ma. Mary looked a million dollars and wore plenty of expensive jewellery, but the thing she was liked most for was that she was down to earth with everyone.

The night before my release I couldn't sleep and paced up and down my cell. I couldn't wait to be free. As the door opened to reveal the decent world in all its splendour, I felt great to be alive. I was overjoyed to hear the huge door slam shut behind me and to walk down the drive away from the 'Big House'. The things that I had taken for granted – like colourful clothes and cars and buses – were now a luxury. It was a great feeling as I headed for 999 Gartoch Road. Ma was up and waiting with my breakfast.

9

More Porridge

Maw was in bed, so I went in and had a talk with her. She was really pleased that I was home again and gave me a hug and a kiss that brought tears to my eyes. She didn't seem to change or age at all, and I thought she would live forever. Ma asked me to get a job and settle down but, despite my promises, I knew I wouldn't: work scunnered me. That same night I went out stealing.

Occasionally Ma's older brother paid us a visit. Uncle Alec was small and wiry and in great physical condition. He played the guitar and accordion and would entertain the family at the fireside. We'd all be happy, especially Maw, who joined in the sing-songs, her feet tapping merrily on the floor.

'Don't you be getting involved in any of these gang fights,' Ma said to me as we stood on our veranda watching people at the quarry screaming abuse, brandishing weapons and charging each other. Ma saw some of my pals hitting other gang members with weapons and shook her head in disgust. She knew I was out stealing, and she got angry with me and said I was taking her for a fool.

When I wasn't stealing I was thinking about it. My dad always said, 'Johnnyboy, as a thief you're hopeless – *get a job*,' but I carried on with a blindness that saw me through. I was gaoled yet again on a shoplifting charge. Broono was with me, but this time he got away and I was again sent to the young offenders' institution in Barlinnie for three months. I never got used to being locked up and it tortured me every day I was there.

Some of the old-timers were allowed to mix with us doing work. They were known as 'jakeys' and 'winos', and they had spent most of their lives in gaols. They always asked us to give them some cigarettes or to keep our cigarette butts for them and they would tell us stories about themselves when they were young. Some of their tales were fascinating, and I loved to listen to them. Although I wasn't much into reading I often wrote lyrics and verses, sometimes about the old jakeys.

Ode to Crazy Joe

'I may be down and out, my boys,'
Said the man called Crazy Joe,
'But young luck was mine's way back in time,
And this hand was never slow . . .
A hand that shook the world
And was raised for Kings and Queens.
I had my words with mayors and lords –
And I drank with the should-have-beens.
Yeah, would you believe I had it all
When the gang was much in debt,
I was there, and quick to share,
Say, give us a cigarette!
Give me a cigarette, boys, to fill my lungs with smoke
There's pleasure in it for a bum like me
Who stands with an empty poke.'
So we gave him up some cigarettes
And he snatched them like a thief
And the hand that once had shook the world
Was now shaking like a leaf.

In the winter the police would round up most of these old jakeys to save them from freezing to death.

10

Back to St Joseph's

Tony Tamburrini, my pal from St Joseph's, had moved to Garthamlock with his family, and when I was released we started going about with each other again. He and I and Gak would go stealing together. One day I suggested that we go back to St Joseph's Approved School in Edinburgh and see how it had changed since we were last there in 1970.

It was really strange to see once again the big mansion building and the fields that I had so often run across when fleeing from authority. Inside we were told that there was only one brother whom we would remember – and remember him we did! We went to his office on the ground floor and knocked on the door. The tall, thin brother with grey hair looked bewildered as he tried to put names to our faces, his finger resting on his lips. One at a time he studied us: 'McGachan?' and then 'Tamburrini?' and 'Steele?'. He invited us in for tea and a talk about our days there. He asked us what we thought of him when we were under his care and we told him he was a bastard. He didn't seem surprised or upset by this, and he told us what he thought of us then. We ended up having a debate about physical and mental torture – not forgetting our Wullie Winkie nightgowns and the little circles. He admitted that a lot of unpleasant methods were used that shouldn't have been. This was a man who used to tell me that it was time I came to my senses and now it seemed he had finally come to his.

11

A Bad Gamble

Ma occasionally went to the bingo hall to try her luck, as did Tony's ma. I was talking to my Ma there one day; she wasn't too pleased to see me with Tony, whom she disliked, and she couldn't hide her feelings. I stood in front of her so that Tony wouldn't see her face. As we left, Tony had a shot at the one-arm bandit that stood in the entrance of the bingo hall. I tried to get him away, but up he went to the cashier's window for change so that he could play it. We started arguing. I said if he wanted the money that bad why not steal the fucking bandit! But he wanted to steal more than the bandit; when he went up for change at the cashier's window he spotted the money bags which contained the prize money. I went to have a look and there it was, just as Tony said. The woman gave me some change and we stood talking, pretending to be interested in losing our money to the bandit. The cashier's window was quite long, with a door at the end of it. There were two or three women behind the glass, and an usher on the outside, busy showing people in. We decided to snatch the prize money. We had no weapons, nor did we need any – it was simply a case of kicking in the door. From inside the bingo hall we could hear men and women having a good time, and occasionally the door would open to let people in and out. I had just put my first ten pence into the machine and pulled the arm when a wee old woman wearing a headscarf came up and said she would wait her turn for a shot. We had to get her away somehow. Then I won the jackpot. I couldn't believe it – I'd never won a thing in my life. The wee woman was hooting at my good fortune and said she only hoped she had the luck I'd had. I told her to take the money and keep it. She must have thought I was joking, but when I put the silver into her bag she bolted out the door in case I changed my mind.

Tony crashed in the door and went in, with me behind him. The three women screamed for the police while we grabbed the money. Before I knew it we were on the street, Tony running in one direction and me in another. I could hear women shouting from the bingo hall that some bastards had stolen the pay-out money!

We were chased by the police, caught and charged with robbing the bingo hall of several hundred pounds. Next morning we were taken to court and remanded in custody at Longriggend.

Probably more than a hundred prisoners passed through Glasgow Sheriff Court each day. It is said to be the busiest in Europe. I was sentenced to six months in a young offenders' institution and Tony was sent to borstal. I said goodbye to Tony.

At Barlinnie I was put through the usual routine. When the doors opened I noticed many familiar faces and I was asked what I was in for by those I knew. Everybody was happy, in a sense, to see someone they knew – it was a feeling of security in an insecure world. My brother Jim and Broono were in, each serving an 18-month sentence for robbing a bookie's shop, and Jim had an outstanding charge to go up for at Glasgow High Court, along with my Uncle Billy, for holding up a jeweller's shop and serious assault. He and Uncle Billy both got six years. My dad was home when we were in the young offenders, and he came to see us. He looked as if he had just come back from Spain rather than a six-year sentence. He was very tanned and, as always, smartly dressed. He sat there and preached to us both about not getting involved with crime, and how I was to get myself a job when I came home. As usual, he told us that if any of the warders were messing us about we were to get their names and let him know as soon as possible.

I was sent to work in the cobblers' shop with Jim. It had a few bench tables scattered here and there, and it looked empty compared to other sheds in the gaol. The warder who ran the shop was a fair and decent enough guy who knew my dad. He never bothered with anyone as long as we did our work and looked as though we were busy. He didn't mind us smoking as long as it was out of sight. He was the sort who was only in the job for the money, a happy-go-lucky man, always smiling and talking to us like human beings, and he told us that he disagreed with the brutality of the system.

I wasn't a cobbler, and I was put onto a machine which seals plastic bags. It was crazy. There I was working for a wage that would hardly buy me an ounce of tobacco, yet I wouldn't work for a good wage when I was out!

One of the decent warders pulled me up on Friday just before tea and told me I was in serious trouble as one of the warders had found a sealed bag of glue which someone had dropped on the dining-hall floor. Because the bag was sealed and I had been working on the sealing machine with another guy, we were being blamed. I didn't think it a serious matter, nor did I remember sealing the bag. As far as I was concerned the machine was there for anyone to use whenever they wanted. Many prisoners made fancy tobacco tins and jewel boxes, and they needed glue to stick the wood.

That night I heard through the grapevine that an older con in another hall was in the gaol infirmary suffering seriously from sniffing glue!

After breakfast we stayed in our cells, because Saturday wasn't a work day. At about ten in the morning I heard, 'Third flat! Send down Steele!' I could see two warders on the ground floor looking up at me, and it seemed that they were whispering between themselves. When I reached the desk on the bottom floor they took me into a cell they used as an office, containing a wooden desk and a filing cabinet. They asked me what my job was in the cobblers' shop, and I told them I was on the machine which sealed plastic bags.

'And what do you know about this here?' one of them said, showing me a sealed bag of glue. They were standing on either side of me in an intimidating manner, but I told them the truth: that I knew nothing of it and that I wasn't the only one who worked the machine. They said that they had spoken to the other guy and they believed him when he said he knew nothing about the glue; but they wouldn't believe me. I realised then that they were only wanting to blame me, and that my denying it wasn't what they wanted to hear. The cell door was closed over so that no one could see in.

'It was fucking you who sealed this bag!' they kept shouting, showering me with saliva. I told them it wasn't. 'It fucking was!' they screamed and, taking off their hats and putting them on the desk, they pounced on me, punching and kicking me to the floor. 'Admit it!' they said as they kicked me on the legs, body and head. I wanted to scream for help but knew that would be pointless. I kept throwing my arms up to protect my face and head, and each time I did they would kick my belly and chest, and when my hands came down to protect those parts, they aimed for my head. They made contact, yet they never hurt me. The thing that hurt was the thought of dying there in that cell. I could feel the crunching of their boots on my head and body.

They put me into one of the punishment cells, not far from their desk at the bottom of the hall. There was no bed, no table and no chair – nothing except for me and my thoughts. I was not the hard case they now thought me to be. I cursed myself for not admitting it and getting it over with. I promised myself that when they came back I would tell them I had sealed the bag of glue. My body was aching so I had to sit down in a corner. With each move I made it hurt, sending sharp pains through me. Outside my cell door I could hear activity and of course there was the usual yelling from the warders from one end of the hall to the other. I could hear my pals and my brother Jim calling my name from their cell windows, but I couldn't answer because I was so sore that it would have been hard for me to climb up to the window, some six feet above the floor.

The door opened and the same two warders came in. 'Are you still going to deny it, Steele?' – and so the beating started again. They were like two madmen as they kicked me and, what's worse, they had a licence to do so. No one tried to stop them, no one came to investigate the noises that came from the cell. They left saying they would be back, and that sooner or later I would admit it.

They came back again after dinner, only this time it was two different warders. I knew one of them had a bad reputation as a 'dog'.

'Maybe you wouldn't tell the others, but you'll certainly tell me,' he said. I didn't want another beating and decided I would say what they wanted to hear, yet I denied it again, and immediately put my hands up to protect my head – but no blows came, and when the warder stood up I thought that he had given up. That was until I saw him unbutton his jacket and take it off and give it to the other warder to hold. He didn't seem to be in any hurry. With each punch he shouted 'Admit it', and I took great pride in saying, 'Never!'. I could see the expression on his face change each time I shouted 'Never!'. It got to the stage that I was daring him to have another punch, and another and another. I was like a madman standing there under a rain of blows, blinded by the tears that were streaming down my face. I was still shouting 'Never!' when they closed the door on me. I had my mouth to the bottom of the door and kept up the shouting. 'Bastards!'

My cell door opened and a warder put in a pisspot which was filthy and had urine in it. 'See you in the morning, cunt!' he said as he slammed the door. As soon as they had left, my brother and my pals were shouting down to me asking how I was and wanting to know what cell I was in so that they could pass me down tobacco. I was really glad to hear their voices – it was great to have people who cared for me in this hell-hole known as the 'Big Hoose'. It was agony climbing up to the window. I thought that my ribs were broken; each time I jumped and grabbed hold of the bars I had to let go again because of the pain. I finally managed to hold on long enough to answer a few of their questions. I told them I was fine and what cell I was in. They passed tobacco along the cell windows by string, each guy passing it on to the next till it reached the cell above me, and from there it was passed down to me. This was a luxury and I thanked them and jumped off to roll myself a smoke. I never slept a wink the whole night through, and by morning I hadn't a smoke left.

The door opened and I knew they meant business. There were about a dozen of them, all looking at me. The PO told me to get to my feet, and I was shaking all over with fear. 'Still sticking to your same story?' he said. When I said I was he drew back his fist. I turned my head to the side so that his fist wouldn't land square on my face, but 'Get your blankets and get up to your own cell,' he said. It was a reprieve. I was glad to be back in my own cell and to lie on the hard, lumpy coir mattress.

Next morning when I was slopping out and filling my basin with water some of my pals and neighbours came into my cell to find out what happened. When they saw my bruises they shook their heads in disbelief – I was blue all over.

Somehow my dad got to hear about it – word travels fast in prison. We heard that he had made some enquiries about the name of the PO who had been responsible for me getting the beatings. Word was sent out to some of my pals on the estate and they wrecked a few warders' cars and smashed their front windows in retaliation – and even looked for their kids at the local school.

The day I got out my dad was waiting outside the prison gate in his car. It was a beautiful morning, with the sun shining, and I felt that life was worth living. A few days later I was away stealing again.

12

Scotty and the Gun

Most of my pals from Garthamlock had married and settled down or were living a quiet life. 'Get yourself a job and settle down,' my dad said. He told me that he was giving up the life of crime and that we should have a go at it together. I'd never heard him talk like this before. I've never even heard him talk about his crimes. Maybe he was tired of it all . . .

I never thought about the damage that all his gaol sentences may have done to him. I wonder now if he was in as much pain as I was when I was locked up, or whether for some reason he too found it hard to stop being a crook. He said he was going to settle down and grow old along with Ma, who deserved a better life than the one he had offered her.

The phone seldom stopped ringing for my dad when he was home, and nearly every day people came to see him. He was very popular and well liked. His pals came from everywhere, and were every colour under the sun. They told me that he was a 'diamond': sometimes I wondered if we were talking about the same man.

I was staying at Lana's house and I went round to see my Ma and the family. My dad had fallen out with Ma, so he was staying with one of his friends. Ma wasn't looking too good so I tried to cheer her up. Scotty, the cairn terrier Dad had bought for Brenda, jumped all over me when he saw me, and Ma asked me to take him out for a walk in the fields. I had to be careful in case the police came by and spotted me – it was best for me to keep walking or they might pull me for loitering. Scotty disappeared in the long grass, so I had to hunt for him. I could hear him growling, and I thought perhaps he had caught a mouse. Then I spotted him. He had something in his mouth and was shaking it wildly. It was a bag of some description.

We were a few yards from the social club on the Gartloch Road when I caught hold of him and took the bag from him. I was for throwing it away but something made me look inside. I thought I was seeing things at first: this was the first gun I had ever held in my life. Something told me it was real, and I put it back in the bag. I was frightened to mess about with it in case it was loaded and went off. I looked around to see if anyone was watching me but the only people I saw were going to the social club. I searched all the other bags that had been dumped there but only found empty cans and bottles.

I decided to take the gun home with me to show my pals, and find out what they thought of it. My dad had always warned me and Jim never to bring anything stolen into our home and I seldom did, but this was different. I wanted to know if the gun worked, and I didn't want to hide it anywhere else in case someone found it.

I carried it under my jacket and once I was home I went out to the veranda and hid the gun under some old lino. Ma never went near this part of the veranda which contained much of our junk.

A few days later my dad said that he had seen police in plain clothes sitting in a car in the Gartloch Road, and it looked as though they were watching our house. 'Are you sure you haven't been up to anything?' he asked, looking me in the eye. Then he asked me if I had anything in the house that I shouldn't have. I thought about the gun in the veranda but didn't say anything about it, even though I was worried. My dad was getting his clothes from his bedroom when there was a knock at the door. He opened the door and pandemonium ensued, with him cursing, threatening and demanding to see a warrant. He wouldn't let the police in, and I could hear them saying, 'If you've nothing to hide, Andy, then you've nothing to worry about.' I hoped that he wouldn't let them in till they'd got a warrant, so that I could throw the gun into the canal or somewhere safe.

My dad finally let them in, thinking he had nothing to worry about. There were only two of them at first but soon there were six, with some more standing below our window, and they searched every nook and cranny in the house. While this was going on my dad was cursing and threatening the police, and warning them not to plant anything in the house. I recognised some of the crime squad from previous raids on our house and from the police station.

My dad and one of the policeman disappeared onto the veranda. 'What's all this, Andy?' the policeman asked and my dad told him it was old wax cloth and some junk belonging to his sons. He was searching through the junk himself and passing it on to the policeman. I expected to hear a shout from my dad at any moment – he would automatically have assumed that they had planted the gun there. But the shout never came, and I was still in the living-room when another member of the serious crime squad came to our door, holding the gun with a pencil so as to keep his fingerprints off it.

Only later did I find out exactly what happened on the veranda. When he saw the gun, my dad knew straightaway that I had brought the fucking thing into the house. He panicked and threw it over the veranda and into the garden below, where the other police were standing and saw it come down. He hadn't realised that the police were there as well.

My dad was remanded in custody at Barlinnie on a firearms charge. When Ma came home I told her that he had been arrested: she was shattered and turned very pale.

My conscience was bothering me at the thought of his being locked up because of my stupidity, and with that on my mind I made a statement to the police, who came to Ma's house. Maw sat with me so that she could be a witness to the facts. They asked her to leave, but she refused, saying that she might be blind but she wasn't stupid. Maw was scared, as I was, that the police would make a false statement to incriminate my dad.

My dad pleaded guilty to throwing the gun over the veranda in the High Court in Glasgow. I didn't know whether to laugh or cry when I picked up the newspaper the following day to read of his 18-month sentence and saw the headlines 'Scotty the wee wiry cairn terrier finds his master a package of trouble!'. It told the story, ending with how Scotty was run over shortly after finding the package.

13

Dear John

One night in December 1976 I met Tony, whom I hadn't seen for a few weeks. Tony was on his way to steal some money when I bumped into him; he said he was going to take the 'takings' off the driver of an ice-cream van, and he even had a key that fitted the door of the van. He had another two guys with him, and he asked me to go with them. I went, but it was decided that I should watch for the police as I was too well known in Garthamlock and might be seen. So I stayed in the shadows – for all the good it did me!

Tony and the others got the money, which wasn't much, and I was arrested soon after. In the police station I was messed about by the police because I wouldn't tell them who was with me.

I was called for trial in February or March 1977: I pleaded guilty to assault and robbery and was sentenced to 18 months in gaol.

My girlfriend left me during the beginning of my sentence. I was shattered and felt like taking my own life, my emotions were in turmoil and it hurt more than the sentence to get a 'Dear John' letter. I spent so long looking for an easy way to kill myself that by the time I got round to it my sentence was over.

14

A Big Mistake

When I got home my dad was there. He wouldn't talk to me because of the gun incident and it was quite clear he didn't want me in his house, so I went to live with Lana.

I didn't know what to do with my life. I was too shy to get a job. I found it hard to work with strangers and couldn't even ask for a job without feeling awkward. Henry Healy's store job had been enough for me. I lacked confidence. I would have loved to be a singer but I didn't have the confidence even to hum in front of a stranger.

I met Tony a few days after my release. All he could say about my misfortune was 'Sorry'. I had to accept it as bad luck and held nothing against him – and we went on stealing together. His ma had moved to another housing estate called Ruchazie. He told me that she had a debt collector who came to their house and that he always carried large amounts of money with him. It sounded easy enough and I agreed that we should rob him. Tony said that since the guy knew him and could identify him, he should stay out of it and leave it up to me and two friends of his, Joe and James – one of whom had a fish knife which he intended to use as a frightener and nothing more.

When the debt collector came out of Tony's ma's house we were waiting on him in the stairway. The plan was that Joe and James would hold his arms while I took the wallet from his pocket, but that wasn't how it turned out. As soon as the guy saw the three of us standing there in masks, he panicked and started to lash out. The other two ran off and left me to fight with the guy, who refused to hand over the money. Every time I tried to put my hand in his pocket he kicked and punched me. One of the two who had run away had dropped the knife on the landing, so I picked it up and pointed it at the guy and demanded the money. I had no intention of using it on him, but he grabbed the blade of the knife while trying to pull it out of my hand and cut himself. When he saw the blood he told me to take the money and leave him, and I did.

On the way downstairs I ran into the other two and raged at them for running away. We met up with Tony and split up the money, which came to about £100.

Tony and I met a guy in Garthamlock whom I knew quite well. He had heard that we had robbed the debt man in Ruchazie and he gave us some advice on doing robberies. He told us we should go for people with plenty of money, and that some people living in a house nearby who owned taxis and a café kept their takings in a wardrobe. If we struck on the night he suggested we might make several thousand pounds. Of course he would expect something for himself . . .

Once again Joe and James were involved. On the night of the robbery we put masks on and each of us had a knife. As we stood in the dark in the back court we were more nervous than excited. I was selected to go up to the top landing and knock on the door. We could hear sounds coming from the street below, people talking and laughing, and televisions from the nearby houses. My heart was pounding as I waited for the knock to be answered, and when I heard someone coming I was ready to run. This was the first time I had ever been in a situation like this, and I didn't feel right. I don't know why I didn't turn around and get away from there. It turned out to be the biggest mistake in my life.

The door opened and a woman stood there; she was in her twenties and wearing a house-coat that came to her knees. For a split second it didn't dawn on her what was happening – then I saw her eyes shift quickly from one point to another and terror set into her face. Someone from behind me dashed into the house, pushing the woman into the middle of the hall; I followed, and then the others, and we closed the door behind us, still not knowing who was in the house. But there was no time to worry now. I ran into a room and searched the wardrobe. Tony ran into another. I heard him say there were two guys in the bed. 'Don't fucking move!' he told them threateningly, and they didn't. Joe asked the woman where the money was, but she told him there was none in the house. I searched the wardrobes again and chests of drawers, but I found nothing. The woman repeated that there was no money in the house, but I said we had information that it was there. She said that whoever told me was lying. She began to argue with Joe, and he told her that if she didn't stop being cheeky he'd beat her up. But she wouldn't let him bully her and gave him a mouthful of abuse.

I decided it was time to leave and get as far away as possible. I was really sick at the thought of having gone to all this trouble without getting the money we were after. The others wanted to search again, and started taking jewellery and the little money there was lying about. One of them even stole the television meter.

I felt better going down the stairs than I had coming up, and I felt even better when I was in the dark back court with the cool breeze on my face. Pulling off my mask felt good. It was horrible to be under the fucking thing. I was sorry for what I had done back there.

Tony knew some people who would buy the jewellery we had taken, and then he took me to another house in the Parkhead area belonging to a friend who knew people who would buy stolen goods. I was introduced to the family, who seemed okay. The son was a thief and had done time. Tony said he was 'solid', meaning he wouldn't tell the police a thing, but before long the police had caught up with us and we were all arrested and taken to a police station.

The CID told me to give them a statement. I refused to do so, and was kicked and punched. 'Come on, Johnnyboy, the others are giving statements,' one of them said. 'Come on, son, co-operate with us and we'll put a good word in with the judge for you.'

Although they didn't know it, I felt like giving them a statement: it's just that when I get caught in a situation like this I cut myself off mentally and can't talk to anyone. They moved me to another room and removed my trousers for forensic tests. I was handcuffed to a radiator while a policeman in plain clothes spoke to me nicely and tried to persuade me to give him a statement.

Once the CID man realised that he wasn't getting anywhere he left the room and another took his place. He eyed me while he took off his jacket and glasses, and told me to start confessing or else I would be a sorry boy. I didn't answer, so he started doing karate on me and screaming. I had had beatings before from the police, but I had never witnessed anything like this.

I was eventually uncuffed from the radiator and, still half-naked, I was taken into the room where Tony was. He too was handcuffed by one hand to the pipe at the bottom of the radiator. He was kneeling on the floor watching the blood pour onto the lino from a deep gash in his face, just below his eye.

Then we were taken down to the cells. After a while the cell door opened and a turnkey told me I was to be fingerprinted. I knew this was untrue, because fingerprinting wasn't done in this station. I was taken upstairs to a room in which there were six or seven CID men. I knew at once that I was in trouble, still more so when I heard the door click shut behind me. One of them was sitting at a desk with pen and paper, which he pushed towards me. When I refused to sign a statement one of the CID men got up and pulled down the blinds on the window – and then they all started kicking and punching and screaming at me to sign and save myself a lot of trouble. I could hear their grunts as they kicked and punched me. I was terrified by the thudding of their boots and by the black flashes in front of my eyes. The old fear was there, but no physical pain. I never attempted to hit back, and this only encouraged them. I heard one of them ask for a truncheon. He held it in his hand, beating his open palm. Two others pulled me to my feet. There was a silence as the one with the truncheon asked me to give them a statement.

I felt the blood drain from my head and the coldness in my skin that told me I was going to pass out. I felt like retching. I could feel my face being slapped as I stood there with my eyes closed, the tears running down my face. Maybe they thought I was crying because I had had enough, but I was crying with rage more than anything. Then the one with the truncheon told the others to put my penis on the table top, at which I panicked and lashed out. I began screaming abuse and challenging them to fight. My only concern was that they didn't get my penis on the table top. I wriggled and squirmed and tried to crawl away under the tables and chairs. They told me to calm down, and that I would rot in gaol; after which they began to talk to me as if I was their friend. One of those who had beaten me gave me a packet of cigarettes just before he closed the door of my cell.

At the ID parade I was picked out by the debt collector as the one who had assaulted him. The woman from the house came to identify us, but she failed to recognise me. The police charged us with 13 robberies and one conspiracy to rob a post office. When we saw the charges we couldn't believe them: I had committed two of them, the debt collector and the robbery in the house. Joe and James gave statements to the police saying I had been involved in both: the police told me I should get my own back by giving them a statement incriminating Joe and James, but I refused to do so.

I was taken to Barlinnie to await trial at Glasgow High Court – my first High Court appearance. I met some pals of my dad's there, and they tipped me for anything up to four or five years in gaol. My only hope was to deny the charges and be acquitted.

My trial was set for June 1978. I was charged with robbing the debt collector and the house, robbing an ice-cream van, attempting to escape from police custody, assaulting police and conspiring to rob a post office.

We were all taken away downstairs to await the ringing of the bell that would tell us that the jury had reached their verdict. In the cells I spoke to Joe and James, who said that the police had beaten them to extract the statements. I blamed myself for getting involved with them in the first place. What angered me was that when they gave their statements incriminating me, they never admitted to threatening the woman, nor said that I had put a stop to Joe's threats.

While I was talking to them the bell of the south court rang and the four of us were taken up the narrow stairs to the dock in the courtroom. I was found guilty on two charges of robbery, Tony on one charge, and James and Joe on three charges. Passing sentence, the judge said he had no doubt I was the ringleader. Something inside me died when I heard him say I would go to gaol for 12 years.

I remember hearing a cry from the balcony at the back of the courtroom.

I then heard the judge sentence Tony to six years in prison, and Joe and James to five years each in a young offenders' institution, but while they were being sentenced I stood there in a kind of daze, looking at a world that had collapsed around me. I didn't even have time to hate the judge or the police officers laughing at the back of the courtroom – there'd be plenty of time for that. My thoughts were with my family, and those close to me. My dad's words kept coming back to me: 'They'll fucking crucify you, son.'

15

The Appeal

My appeal was heard at the Edinburgh High Court by three appeal judges. Two of them had bad reputations amongst the criminal fraternity, but my lawyer and the Queen's counsel were optimistic that I'd get my sentence reduced. There were a few prisoners up on appeal that day. Everyone – warders included – thought I would be the only one to get a result. As soon as I entered the appeal court I was aware of an eerie silence, and the staring eyes of the three judges upon me as if I were some sort of subhuman. My QC said my sentence was far too long and asked the judges to reduce it . . . but naw, they didn't seem to think me too hard done by. I left the courtroom with my hopes shattered. My QC said he was sorry for me and that somehow I'd just have to get on with it; then he shook my hand and left.

It was like being sentenced all over again. I wept, and almost cracked up – then I thought about escaping, and it made me feel better and helped me over my depression.

Part Two

16

The Draft to Hell

Peterhead Prison stood alone and dreary looking with its twisted granite walls and a high security fence – and I wished my dad and Jim were there to get me out. Before I knew it the massive electronic gate had closed behind us, cutting us off from the outside world. The turnkeys began removing the shackles from the prisoners as we drove through a series of prison gates to one of the halls. Country music was playing somewhere – I could hear guys singing and playing their guitars at their tiny cell windows. As we stepped out of the bus there was an exchange of banter before the turnkeys could silence it with their threats. They shouted to the guys to get back from their windows. A turnkey ran over to where the shouting came from, his face screwed up like he was giving the world a dirty look and defying someone to shout at him at close range. His eyes swept the row of windows, but no one answered him. He seemed satisfied, and walked back to where we were standing. Another steel door was opened and we were taken through to the punishment block and put into a small cell.

The cell into which six of us were locked was about eight feet long and six feet wide, with one piece of wood on hinges attached to the wall to form a bed. Someone nearby was screaming a torrent of abuse at the world. The cell door opened and I was taken to a small reception area and made to strip in front of six warders. They told me to bend over and spread my cheeks, which I did to mocking laughter. After we had changed and fed we were taken through to B Hall by some warders. It was decaying and haunted looking.

I heard a voice calling my name. It was one of my dad's friends, Big George. Big George was one of the guys who came to St Joseph's along with my dad when I was being abused by the brothers. He got one of the warders to open my door so that he could talk to me as I was his pal's son. Big George was powerfully built and as strong as an ox. He hadn't changed much since I first met him when I was 14 years old, back in 1970. As I was talking to him some other guys looked in and asked me how long I was doing and where I came from. Many of the cons knew my dad and had known me when I was a wee boy. 'How is your dad?' 'Is your wee maw still alive?' 'How are your uncles doing?' 'How is your Ma keeping?' 'Twelve years, you said?' 'Who did you kill?'

George, who was the bookie at Peterhead, got me a huge bag of sweets and some tobacco and soap and toothpaste. I was warned that the place had informers, and to be careful what I said to others. My dad had no enemies amongst the prisoners, he was well liked and respected, but he wasn't too popular amongst the warders, as I came to know. Coming from Peterhead and Aberdeen, the warders mocked prisoners from Glasgow for thinking of themselves as 'hard' men.

B Hall had been condemned and was out of use for years used only as a store, but now it held its human stock to full capacity. My cell was badly lit, and badly in need of a wash and a coat of paint. The concrete floor was cracked with age. On my first night I never slept a wink, but spent my time looking out of my window.

Some cells were known as 'iron lungs' – they were only seven foot long, and if you stood in the middle of the floor you could touch the walls on either side and the ceiling. Other cells were called 'Peters' – the code name for a safe or vault.

After a few days I was moved out of B Hall into D Hall. D Hall was much the same as B. In the middle of the floor was an old table-tennis table and a television set, and there was a hotplate from which food was served. That night in my cell I heard the wall next to my bed being knocked on. I went down to the pipe which ran through all the cells and called through the little gap. 'Is that Andy Steele's son?' a voice asked. Its owner's name was Rab, and he was a good friend of my dad's. He was in an 'iron lung' and had been since he arrived there.

The next day I was taken in front of an induction board to be allocated to a work party. The board consisted of the governor, a welfare officer, a psychiatrist and a few others. When I was asked where I would like to work I said the cookhouse, but was refused. They told me I would be going to Number 5 work party, the tailors' shop – the security party where the potential 'troublemakers' were housed for their work duty.

When the time came to go to work we were taken out to the exercise yard and lined up in our work parties. The warders shouted at us to get our hands out of our pockets, whether in hail, rain or snow. As each party was marched across the yard we were counted and re-counted. To get to work we had to walk in twos through a huge gate manned by warders, and past the football field. Next to the field was a hilly piece of land like a dump, and behind it was a brick shelter housing the toilets. There were little sentry boxes at strategic points around the field. The dirt road we walked down was known to all as the 'Burma Road'.

Some prisoners couldn't do their time and were put on the sort of medication which is given to psychiatric patients. They walked about like zombies, hardly knowing where they were or who they were. They were laughed at by others, but it was their way of surviving.

One day while I was brushing the floor in the tailors' shop a warder asked me if my dad had been in Aberdeen gaol. He then told the other warder who was with him that my dad was a fucking animal, and that he had put his finger up a warder's arse and run him around the gallery to humiliate him. During my tea break I asked the older cons if they knew anything about what I'd just heard. It was true, and there was more. I was told that he had made a spirits bomb and left it inside the hotplate where the warders dished out the food because they were giving such small rations to the prisoners. The bomb was meant to go off when the warders were standing round the hotplate, but there was no one near when it exploded.

They knew it was my dad, but they couldn't prove it. I

learned that he hated the warders and was forever threatening them with gelignite bombs. They seldom went out of their way to hassle him because they knew he meant what he said, and they feared him as a result. I was told that my dad had blown up a few places when on the outside, including a house on the South Side of Glasgow belonging to an informer who was giving evidence against one of his pals. A gelignite bomb was planted on the window ledge, and although it did terrible damage no one was in the house at the time. They said that if anyone needed explosives or guns and ammunition, my dad was the man to get them.

Some prisoners said the food at Peterhead was better than at Barlinnie, but that didn't mean it was any good. It was bad, and by the time it came from the cookhouse it was often cold. This used to cause trouble for the warders, and sometimes resulted in fights or a hunger strike. There were many work strikes as well: the prisoners would walk out, sometimes because there was no heating on the coldest of days, sometimes because a prisoner had been put on report by one of the warders. Strikes were common, and every day off work meant the loss of one day's remission or the cellblock for a spell. Other work parties would come out in sympathy and the warders and governors would brace themselves for serious trouble.

The warders often threatened us with 'Yi'll be ganging ben the hoose, loon!' – what they meant was 'You'll be going to the punishment block, lad'. The cellblock was their pride and joy, and if anyone stepped out of line they were sent there. Some guys were terrified because of its reputation. It stood on its own, a two-storey granite building with cells on one side only, eight cells on each floor. Solitary confinement was the main part of the punishment. It was a prison within a prison. It was rumoured that blood coated the walls from the beatings handed out there.

If we wished to make complaints about a warder or conditions, we had to request to see the governor, who would then investigate – and, if need be, give us a petition so that we could write to the Secretary of State for Scotland. Making such complaints could mean being locked up for making false allegations – even though they weren't false. There were often fights between prisoners and warders. If one was prepared to fight – or rather 'assault' – a warder, one had to accept the consequences: being charged with assault and beaten up by a gang of warders.

Tony Tamburrini was transferred to Peterhead and put into my hall. It was great to see him again. From my cell window on the fourth gallery, I got a great view of Peterhead harbour and the sea. I'd stand there for hours watching the ships in the distance and wish I was on them. But Tony and I soon started arguing over trivial things, and I decided it was best we parted friends rather than enemies.

Derek had a letter from my dad asking him to look after me and make sure I didn't get any hassle from anyone. He did his best to put some happiness into my life. He'd come into my cell with mugs of tea and ask me to sing the country songs he liked. We'd look at each other's photographs: like me, Derek was sentimental and whenever he spoke about his friends and family I could see the beggar within him come to the surface. His eyes would fill with tears, and mine would well up too. Derek made fun of it later by saying, 'We were sitting there crying like it was the end of the world.'

Derek was due to go down to Barlinnie on accumulated visits to see his missus and twin sons – in Peterhead a prisoner could save up enough visits to go to a gaol nearer his home and stay for a few weeks, and once the visits were finished he came back to Peterhead. The night before Derek left we swapped photographs: I gave him pictures of Ma, Maw, Brenda and my dad in exchange for pictures of his sons. Next morning he came into my cell with my mug of tea and some biscuits and we had a good talk and a few songs together, then he left for Barlinnie in his usual happy-go-lucky mood.

I never saw Derek again. He committed suicide in his cell soon after arriving at Barlinnie. It was hard to imagine that someone like Derek could hang himself. Most guys in Peterhead were shocked and saddened. I cried when I learned of Derek's death. The prisoners gathered a collection, donating money from their weekly earnings to help pay for the funeral as a sign of respect for Derek, but the governor refused to let the money out. A year later Derek's wife hanged herself in her home in Carntyne.

I was locked up in solitary confinement in December 1978 for attempting to escape. That weekend I had been out to the football field to see a guy I knew who was in another hall. He was playing football and I wanted an opportunity to talk to him before Monday morning. The football only lasted about half an hour because it was too cold. I came out of the granite toilets to find that the park was empty except for a few warders. They were relieved when they saw me.

'Where the fuck hiv you been, loon?' said one.

I was asked my name and when I said Steele I wasn't surprised to hear a warder say, 'Andy Steele's son?' They searched me and made me strip to my underwear. When they didn't find anything they took me to the punishment block.

They didn't know which cell to put me into – someone said I was to be taken upstairs, another asked who I was and why I was there. The place was deadly silent, but I knew there were prisoners around because I could see their bedding outside their cell doors. I was taken into a cell with two doors. The warders again stripped off all my clothes and searched them outside the cell, locking me in and leaving me naked.

The window in the cell was some six feet off the ground; the walls were damp with condensation and the paint peeling and bubbly; the roof was shaped like the roof of a wagon, resting on massive granite walls; the wooden bed was worn with age.

Every so often my cell door opened and the warders looked in and said that if I'd dug through the walls of the tunnel, I'd have been eaten alive by rats or that I'd have been suffocated by the gases from the sewer. Eventually I was told that I was on the governor's report for attempting to escape by digging a tunnel in the football field behind the toilets. Then the door opened and in came the governor with his warders.

'I've no doubt your father and the Paddens have put you up to trying to escape,' he said to me through clenched teeth, one hand gripped tightly round my arm. I denied their having anything to do with it, but he said he didn't believe me and that he knew what kind of family I came from. The governor said that I wasn't to have any books in my cell during the day. My bedding was taken from me during the day and given back at seven in the evening. I wasn't allowed my photos, nor any soap or shampoo. I was kept locked up for 23 hours a day, and it began to get to me.

'On yer feet, loon, for the governor's visit!' I stood to attention, which seemed to please the governor, who looked on with a grin.

I was taken before the prison visiting committee. Two men in their fifties and an older-looking woman were seated behind the governor's desk. I was made to stand before them and give my name, number and sentence. A warder stood on either side of me to restrain me should I make a wrong move. The woman had a hat on, which gave her a snobbish look – a typical little granny. Her wee beady eyes were all over me as I stood there in my slippers and grey uniform. I thought that she was eyeing me up for the kill . . .

The warders gave evidence that I had been attempting to escape, yet not one of them said he had seen me come out of or go into a tunnel, nor was a single witness produced to say that I had. After the evidence had been given I was told to wait outside while the committee came to its verdict! I hadn't been allowed to cross-examine any of the witnesses, and I was refused a lawyer to act on my behalf when I asked for one. It was all cut and dried, and I knew I would be found guilty. I was sentenced to 28 days' solitary confinement with no privileges, and forfeited 60 days of my remission. I asked for a petition to the Secretary of State, but was refused.

They had me on strict security; my clothes were put outside my door every night, and a light was left on. There were two ventilator systems in the cell, one of which was supposed to bring in hot air, the other fresh air; the vents had steel grilles over them and there were dead birds behind them which had fallen down from the loft above. I was allowed one blanket during the day to keep me warm. My shoes and jacket weren't allowed in my cell at any time. There were three exercise yards outside my window: each 'pen' had 16-foot-high walls with rolls of razor wire along the top.

In the halls prisoners are exercised indoors during inclement weather, but in the punishment block it's outside or nothing. We weren't allowed to talk out of our windows or to each other during exercise. The warders made a point of being strict so as to put us off going back again. During slop-out a group of warders watched me at all times and followed me wherever I went. 'Hurry up, loon!' they'd say as I filled my basin and slopped out my pisspot, but I always took my time because the longer I was out of the cell, the better I felt.

One morning the warder who had told me about my dad putting his finger up his pal's arse in Aberdeen gaol told me to put my bedding and blankets outside the door. I folded up the blankets neatly and hung them over the railings. The warders pulled them off and threw them onto the floor, saying they weren't folded well enough; then they stood in front of me, chewing gum in an exaggerated way. I picked up the blankets, threw them over the gallery and told them that they could fold them themselves if they weren't satisfied. Other warders came running up to see what was going on, and they all attacked me. After this I refused to take in my mattress and blankets. They were furious about this because they wouldn't be able to come in at six in the morning to take my bedding off me. I was freezing that night.

When Ma wrote and asked me how I was keeping I told her I was fine and that she wasn't to worry. Sometimes I got a letter from Maw which was written for her by Brenda, and I always became emotional and had a good cry fearing that I would never see her outside again. My mind was made up. I couldn't possibly get through this sentence in one piece, it was fucking killing me. At nights I would get up and pace the floor in my bare feet and smoke one hand-rolled smoke after the other, plotting or reminiscing about my past.

A few days after I came off punishment, Archie, who'd been suspected of trying to escape, was thrown into the security party. We sat together in the tailors' shop and discussed our experiences. Like me, he had been brutalised in the cells, so we decided we would do something about it. Archie, Davy, Wee Smiddy and I decided to wreck the punishment block, which was the warders' pride and joy, and so ruin their cushy job of locking up and beating up the prisoners. All the others in the security party were aware of what was going to happen and helped in whatever ways they could, giving us tobacco and sweets and biscuits and other odds and ends that would come in handy in case we were up on the roof for a few days. Some of them encouraged us to burn it to the ground, others thought we were crazy for doing something that would only get us into serious trouble.

It was six below zero when we stormed the cellblock through the roof. The snow made it difficult to walk on the slates with our haversacks on our backs. Once on the roof we started smashing the skylight windows with iron bars and ripping up the slates and throwing them down into the yard below. It felt great. Through the broken skylights I watched the warders panicking and shouting, unsure what was happening. It must have sounded as though there were a hundred men on the roof.

We smashed through the wood under the slates and climbed down into the loft to shelter from the warders in the yard who were throwing bricks at us, and we lit a small fire there. We could hear the others shouting from their cell windows, roaring at us to burn down the torture chamber that so many of them had suffered in.

We stayed up there for three days and nights, tearing the place apart, like madmen, and doing as much damage as we could. At night we gathered round the fire and talked about our families and our pasts.

The main governor had been away when we first went on the roof, and only came back a few hours before we came down. In fact it was he who talked us down. We had taken down the barricades, and were throwing boulders at anyone who tried to come in, when he came walking in shouting, 'Hold your fire!' We did, and he marched up the staircase and onto the gallery, looking up at us looking down at him through a huge hole in the wall. He told us to come down and give him a list of our complaints, but we refused, thinking it was a trap. He then told us to come down one at a time and talk to him. There were no lights working in the cells, but a warder who was with the governor had a torch which he shone on our faces as we went down to say our piece, climbing down a makeshift rope onto the mountains of rubble and bricks on the gallery.

We sat together on the rubble, and I told him that I was rioting because I'd been framed by the warders over the escape charge, that I couldn't cope with the length of my sentence or the prison regime, and that it was easier and less painful for me to rebel than accept.

When we'd all seen the governor we sat round our little fire and decided what we should do; and then, late at night, we came down. They took us over to the surgery, where we all shook hands as we parted, never knowing if we'd see each other again. It was the parting that hurt, more than surrendering. For the three days and nights that we were up in the loft we had all four become really friendly and close.

The governor had told the warders that if anyone put a hand on us they'd be charged with assault. He meant it, and they knew it and were furious, but they were too scared to say anything to him — which was why many prisoners liked and admired him. I heard the warders complaining to each other about the governor's attitude: they wanted to break our bones for what we had done, yet this man prevented them. He told the warders to make sure that we were all bathed and fed; he put a special guard on our doors, and warned the warders that if anyone got into our cells to beat us up the warder in charge of the cells would be held responsible. The warders had to make us ham, eggs and tea at three o'clock in the morning!

We were guaranteed that there'd be no beatings, but as was only to be expected, they kicked me about the cell over in the surgery. Before I was beaten up I was given a medical examination by the surgery warder, who was looking for cuts and bruises that I may have got when I was on the roof. Then I was taken upstairs to join the others. The cells in the surgery had steel grilles as well as thick wooden doors, and as I was dragged to a cell I passed Smiddy and Davy, naked and filthy black, standing behind their steel grilles, looking out at me. Smiddy had his leg through the steel grille, trying to kick the warders.

Every day in my cell I sat by the window and looked out to sea, reminiscing as usual. I imagined I was at home and sitting at the fireside with Maw and Ma, and I'd sing to them too – it helped me through the hard days. When I wasn't singing I was plotting and scheming as I paced up and down the little cell floor, my hands behind my back. I must have walked miles this way: I'd take six paces forward and stop inches from the wall, turn around and take another six paces back. I became so used to it that I could do it with my eyes shut so I could rest as I walked. I ate even less, and I only picked at my food.

Every now and then an urge to commit suicide would come over me while I was eating, or reading a newspaper, or thinking about home. It was like something clinging to my back: I'd try to shake it off in a blind panic, and a voice in my head would be shouting, 'Naw! Naw! Naw! Don't do it!' I'd run back from my cell window so that I wouldn't hang myself with my sheets. I couldn't get away: I was trapped in my little cell, which seemed to get even smaller. A voice in my head was shouting for me to press my bell and alert the warders, but I knew that if they saw me in this state of mind they would send me to a mental hospital. I panicked even more at the thought of going there to vegetate and die inside. I only managed to come to my senses when I thought of escaping – it was like a safety valve.

The visiting committee came to see us in the surgery in January 1979. The chairman was a youngish-looking woman and they all eyed me as I came into the room. Again I was refused a lawyer. I listened to the warders giving their evidence, indifferent to what they said about me. The whole exercise was pointless, as I knew I would be found guilty. I even thought it was funny to hear the warders take the oath on the bible and swear by almighty God to tell the truth.

I was found guilty. The chairman thought it terrible that I had recently been in front of a committee for attempting to escape. I would have to suffer the consequences of taking part in a riot which had caused some £30,000 worth of damage to prison property. I was to forfeit 365 days' remission and sentenced to a further 28 days solitary with no smoking or wages, and a fine of £25. On my way out one of them said, 'Let this be a lesson to you.'

We all got the same sentence, and they took us back to the cellblock to serve out our punishment. It didn't take long for them to repair the cells, as they felt insecure when they were not in use. The noise of hammering and drilling was deafening.

One morning the warders came in and held me spread-eagled on the concrete floor. One of them stood on my belly with all his weight and told me I was just a silly little boy. The madness came over me and I laughed in their rotten faces, and told them I would get the last laugh. I heard Archie, Davy and Wee Smiddy shouting and banging on their doors and the warders left me to attend to them.

Whenever they brought me my food one of them would hold the plates while the others stood by, ready to attack if I made a move. 'Thanks, arsehole,' I'd say, so they stopped handing me my food and left the plates on the ground. I knew they sometimes spat in my food as I could see the spittle. They probably hadn't been too pleased when they recovered their kettle from the loft to discover someone had shat in it.

A few days later the governor came on his rounds, and I heard him screaming from one of the cells above me. Apparently he was attacked by and had got into a fight with one of the prisoners, and had been slashed on the neck. I could hear all the warders shouting and kicking the guy. There was pandemonium in the cellblock, and warders were running in and out in a panic. We all began banging and kicking on our cell doors, yelling at them to leave the guy alone. The governor was shouting at us at the top of his voice to shut up. The prisoner had to have stitches in a wound on his face where he had been slashed during the fight, and the governor had two butterfly stitches in the back of his neck. The governor then came to my door with a mob of warders who looked as if they were dying to give out more beatings. He had his battered hat in his hand and his tie was open as if he needed air; he was shaken and white looking as he screamed at me, 'Don't you imagine that your dad or the

Paddens frighten me, Steele!' He started shouting that he would fight anyone – he was getting more furious by the minute. Then he went away and threatened a few others in the cells nearby.

For weeks all the talk in the gaol was of the incident, but the whole thing was hushed up by the authorities.

17

Back with a Vengeance

Back in circulation with the other prisoners I didn't feel any better; this seemed just as bad as solitary confinement. I couldn't go anywhere without guys commenting on how pale and thin I was. One of my dad's pals gave me some vitamin pills, saying they would help.

About this time, Jim had been tried for shooting a guy with a sawn-off shotgun in the pub in Garthamlock. There had been an argument in the pub which led to him being shot. He was found guilty and sentenced to 12 years. I was in the exercise yard when I saw him come out of the hall towards me. I was all choked up, but I tried my best to hide it.

I told him what had happened to me since my arrival, and he said he wasn't going to stand for their bullshit and their wanting to torment us because of what our dad had done in the past. Although he was only 18 months older than I was, Jim tended to treat me as though it was 18 years: he was the typical big brother.

One evening the warders were in my cell going through everything twice while I stood in the gallery being searched. All the other prisoners were locked in their cells. One of the warders told me to take my clothes off and bend over so that he could look up my arse. I refused and the other two came out of my cell and threatened me with violence if I didn't do what I was told. I wanted to attack the bastards but I started laughing at them and they went back in again. When they came out of my cell smiling deviously I knew I was going to the cellblock for something – and that 'something' was a prison rules and regulation book.

The next morning the governor asked me what I was

doing with another prisoner's rule book, and I said I was reading it. 'You can't even cope with the rules in society,' he bawled. 'What chance do you think you have of coping in here?' I never answered.

The governor was transferred to Barlinnie Prison as the number one governor of Scottish gaols. Before he left he told me that he was a specialist in breaking the spirits of would-be hard men like me.

There had been a lot of tension in the gaol – many of the prisoners were getting unnecessary hassle and there was much talk about rioting and killing the warders. At first Jim, Archie, Smiddy and I thought of escaping, but then we decided to riot and try to stop the brutality and witless persecution.

I went to Big George, the bookie, and asked him for 20 ounces of tobacco for the 'hold-out' in the cellblock after we had stormed it. Most of the prisoners knew what was going to happen and, as before, many of them wished us luck and offered to help in any little way. We were given iron bars, sweets, tobacco and tinned meat. The gaol was alive with excitement and I felt good – this was better than bare existence any day. At slop-out I talked to Archie and Frank and Jim in my cell. We had all we needed and were satisfied with the way things were going.

When we met in the exercise yard we all had iron bars under our coats. Even the gaol informers wanted us to destroy the cells, and some of them even wished us all the best!

As soon as most of those involved in the riot were in the yard, about ten of us pulled out our iron bars and chased the warders away while we walked round to the back of B Hall to get onto the roof of some sheds there. The warders ran away in terror, screaming, and it felt great to watch them go. There were rolls of razor wire behind B Hall to prevent anyone from getting onto the roof, but I got through them without much difficulty and the others threw their coats and jackets over them and walked across. By now riot bells were ringing in every part of the gaol and all the warders had come rushing

to the yard, but when they saw our weapons they kept their
distance. We climbed onto the long workshed roof alongside
B Hall, which led to the corridor roof and the punishment
block. Everyone was at their window, cheering us and
dropping food, sweets and woollen jumpers from their
windows. Some prisoners became so excited that they broke
their windows and furniture. We started smashing the shed
roof and the old picture house which contained the church,
the chapel and the gymnasium. Jim and Archie were on the
punishment block roof, and I could hear them shouting down
to the warders in the exercise yard and throwing slates at
them. I climbed up a drainpipe onto the roof of B Hall –
somehow I got through the rolls of razor wire that were
wrapped round it without a scratch. Once on the roof I could
see the warders in the yard, who were furious when they saw
me up there with my iron bar, smashing the skylight windows
and slates. I could hear guys shouting, 'Johnnyboy is on the
roof!' and a cheer went up from the guys who were locked in
their cells in B Hall. The warders tried to knock me off by
throwing stones and turning on their power hoses. Breeny
managed to get onto the roof with me. Before I knew it, it
was getting dark. The warders, in their protective gear, were
everywhere, even on the corridor roof below, and they had
trapped the others in the loft of the punishment block, pelting
them with bricks and stones and concentrating their power
hoses on them if they tried to come out of the hole they had
made on the roof.

Breeny and I had no food or tobacco with us, and we
couldn't get off the roof to join the others. We couldn't even
get into the loft in B Hall because it was full of warders.
They came to the loft door and tried to sweet-talk us down.
Breeny wanted to give himself up, but I tried to discourage
him by telling him they would smash his head in. The
warders heard me say this, and they told him not to pay any
attention to what I was saying. I could tell Breeny was in two
minds. He decided to give himself up to the warders in B
Hall at the loft door; we shook hands before he left, and he
gave me his jacket. I could see over the wall to the quarters
where the warders lived: I could see their families at their

windows, and some even sitting on the roof to get a better view of what was going on. They also had flash lamps which they shone on the roofs so as to keep an eye on me.

'Okay! I'm surrendering!' I said, jumping up and raising my hands above my head to let them know I had no weapons. As I climbed onto the top of the drainpipe, which was well greased to prevent anyone climbing it, I saw warders coming out of the loft door to try to stop me, so I slid down till I reached the rolls of razor wire. I got tangled up in the wire while the warders below were laughing and rubbing their hands with glee, but I managed to get back onto the drainpipe and tore my clothes from the wire.

I walked along the ridge of the workshed roof, trying to look defeated and dejected. To my left were the prisoners and to my right the warders. I told them that I was giving myself up to them as I didn't trust the others. This seemed to please them, and they coaxed me on. I kept walking till I reached the end of the long roof and then stepped onto the corridor roof. I could hardly contain my laughter as the warders made way. I turned to the left and walked to the hole in the roof, where the boys were cheering and patting me on the back. The warders were furious and began shouting at each other for letting me get away so easily – and then they started throwing stones and turning the hoses on us.

I was livid when I heard there were still guys locked in their cells below us, and that the warders had no intention of letting them out. There were about 60 warders in riot gear on the bottom floor, waiting for us to come down. I climbed down to the gallery and barricaded the stairs so they couldn't get up, then I looked in at the cell doors to see who was there. The guy who had slashed the governor was still there, and another guy was up to his knees in water – the warders had aimed one of the power hoses through his cell window after he'd smashed the glass with an iron bar which Smiddy had passed him through the ventilator system from the loft. Further along I found a prisoner fast asleep, so I banged on the door to wake him up. He was known as 'The Bear', and he had been getting treatment from the gaol doctor – something called Largactyl, which leaves people like zombies. It took me about ten minutes to wake up this poor guy. He had a massive beard, his hair was unruly and matted, and he didn't even know there was a riot going on. I told him I would break him out of his cell but he didn't want out, all he wanted was some tobacco, and when I gave him some through the spy-hole he thanked me and went back to bed. I felt sorry for him – he was mentally dead inside. I then went to help the other guy out of his flooded cell. I smashed away at the door from my side, while he did the same from his.

Jim shouted at me to come back onto the roof as the new governor was in the yard and wanted to talk to me. He was standing in the yard below there with his umbrella, looking like he was posing for a photo. We threw slates at him and at the warders, who galloped away across the yard, then we started singing 'I Belong to Glasgow'. The warders turned on the power hoses, so it was back to work inside for me. I managed to get the guy out of his flooded cell, and we took his cell door off and threw it over the gallery. Up in the loft, we fed him and gave him some dry clothes. Then we went out onto the roof to let them see that we had broken the guy out of his cell, displaying him like a trophy.

Again I looked over the gallery and saw the warders beneath us in their riot gear. They had commandeered an empty cell on the ground floor where they made coffee and tea. I edged down the stairs so as to count them, and they stared at me in disbelief for having the audacity to venture so close to them. Jim and Archie told me to be careful in case they got hold of me, but I knew that if they tried to rush me I'd have been back on the roof before they were halfway up the stairs. To get back into the loft I climbed a sheet rope that hung from one of the rafters through a hole in the wall. We decided that the only way we'd get the warders out of the cells was by hurling down at them the thousand or so bricks we had at our disposal.

Most of our food had been ruined by the hoses or was underneath the rubble. I suggested to the warders that they could have the remaining prisoners in the cells in exchange for food and bandages and some antiseptic lotion. They said they would have to phone the prison department to ask permission and would let us know later.

From the roof we could see a dozen or so newspaper reporters and cameramen outside the gaol, shouting up to us to ask what it was all about. We shouted back that we were rioting because of harsh conditions and brutality – but we couldn't talk to them for long because the warders kept throwing stones at us. A light airplane was circling overhead, and we could see a TV camera in the window. We listened to radio reports, according to which the authorities had estimated the damage at £1 million.

The warders told us they could agree to the exchange we'd suggested. We demanded the food and medicine first, and it was delivered to us. A surgery warder brought over the bandages and lotion and had a good look at my bruises and cuts. He told me I needed an injection in case I had poisoned my bloodstream, but I refused, so he cleaned up my wounds and bandaged some of the deeper ones. All the time he was cleaning my wounds he kept telling me what a nice guy I was and how silly I was to be rioting.

We let two warders come upstairs to take the guys out of their cells. They were obviously terrified, but we assured them they would come to no harm as long as the others below didn't try anything. The Bear came out of his cell and laughed when he saw the mess the cellblock was in.

After this we got ready to attack the warders on the ground floor with bricks, iron bars and anything else that was handy. It felt as though we were in some housing estate doing battle with another gang – the only difference being that we knew we wouldn't win.

Jim, Archie, Frank, Joe, Wee Smiddy and I climbed down the sheet rope quietly, our iron bars strapped to our bodies. I was the first down and I crept along the gallery, straining my ears for the warders below me. They were boasting about the overtime they were getting from our misery and bragging about what they were going to do to us once they got us down. As soon as we were all down from the loft, we leaned over the railings of the gallery and started hurling bricks at the panic-stricken warders, who ran back and forth with their shields above their heads to protect them. The noise was deafening. Some of the warders tried to fight back, but many of them ran out of the double doors and stayed there. When we saw this we headed for the staircase and made our way down, swiping at the warders as we went. We didn't know it then, but it seemed that the whole gaol could hear the battle, including the reporters on the other side of the wall.

Eventually we drove all the warders out. In their hurry to get away, some of them dropped their riot shields and sticks and we took them onto the roof with us to show them off. About half an hour later a newsflash on the radio reported that we had been seen on the roof with warders' riot gear. The authorities told the reporters that we must have found the riot gear in a cupboard, and we had a good laugh at this.

To our surprise, about 60 guys in B Hall began rioting when they were opened up for exercise. They threw furniture over the galleries and barricaded the one set of stairs in the hall, and they planned to get on the half-wrecked roof and destroy it completely. They forgot to barricade the doors on the galleries that led through to the adjacent hall and the riot squad stormed in and beat up anyone in sight.

The first we knew of all this was when Joe, who was watching the warders through a hole in the loft with a pair of binoculars he had found, told us that Ronnie and others were on the roof of B Hall. We were all really glad to get some support – particularly as the warders had told us earlier that the other prisoners weren't interested in us and were all perfectly happy. Although some of the guys in my loft hadn't got on too well with some of those in B Hall, the guys on the B Hall roof were suddenly our best pals in the world.

One of the double doors below us was open and the warders were hiding behind a steel mesh, shining powerful lamps through into the darkness. They had a power hose on, which made it almost impossible to get down the stairs. I managed to climb down with some others, and we crept along the gallery until we reached the far wall, directly above the double doors. I was carrying an iron bar shaped like a golf club, and I leaned over the gallery railings and smashed at the lamps through the steel mesh. Frank held onto my legs to stop me from falling as I swung wildly with my club.

At the far end of the ground floor, near the reception door, was a huge wooden cupboard in which the warders kept property belonging to the prisoners who were on punishment. We needed it to barricade the double doors and prevent the power hose from hitting us, so that we could get into reception and collect our personal clothing which was stored there. Jim, Frank and Archie agreed to try to move the cupboard provided I somehow kept the hose away. So, with Joe holding onto my legs, I hung almost upside-down over the railings, and swung my iron club at the observation panel through which the warders aimed the hose. I don't know whether I hit the warder behind the panel, but he dropped the hose, which fell inside, soaking them. Then I jammed a plank of wood into the observation panel and held it there till the others had managed to move the cupboard. I laughed when I heard the warders cursing and trying to smash the plank of wood so as to get the hose through the panel. When I looked to see what the others were doing at the far end, all I could see was a huge cupboard moving towards me. I heard the warders grumbling when they saw what we were up to: they withdrew the hose and we put the cupboard door in front of the double doors.

Negotiations began and we were promised a public inquiry into brutality if we came down. Some of the guys wanted to agree, but others, including me, told the warders to fuck off and said that they should get our MPs and lawyers in to see us first.

We put on our own clothes and felt like human beings again, but before I changed I had a bath in the huge water tank in the loft, washing myself with a bar of gaol soap and a floor scrubber and singing for all the warders to hear. I was joined by Wee Smiddy, who came for a swim. After my bath I went onto the roof with the others.

The new governor asked to speak to us on the roof, so we went out and listened to him. He told us that he might be able to get a lawyer in from Peterhead to see us, and that he would be there when we came down to make sure there was no brutality. I told the governor I wanted my own lawyer from Glasgow and Jim shouted that he wanted Perry Mason.

Some time later the lawyer from Peterhead came into the exercise yard to speak to us and listen to our complaints. He said he could guarantee that there'd be no brutality if we came down now, and that he'd talk to us in our cells. We went back into the loft and argued amongst ourselves. For four or five days we'd been in control of the cellblock – the guys in B Hall had given themselves up earlier because they were cold, wet and hungry. Brian, who was serving life, wanted to give himself up, reckoning enough damage had been done, and Joe thought the same, and then Jim, then Frank . . . I wanted to stay: I knew I'd get a beating from the warders, and it was better up here than down below. Smiddy also wanted to stay, as did the guy I'd helped to break out, and Archie and Mac, whom I'd known in Larchgrove, and Tam, my wee pal from St Joseph's. There was no vote taken on it – we each just made up our own mind – but the atmosphere on the roof had changed now that some of us were going down.

We went back onto the roof and Jim told the lawyer they were coming down with the assurance of no brutality. The lawyer sounded pleased at this, and must have assumed that Jim was speaking on behalf of all of us. A ladder was put up against the front of the building to enable us to come down into the exercise yard. We all shook hands and wished each other the best. I had tears in my eyes as I watched Jim going down the ladder. When those who wanted to go had disappeared from sight, we went back into the loft and sat about smoking, straining our ears to hear any screams – but they never came.

'What about the rest of you?' the governor called up to us. I went out onto the roof and there he was, standing in a military posture and holding his umbrella. I told him to fuck off, and he told the warders to take up their positions again.

Back inside, I began smashing everything in sight. The next thing I knew thick smoke was making its way into the loft, suffocating us. I could hear the warders shouting, 'Die, you bastards!' I wrapped a wet rag around my mouth to prevent me from inhaling dangerous fumes. The smoke was so thick I could hardly see in front of me as I staggered about, groping for the hole in the roof. Archie and the guy I broke out of the flooded cell with managed to get out and surrendered to the warders. I eventually found the hole, but when I tried to climb out the bastards started throwing stones at me and turned on the hose. I was choking in the smoke; I could hear Smiddy choking too as he groped for a way out, and I pulled him to the floor where the smoke wasn't as dense. By this time the warders were on the roof above, shouting that we weren't so fucking tough now. We crawled under the huge water tank, hoping the smoke wouldn't be so thick there, but it was; I could feel pains in my chest when I breathed in, and I was afraid I was going to die.

I don't know how long we were trapped up there in the smoke, but eventually I felt myself being dragged through water and onto the rafters. I felt I was dreaming when I opened my eyes and saw the warders holding me, and I felt so tired that I only wanted to rest. It hurt to breathe, and although I could feel the breeze on my face, that high-pitched sound in my ears warned me that I was going to pass out.

When I reached the bottom rung other warders in riot gear put my arms up my back and frog-marched me towards B Hall. Suddenly I was sorry for having got involved in the riot, and I wanted to scream that I was sorry. As I saw them all standing there in the gauntlet fashion, I panicked at the thought of what lay ahead for me. I saw them raise their riot sticks and move towards me. I cursed them and challenged them.

I came in to an empty cell. I still had my own suit and shoes on. They came crashing in on me with their sticks and shields. I thought I was in for another beating and I panicked. Two of them were hanging over me with knives, while the others held my legs and hands. I thought they were going to kill me. I tried to move but I couldn't. They started slashing my suit with their knives, ripping at it as though they were plucking a chicken.

That night there was much talking and shouting under cell doors to each other. I heard Jim, Archie, Joe, Frank and the others calling my name, and it echoed throughout the hall.

I got myself to my feet and limped up and down the small cell holding onto the wall for support. My legs were black and blue and covered with cuts. Painful as it was, I kept on moving. I had hardly slept all the time I was on the roof, and had seldom stopped smashing walls. My body was wrecked, but my mind wouldn't let me rest.

A few days later Mac called me to the pipe and told me that Ma was on the front page of the newspaper, claiming her sons had been brutalised. I got the newspaper from him and there was a photograph of Ma below huge headlines. I loved her for this and felt sorry for her at the same time; I cried as I read her words: 'I know my boys are no angels,' she said, and then went on to say that we weren't animals either. The warders were furious at Ma's allegation. Some of the guys said they could taste the piss in their soup.

We were taken out to see the prison doctor for an 'examination'. He sat at a table in the middle of the hall, surrounded by rubble and broken glass. 'Any complaints?' he asked as I limped towards him, but before I could answer the warders took me back to my cell. He did the same with nearly everyone that day, yet there he was in the newspaper next day denying any evidence of brutality!

A few weeks later the visiting committee came to the gaol and gave us a mock trial. Just before the visiting committee arrived, one of the governors had put notices up to the effect that the rioters on the roof were responsible for destroying the prisoners' property. This didn't bode well for our getting a fair hearing from the visiting committee. The notice was later taken down and smuggled out to my dad, who took it to his lawyer along with other complaints.

When it was my turn to go into the orderly room to face the charges, I asked for a lawyer to represent me, and again I was refused. The charges were read, but I shut my ears to them and to the evidence. I knew what the outcome would be. I lost a further two years' remission from my sentence, which meant that I would have to do 11 years out of my 12. I was also locked up in solitary for 28 days and told that Rule

36 was to apply after that. Rule 36 means that a prisoner is kept locked up in his cell for 23 hours a day.

The Procurator Fiscal set up an internal inquiry into the allegations of brutality, and some warders were charged with assault. My dad visited me, but there wasn't much I could say because warders were standing behind me listening to everything we said. Jim was there too, and we both sat in the same box talking to my dad, who couldn't conceal his rage and hatred for the warders. He threatened them with murder and mayhem, but they only smiled. This so antagonised my dad that he turned to his pal and said, 'If you see any of their subhuman kids in the street, just run the bastards over!'

They weren't laughing now – one of them ran to get the governor. They asked my dad to step outside for a moment, and we could hear him telling them they had made a mistake in fucking his sons about. A senior warder stormed into the visiting room shouting, 'Terminate this visit!' and called Jim and me 'bastards'. Jim spat at the warders, picked up a chair and tried to smash the unbreakable glass to get through to the governor. I started trying to kick in the glass too, but I soon stopped to help Jim, who was being attacked. One of the warders pressed the riot bell and the visiting room was filled with their pals, who dragged us away and kicked us down the corridor.

I woke up in my cell and could hear Mac calling through the pipes, 'Are you in there, Johnnyboy?'

I was covered in blood from my nose. At first I thought I was bleeding elsewhere, so I stripped off my clothes and looked my body over, but there were only bruises. Mac told me I had been screaming in pain and had been lying there for several hours. A warder gave me a basin of water and soap to clean myself up.

I was taken in front of the governor, who took more remission from me and told me I would not be allowed visits at the same time as Jim.

One night I felt an uncontrollable urge to kill myself. I thought it was all over for me, then I snapped and pressed the bell, desperate to get out of that cell. In a blind panic, I wrecked the windows and what little furniture there was, and

I tried to smash down the door, like a man with superhuman strength. Once I had calmed down, the warders took me to the cellblock, where they threw me into a cell and slammed two thick doors behind me. This was the first time I had been in the notorious silent cell, and I stood there in the dark, straining my eyes. It was different from any other cell in that the window was on the roof and hardly let in any light. I could hear my own breathing, but nothing else. I felt my way around the damp-smelling cell until I reached a block of wood, rotten with age. That was my bed.

When I was moved back to the punishment block we made the best of the worst and rioted in our cells and threw our piss and shit out the doors for the warders to clean up. After a while the riot squad was sent in, and I heard them going from cell to cell; I listened to the screams and thuds and threats. When my cell door opened, I saw only a mattress – behind which the warders rushed, pushing me up against the wall while others cleaned out my cell, throwing broken tables and chairs and glass over the gallery. I tried to get out from behind the mattress but they held me all the harder, almost embedding me in the wall. They kicked me on the legs till I fell to the floor, and then handcuffed my arms up my back. My only weapon was my tongue, and I used it. They made me pay for that too. Before I passed out I heard one of the warders shouting that they should leave me alone or they'd kill me.

My fingers were numb from the tightness of the handcuffs. Whenever I moved my arms or hands, I cried out in pain. My handcuffs were removed at dinnertime; my hands were swollen, and I rubbed them gently under my armpits till the feeling came back into them.

The smell in my cell was really bad. I had been peeing and shitting on the floor and leaving it for the warders to clear up. They had to hold their breath when they opened the door.

I had been kept locked up for six months, like most of the others. The governor told me I would be going back into circulation and that I would have to go into an 'iron lung' until a larger cell was available. A Hall was closed for renovation, so I was put back into D Hall. I was glad to see some guys I knew and to talk to them again, and I was given sweets, tobacco and the like by my pals. I was shown to my 'iron lung' by a warder who laughed and joked as if I was his best pal. I took the chair out of the 'iron lung', left it in the gallery outside my door on the second floor, and refused to take it back: the cell was small enough without a chair in it.

I became pally with a new guy called Thomas, and before I came off security we were sawing through his cell bars with a hacksaw. Thomas had no intention of escaping, but he wanted to help us escape and was prepared to cut his bars. The warders told me they needed my cell for someone else, so they moved me into Thomas's cell, where the two of us worked slowly and carefully on the bars at the weekends and sometimes during recreation, when the hall was noisy and busy. The hotplate was outside our cell door and the warders would often sleep on top of it to keep warm. We tried rubbing oil on the blades to keep down the noise and that helped some. The guys in the cells nearby knew what we were up to, so they'd play their music loud to cover the noise of cutting. On one occasion I asked Thomas if he was prepared to come out into the hall with me and bring our guitars to sing for everyone, and all the while we could have one of the guys sawing the bars for us and the warders would be none the wiser. He thought it was a great idea and so we dressed up like western singers and went out and mingled with the other prisoners while Frank sawed away at the cell bars. It was working fine, for all the prisoners and warders gathered around and laughed and cheered. But the warder in charge of the hall became suspicious, his eyes everywhere. I noticed, as I sat there singing, that he told the other warders to keep their eyes open and then they too moved about the hall suspiciously. So that was the end of our concert.

A fight broke out early one morning in which Frank and Thomas were involved. When they were taken away to the cells I was left to cut the bars by myself. The day after the fight the warder in charge of the hall came into my cell and told me he was glad I was settling down. I played along with him, though it was hard to keep myself from laughing: little did he know that he was sitting in a cell with half the bars cut through. He was even sitting on the hacksaw blade, which was glued to the bottom of the bed. I had to lower my head when I felt a smile spreading over my face. The governor and the warders thought that my not getting involved in the fight was proof that my spell in the punishment block had paid off, and that I was settling down.

18

Homeward Bound

Jim and Archie were going to Barlinnie on accumulated visits.
I decided I would go with them, if I could, and come back
with some new hacksaw blades. Before I left I painted the cell
bars and filled in the cuts with woodfiller. I did a good job and
I felt sure it would pass inspection.

It was great to see Ma again with my sisters, Lana and
Brenda, and of course my dad. We had a family reunion in two
small cubicles, smaller than telephone boxes, with a sheet of
armour-plated glass and wire mesh to separate us. Soon after
we arrived at Barlinnie and I got some new hacksaw blades
from my dad, a guy from Peterhead was brought down. At
Peterhead Big Tony did repairing jobs – mending and painting
and rewiring – and even though he was a trustee we trusted
him and knew he would never grass on any of us. When we
met he looked kind of worried, and then he told me that the
warders at Peterhead had found my half-cut cell bars – he had
been there when they welded them back together. My heart
was in my mouth and I expected a hand to fall on my shoulder
at any moment. I felt much better when Big Tony told me that
he had learned from some of the warders that they weren't
going to have me arrested at Barlinnie; they'd get me when I
stepped off the bus back at Peterhead. I was going to have to
escape from Barlinnie.

With a few others we could trust we tried to figure out the
best way to escape. I knew there was a hatch leading onto the
roof in a cupboard-like room in the top gallery showers. The
door had only a Yale lock, and sometimes it was left open so
that prisoners could regulate the water. In the ceiling was a
steel-barred gate with a security padlock on it. Above that was
a wooden door leading to the roof. To one side of the room

was a shaft with pipes going down to the ground floor.

We had found a way out – now we had to figure a way off the roof and over the wall. There were many ideas bounced about and rejected.

We told my dad what we had in mind and he said he would help us, though he wasn't too happy about me and Jim wanting to escape. Broono came to see us with his wife, and he too wanted to help get us out. We saw and spoke to Alex Howatt each day. It was great to hear that Alex, a pal from way back, had started cutting through the padlock on the steel gate. During recreation he and his pals would say they wanted a shower, and while the shower was running one sawed the padlock, another watched out for warders while pretending to wait his turn at the shower, and another pretended to be mopping the floor. But the teeth of the hacksaw blade wouldn't grip and it kept slipping, so Alex decided to burst the padlock off with an iron bar. He took most of its insides out, but still it wouldn't budge.

Although they sometimes only got five minutes' work done in one night, because other prisoners were in the vicinity, Alex wouldn't give up. He was aware that the warders at Peterhead would be waiting for us on our return. In the end he told us the padlock wouldn't come off – his hands were almost raw from handling it – and that he would have to saw through one of the bars on the steel gate.

The day before we were due to escape we came back from recreation and went into the dining hall for tea. My heart was pounding and my belly turned at the thought that Alex and his pals might have been caught. Then I saw Alex come in and as he passed our table he gave us the thumbs-up sign.

'God bless ye, Alex,' I thought as he passed by. We were all happy now and winking at each other. I couldn't eat a bit of food.

Next morning – Sunday, 22 June 1980 – I was up and waiting when the warders opened my cell door. The sun was shining brightly and the world wasn't such a bad-looking place after all. I brought my clothes in and got ready fast. Jim came in to ask me if everything was okay, and I said it was. He had decided to walk upstairs to the top floor: I couldn't risk following him in case the warders stopped us, so I had to rely on him or Archie coming down the shaft from the top floor and opening the Yale lock from the inside.

Jim went upstairs and I joined some other prisoners who were carrying their pisspots and towels and shaving gear. I stood by the cupboard door, and after a while I heard a slight rapping. A warder was standing nearby with his legs apart and his arms folded, chewing gum. He kept looking at me, and I was worried that he would stay there till slop-out was over. I hadn't much time left; in a few moments breakfast would be brought into the hall. Prisoners were coming and going with their pots, and still the warder stood there. I saw my pal Aldo at a sink, pretending to shave, and I asked him to distract the warder. Aldo stood up and stared at the warder, who began to shift nervously from one foot to the other. I threw a tantrum and told him to go and get me the fucking governor as I wasn't taking any more from him and his staring. It worked, and the warder walked away. I shook hands with Aldo and entered the cupboard, locking the door behind me.

It was pitch black in there. I could hear sinks being filled and prisoners talking, Jim's and Archie's voices coming down the shaft. I climbed into the shaft and went up fast, groping for holds. The dust almost choked me. I could smell the dry wood as I climbed up. When I reached the fourth gallery, Jim and Archie pulled me out and into the cupboard. I squeezed through the cut bar; then I crouched on the steel gate and put my back to the wooden door a foot or so above me. I managed to open it, and the sun lit up the little cupboard.

I climbed out onto the flat roof at the end of the hall and could see for miles and miles. I sat there marvelling at the view, waiting for Jim and Archie. Jim came out, but Archie was in a panic. He looked up at me and told me that he couldn't get through: he would have to go back inside so as to give us a chance to get away. He had both his arms and his head through the hole in the bars: I pulled one arm and Jim the other, but for a long time we couldn't budge him. Eventually we pushed and pulled him through onto the roof.

We kept as low as possible so as not to be seen from the warders' houses in the street below. I crawled to the edge of the roof and looked over. Below me was the huge, thick prison wall that kept us in. We were at a great height, above the security camera which was looking down along the bottom of the wall, watching for anyone trying to scale it.

I stood up to my full height, walked to the end of the building and looked up and down the street, like a pirate looking for ships. Suddenly I spotted a black car creeping round a corner. It was them! There were four of them and the driver waved up at us. The car stopped and the guys got out.

We had stolen a roll of tape from the textiles shed, which we would throw over the edge so that they could tie the mountain-rope to the end of it. One of the guys had a white rope with him, and we threw him down the tape and pulled the rope towards us. Jim and Archie were shocked to see how thin the rope was, and doubted if it would hold their weight. I took hold of it and told them to hold as tight as they could.

'I'll gladly be the guinea pig,' I said and climbed over the edge of the building and onto the rope, which went straight over the top of the wall and into the warders' garden. It was almost a straight slide down, clearing the wall as I went. I landed in the arms of the guys below, who congratulated me and told me to get into the car and change my clothes. I looked up at B Hall roof and saw Jim and Archie tying the end of the rope to a concrete frame. Archie slid down into the garden and Jim followed. As soon as they reached the car, the other three walked off in different directions and disappeared.

The driver took us to a house in the Haghill district. He wished us luck; we couldn't thank him enough for what he had done and the risks he had taken. We danced and sang with happiness once we were inside the house, and roared with laughter when we thought of the warders waiting for me at Peterhead. It was great to be free.

It was then we noticed that the owners of the house were there, and they were both in bed and steaming drunk. They were expecting us and they got up and made us welcome. They couldn't believe I was in prison: they said I was only a 'wee boy', and the woman cuddled me like I was her lost kid and told me I could stay with her for ever. Jim and Archie laughed at my being pampered by this little woman, who was just like my Ma in many ways. It didn't take long for us to feel at home and the woman made us a nice breakfast.

On television we watched newsmen and police describing 'Scotland's most daring escape'. The police warned the public to watch out for us and our photographs were shown. All police leave had been cancelled and a massive operation had been set up to catch us. The public was advised not to 'tackle' us should we be seen.

The driver and the other three came back to the house with food and fresh meat, and some money for us to buy cigarettes and drinks. They told us to lie low for the time being as the police were searching half the houses in Glasgow, dragging people in and demanding to know where we were. I couldn't even send word to Ma to say that I was fine – I knew she'd be worrying herself sick. So we stayed put and hoped things would settle down soon.

It was great to look out of the window and see people walking about in colourful clothes and women hanging out their washing; I reflected that I too could have been out there, enjoying life. I always seemed to see the best in life through a window. Jim, Archie and I scrubbed the house till it was sparkling, not just to pass the time, but because we wanted to. We joked about making good pass-men back in gaol. We burned our grey prison uniforms, and our shirts, underwear and shoes. We cooked meals and made sure the couple's kids were fed and washed. I'm not saying they were neglected – they looked healthy enough – but their folks being alcoholics didn't help matters. One of the boys told us that he was going down to the Barrows Market to steal a bike, and that he went there every Sunday with his pals to steal. He was a handsome kid of eight or nine with short fair hair, and he was all excited about venturing into the world of crime. We tried to give him good advice, telling him he would only end up being taken away from his family if he was caught stealing, and we managed to talk him out of going stealing that Sunday. They were great kids. When they were tucked up in bed we had to tell them stories before they'd go to sleep.

News came fast, and we learned that many of our pals had been pulled in by the police demanding to be told of our whereabouts. The police had offered to drop serious charges against some people if they told them where we were. From those of our pals who managed to slip in to see us, we learned that Alex Howatt had been locked up in solitary for helping us. They couldn't prove it, though, so he couldn't be charged. Jim and Archie sat by the fire drinking vodka and saying, 'This is one for Alex.' The wee woman got drunk, and she kept filling her glass saying, 'Here's tae Alex, and the boys who helped ye's!' before swallowing the glass in one gulp. Then they had a sing-song, seated around the fireside. I didn't touch the vodka, but I had a can of lager and sat there enjoying the company and singing country songs.

That night another couple came to the house. The couple who owned the house assured us that we had nothing to worry about, and we chatted away like old friends. They told us that we could stay with them for the time being, in their house in Carntyne, and we accepted their offer. We were frightened to stay where we were too long and feared it was only a matter of time before the owners of the house got drunk and told somebody that we were there.

Early next morning me and Archie, dressed like workers in hats and overalls and carrying some small wooden steps, set out with the couple. I felt exposed and frightened and wanted to go back to the comforts of the house we'd just left, but we kept on walking. They took us up and down streets, through back courts onto spare ground and along a railway track. Cars kept passing us everywhere we went, and the occasional police van sped by. We passed some teenagers who eyeballed us and, recognising us as strangers in their territory, threatened us and told us to move on. We ate humble pie and did so, though Archie took umbrage at their insults and said he had a good mind to go back and punch their cheeky faces in for calling him 'bald head'.

When we reached Penicuik Street, we were asked to be very quiet, and I found myself walking on tiptoes. The couple lived on the ground floor in a sparsely furnished two-room flat. We were taken to the bathroom to wash our faces, which we had dirtied to make us look like workers, and we were told that we could make ourselves at home while they went to collect Jim.

We checked the doors and windows in case we had to make a quick exit. It was a strange feeling to be in Penicuik Street, for I'd played round there as a child. Archie and I sat on the bed in a room facing the street and waited for Jim, hoping that everything was okay with him. Once he'd arrived we made some tea.

Next morning the woman came back from the shops all excited, saying my Ma was in the papers. There on the front page was a huge coloured photo of Ma looking worried, below headlines that read, 'give yourself up for your own good'. Ma's appeal touched me and I had a good cry. Jim and I were now more concerned about Ma than about anything else, and Archie and the others left the room so that we could have a personal talk together.

Jim asked me to give myself up for Ma's sake, but I told him I couldn't because I couldn't do the time, and the length of my sentence was killing me. I couldn't give myself up, nor could Jim.

At the older couple's house there was a younger man of whom we became suspicious. He said he was more than willing to help us in any way, but he stole from us, and whenever he came back from seeing certain people on our behalf he behaved very nervously. We had asked him to go and see a friend of my dad's and I asked the older guy if he would go and make sure the young guy wasn't pulling any strokes on us, and he agreed to do so. It was dark when they left the house; we made ourselves some tea and got ready to leave when they got back.

When they returned, I noticed that the younger man had a black eye, as if he had been in a fight. The elder guy said he had thumped him for being cheeky. We knew something wasn't right, but the elder guy wouldn't tell us as he didn't want to worry us unduly. He told us that he was to go and see my dad's pal in the morning, and then we all sat round the fire together.

We had just decided that we should leave in the morning when we had an unexpected visitor, steaming drunk and staggering about like he'd been shot. It was an old friend of ours, Shadow, and I've never seen a man sober up so quickly in my life. He stood there in his black coat, swaying from side to side, as he looked from me to Jim to Archie like we were ghosts. He had come to see the elder guy, who was his drinking partner. It was great to see him, and Jim and I rushed up to him and hugged him. Shadow was just like one of our family. He told us that he and T.C. had been questioned about our escape and that his house had been searched by many armed police.

Jim, Archie and Shadow and the others then had a wee drink, and then we had a sing-song to cheer us up. By now Shadow was drunk again: we were worried that he might unintentionally tell someone about us, so we coaxed him into staying and filled him with more drink till he fell asleep on the couch.

After breakfast next morning, the elder guy went to see about the message from my dad's pal. He went alone, and the younger one remained with us. He was acting very suspiciously and nervously, so we watched him closely. The last we saw of him he was going to the toilet – and then the elder guy's wife came running in and said that he had climbed out the bathroom window and was off to get the police. She told us to move fast before they came. She didn't need to say more – Jim and Shadow went one way, and Archie and I the other.

I found it hard to believe that the young guy had really gone to the police – but he had. The police now knew that we were still in Glasgow, whereas some of the newspapers and news reports had said that we had been sighted as far away as Jersey and London. Archie and I ran towards the railway, where we picked up some picks and shovels, hoping to give the impression that we were a couple of workers. I ripped the sleeves off my jumper to make woolen hats. We watched the police cars speeding by in the direction of the house we had left.

We learned later that Jim and Shadow had run out the house and through the back courts. They had heard someone rapping on a window – it was a pal of theirs beckoning them in. They went into his house and listened to police messages about us.

It was a nice day as Archie and I walked off along the railway: the smell of grass and flowers reminded me of when I was young and used to play here in the summertime. I took Archie to where I had once lived, hoping to find Dannyboy in, but the building was empty and the closes had been bricked up.

I stood in the back court and looked up at the house I was born in and had so often run away from. If only, I thought, I could turn back the clock . . . I had often longed to be there when I was in solitary confinement at Peterhead, yet there I was with not only Ma, but every policeman in the country looking for me. It was the best I could get out of life, and I snatched it like a thief.

We hailed a taxi and I told the driver to take us to Shettleston. We agreed that should we get split up, we would meet at the Shettleston bingo hall at ten the following morning. It's a pity we hadn't made such arrangements before we lost Jim – now we had no idea where he was. Once out of the taxi I had to keep my head down while passing people I knew. I told Archie that we were going to the house of a lassie I was friendly with.

Marie looked surprised to see us on her doorstep, but she didn't hesitate for a moment as she ushered us in and closed the door behind us. I gave her a big hug and a kiss after which she pushed us into a room and told us to stay there and keep quiet – her grandmother was in the living-room, but would be leaving soon. She looked lovely as she went to the window and closed the curtains. Then she left us and went back to her granny.

Every time we heard a car stop we looked out of the side of the curtains to see who it could be – only when we were satisfied that it wasn't the police could we relax in the semi-darkness. Once her granny had left, Marie made us something to eat. There she was, sheltering me once again, as loyal and as friendly as ever: I felt quite emotional as I watched her moving about the kitchen. She said she was worried about Archie being on the run for murder – not because she was in any danger from him, but because harbouring a killer was worse than harbouring a robber. Archie was aware of this so he told her that he wouldn't stay long. She said we could stay as long as we had to, and that she wouldn't dream of turning us away, but we could tell she was worried. We stayed the night in the living-room while Marie went to stay with her sister Christine.

Then the door went again, and my heart nearly leapt out my

mouth – but it was my wee sister Lana, crying and rushing into my arms. She could hardly speak for sobbing, and I sat on the bed with her on my knee, rocking her back and forth and patting her back to comfort her. I wanted to scream when I thought of how I had ruined my life and the lives of those I loved most. I had never realised how much they missed and cared for me, nor how much I missed them.

Lana had a pal who took us to a house in Cranhill in the East End of Glasgow, not far from Barlinnie Prison. Whenever we left the house wearing our men's wigs and our new suits we passed some of the warders; none of them recognised us, and we had a quiet laugh to ourselves. Lana and her pals came from time to time to bring us food supplies and cook for us. A guy we knew gave us some money and advice on passports – and a sawn-off shotgun, thinking it might come in handy should we decide to do a robbery. At first the woman who owned the house thought Archie and I were on leave from the oil rigs, but she soon put two and two together. She told us we could stay and that she and her son would go and stay with a friend. We couldn't thank her enough and we apologised for not telling her the truth in the first place.

I went out one night with Lana and phoned Mick and Mary Carroll at a neighbour's house to enquire about passports. Poor Mary was crying when she heard my voice on the phone and kept telling me to look after myself. She and Mick were out on bail, charged with smuggling illegal immigrants into the country, so the police were watching their home and had been listening to their phone calls. All we could do was lay low till things had settled down, only then could we get what was required.

After a while we were moved to another flat on the other side of Glasgow: it was near the top of a skyscraper, which gave us a great view of the city. At night Archie and I would go for a walk in our wigs and suits, strolling about the city centre as if we were entitled to be there. It was better than sitting in a house waiting for the police to come. We went on trying to make contact with Jim, without success. I asked Wullie to get in touch with my dad so that we could get away to London instead of running from house to house each night, but he said it was far too risky – he was being watched closely by the police. We heard through the underworld that both the young couple from Penicuik Street and the elderly couple had given statements to the police, incriminating T.C. and Shadow, and they were getting police protection in case they were intimidated.

We decided to head back to the house in Cranhill, get rid of the shotgun and make our way to London. The gun was in a locked cupboard on the outside of the house. It was about midnight when we got there, and since there was no one in we had to hang around hoping that Lana's pal, who owned the house, would come back. Two guys approached and asked us what we were doing there. We couldn't argue with them or we could well end up in gaol for breach of the peace. So we had to leave pretending to be scared. As we ran we were in fits of laughter. Archie reckoned the whole world was going mad; this was the second time drunken bums had threatened to beat him and me up, and he was getting sick of it.

Lana came round and we decided to stay the night and leave next morning. We learned that the police had arrested Jim. He had agreed to meet some guy in a pub, and when he got there the serious crime squad were waiting. We felt sick at the news. I went to a phone box and rang Barlinnie Prison. When the warder on the gatehouse answered, I told him who I was and threatened murder should anything happen to my brother.

Next morning Archie went out to make a phone call and to buy something for our breakfast. He took Lana with him so that he could pretend he was her husband, and I was left alone in the house. I was in the kitchen pressing my suit when the phone rang. It was Archie. He said that one of the guys who had helped us had been dragged in by the police – and that Archie had given him our phone number on a scrap of paper.

'Johnnyboy, get out of there now!' he said. I told him he was getting paranoid – I couldn't see the guy keeping the phone number on him for the police to find. I told Archie to come back and bring Lana with him. Then I went on pressing my suit. Beside me lay an Adidas bag containing the gun, the wigs and a few other odds and ends.

Through the window I could see two young-looking guys

standing at the foot of the path. A red car drew up and the driver told them to get away.

I grabbed the bag and ran into the bedroom; panicking, I hid it under the bed then ran back into the kitchen. I cursed myself for not taking Archie's advice about getting out of the house, but it was too late now. Suddenly police were all over the street, and cars were screeching to a halt. I could see that the police were armed. They came up the footpath and one of them was carrying a sledgehammer. The neighbours were shouting out of their windows. The street was full of men, women and children – I saw the two guys who had threatened to beat us up the night before. I heard the police tiptoeing down the hall, so I called out to them not to shoot as I was unarmed and in the kitchen with my arms raised. One by one they appeared, pointing their guns at me. I stood stock still in case I made them nervous and one of them shot at me. Then one of them said 'It's Johnnyboy' and they came rushing in and pinned me to the wall. One of the younger ones asked me where Archie was, while the others searched me for weapons. I told him he was in London. He wasn't amused and smashed me across the side of my face with his gun. The madness came out in me, and I asked him if he wanted to have another go at beating me into telling him. But the copper in charge told him I was a tough nut and wouldn't tell him anything; he never bothered me again except to help spread-eagle me on the floor and handcuff my arms behind my back.

They then searched the house. They found the shotgun and laid it alongside me on the floor. Some of the coppers told me that I had pulled off a great escape, and one even patted me on the shoulder as I lay there.

After about five minutes half of them went rushing out into the street to pick up Lana and Archie, who had just got out of a taxi. A neighbour who had seen us in the house had shouted from her window, alerting the police that Archie was there.

Everyone in the street tried to get a look at us as we were taken to the CID cars, and some shouted 'Cheerio!' and 'Hard luck!'. In the police station Archie and I were taken to two different rooms. Almost all the police who came in to look at me congratulated me on making such a daring escape: they were really quite pleasant, much to my surprise. They seemed more interested in the escape than anything else. One of the head CID men said that my dad was the cause of all my troubles. I told him it wasn't so, but he was adamant. When they asked me if I had anything to say, I told them that the lassies knew nothing about the shotgun, but I learned later that Lana and the two other lassies had been charged with harbouring prisoners. Sometime later my cell door opened and about half a dozen CID men came in. They said they wanted to know the name of the Barlinnie Prison warder who had taken a bribe from my dad. I told them they had charged T.C. and Shadow when they had nothing to do with it – and they were wanting me to do them favours? They were quick to tell me there was no real evidence against T.C. and Shadow. I said that I thought they would fit them up for the escape by manufacturing evidence, but they swore they wouldn't. I said I needed to talk to Jim and Archie before I said anything – and when they came back they brought them with them!

We cuddled and shook hands, glad to know we were all fine, apart from my swollen face. The CID told us that we should give the door a kick when we had come to a decision. After discussing what would happen to us when we got back to Barlinnie, we told them we couldn't give the warder's name because that would make life worse for us in gaol. They assured us that we would be granted immunity and sent to any secure prison we wanted. All they wanted was the name of the warder who had taken the bribe. We told them we would give them all the information they needed if they stuck to their word about the immunity and not manufacturing evidence against T.C. and Shadow; they agreed.

We were taken to Glasgow Sheriff Court, where we were remanded and returned to Barlinnie. I hadn't seen Lana since our arrest, but I heard she had been remanded in custody at Cornton Vale women's prison.

It was horrible to see Barlinnie's walls and its huge halls looming up again. We stopped for a moment outside the massive electronic gate; then it opened and in we went. A senior warder came over to me; he was shaking with rage and couldn't open the cuffs, nor could he look me in the eye. I knew him for what he was, and how he condoned violence and beatings. When the cuffs were eventually off, the CID took us through the back door of reception and into a waiting transit van. We were driven to a building near B Hall which was used as an office by the warders. The CID men stayed with us all the time, and there wasn't a warder in sight.

Then we were taken to a room on the ground floor and introduced to an elderly looking man seated behind a wooden desk and told to sit down. He introduced himself as the Procurator of Glasgow and congratulated us on our daring escape. I asked him what he wanted and he said he believed we had something to tell him! He tried again and again to get us to give him a statement, but we refused. He said we had nothing to worry about as he had made arrangements to have us protected against the warders, and that we could be transferred to any other security gaol we wanted to go to. We were thankful for this. We were then handed over to the prison authorities who took us to E Hall – the Barlinnie training hall!

Warders had been posted outside our doors on the ground floor of E Hall. It was just like being put on protection – only this time we were being protected from the warders. The coppers had stuck to their word. We weren't allowed out of our cells except to slop-out and exercise. The hall was run along the same lines as the training hall at Peterhead: no training of any kind was given, yet when the authorities spoke of it they gave the impression that it was all in your best interests! Every time my door opened I expected warders to rush in and do their dirty work, but it never came.

The governor came to see me. He told me he had received a letter from my dad, asking him to stop anyone beating me up. He said my dad wasn't the same man that he had once known – the long-term gaol sentences had affected his head – and that I should think carefully about this. I couldn't guess what the governor was talking about, but I learned later that my dad had threatened terrible revenge if anything happened to me or Jim.

When the governor asked me which prison I wanted to go to, I asked for Dunvagel, which is an 'open' prison. He said no way was I going to an open prison – it had to be a high-security one. So I said Peterhead, because I knew that I would be back there anyway.

We were taken back to Peterhead under a heavy escort of armed police.

After we had changed into prison 'greys' we were taken to the punishment block and locked up. I was to be kept in solitary until I was tried in Glasgow for escaping – which could be anything from a few weeks to a year. The Peterhead warders weren't too pleased with me. I had cut the bars in my cell and made them a laughing stock; one of their fellow warders was in trouble because of the bribery allegations; and they'd been worried about our taking revenge on them for the harm they'd done us.

There was a huge puddle on the floor of my cell, and the walls were running wet. I asked to see the prison doctor, and was moved to a cell next to Joe – but it was just as bad as the other. At about 8.30 each night I was told to take my clothes off and put them outside my door. One of the warders threw in two blankets, but no mattress. I waited till the warders went away and then told the night-shift warder, who was new on the job, that they'd forgotten to give me my mattress. He told me I was on 'guard bed' – a form of punishment in which a prisoner is deprived of his mattress – for seven days for smashing up my last cell.

I managed to break off part of a cast-iron shelf from my cell wall. It was shaped like a machete blade, and after dark I began to hack away at the wall separating me and Joe. Joe started digging from his side. The cell walls were about 30 inches thick and made of huge granite blocks which I placed as quietly as I could on the floor. Eventually I saw Joe's finger appear, and then his head. We laughed and shook hands like long-lost brothers.

By the time the warders realised what was going on, Joe and I had taken half the wall away. I was in Joe's cell and we had barricaded ourselves in with the debris and the huge granite blocks. The warders tried to negotiate with us through Joe's spy-hole, but we just continued tearing the wall down. Joe was like me; he couldn't do his time and we swore we would try to escape as soon as an opportunity arose.

We were so exhausted that we fell asleep, and when we woke up the warders were about to force their way in. They took the cell door down and came rushing in with riot shields and sticks. They dragged me away to another cell, and Joe was taken away to the silent cell. I was kicked and punched to the floor and handcuffed.

There was nothing in my new cell except a concrete block for a seat, and a bed (a thick wooden door) which was bolted to the floor. I took my handcuffs off. The concrete block had been cemented and bolted to the concrete floor, and should I manage to prise it loose it would be too heavy to lift. I tried to budge it again and again. I took a run at it and hit it with the flat of both my feet; it moved a little, and I began to get it loose by running at it and kicking at it. I managed to lift it up and drop it on the wooden bed, which was shattered to pieces. I then tried to smash the cell door down. It made a terrible noise and I could hear the warders outside panicking. They came rushing in to get me, but ran out again when they saw me with the huge concrete seat. They couldn't believe it – they'd been boasting about their new concrete seats and how secure they were. I heard them saying I was a nutter and that I should be in a mental hospital. I was crying with rage and frustration, and when they heard this they took the opportunity to speak to me like a human being, saying that if I came out quietly nothing would happen to me.

I came out without resisting and was put in another cell. They put another set of handcuffs on my wrists – this time of the bracelet kind that can be tightened till they dig in. After they'd gone I removed the handcuffs and once again smashed the wooden door-bed with the concrete stool. They were demented, but they got me out without my resisting or their beating me up. They asked me how I'd managed to get the handcuffs off, but I only laughed and said that if they put them on again I'd take them off again. They then produced a body belt made of thick leather with chains and handcuffs attached to it and tied me into it, taking turns to pull at the belt and chains to make sure they were secure.

After they'd left I managed to slip out of the body belt and chains partly because I was so skinny, but also I'd learnt a trick.

I pressed the emergency bell and when the warder opened the spy-hole I was standing there with the body belt held out like a present, and I said, 'Give these back to that fucking teuchter of a chief.'

The chief told me that he had asked the works to make something that I couldn't get out of, and that until it was ready staff would sit in the cell with me to prevent me doing any more damage. We sat there for about four hours, me in one corner and them in another. They seldom spoke to me, and each time I made the slightest move their eyes were on me. They complained that the works warders were taking too long and that they felt like prisoners themselves, sitting there with a madman.

Eventually I made a deal with the chief and they left me alone with my few luxuries – tobacco and a mattress and a guitar. I was placed on governor's report for damaging the cells. I saw a civilian taking pictures which were to be sent to the Prison Department so that the authorities could see the damage I'd done.

19

The Barlinnie Escape Trial

A lawyer and a Queen's Counsel came to see me about the escape from Barlinnie. They advised me to plead guilty in the High Court in Glasgow, but I refused. They told me they wouldn't be able to defend me since I was guilty no matter what I said. I told the governor I was citing him as a witness, so that he could testify that it wasn't me who had escaped. He asked me if I would like to see the gaol psychiatrist. I told Jim and Archie that the lawyers weren't going to represent me in court. They couldn't stop laughing when I said that I had told the QC that I had been kidnapped by them, and that that was how I became involved in the escape. Jim and Archie's defence was that they hadn't escaped – they had fled for their lives, fearing more brutality from the warders.

It came as no surprise when our QCs stood up in the High Court and asked permission to withdraw from the trial. We were left to defend ourselves. Our first witness was Joe McGrath, but when he tried to describe the brutality the judge told him to shut up. That was the end as far as our witnesses were concerned. The authorities knew that we were prepared to put the system on trial and show it up for the monster it is, which was why they stopped Joe in his tracks and had him removed from the courtroom. The judge told the court that it wasn't the penal system that was on trial, but me, Jim and Archie. We did manage to say something about the brutal regime, and I believe the newspapers carried some of it. We were all found guilty. Jim and I were both sentenced to three years in prison and Archie to four years. Three years on top of the twelve I was already serving only made me even more determined to escape again.

Back in Peterhead, I was determined to find a way out of the hall. I was sitting in my pal Checker's cell on the top gallery one day and I had a good look at his ceiling, which was made of granite. I never said anything to him about it, but I talked to Jim and Archie about having a go at digging through it. They both agreed it was feasible – as long as I did the digging! If we got through the ceiling, it would take us up into the loft. From there we could make our way down the building under the cover of darkness during recreation time – and, with luck, we wouldn't be missed till lock-up at 9 p.m.

I agreed to do the ceiling myself and slipped into Checker's empty cell with an iron bar. We'd thought about asking Checker to come with us, but we knew he would freak out at such a suggestion and he knew nothing of it. I asked one of the cons to make sure that he stayed out of his cell. In fact Checker and a few others were due to play cards that night, and the guys were prepared to give evidence that he'd been out of his cell throughout the recreation period.

I had to stand on his locker to graft his ceiling, and the debris fell onto his bed. I put some blankets on the floor to stop any chunks of granite from falling heavily onto the concrete. I was almost blinded by the dust and my eyes were burning. I had to sit down on the bed for a moment, and I got down on my knees to feel for Checker's basin of water so as to wash my eyes. Archie came in to see how I was doing and he bathed my eyes with clean water. That helped, and I tore into the thick granite ceiling again – but it was obvious that the hole wasn't going to be big enough in time. By now it was only half an hour until lock-up. I couldn't leave the cell as it was, so I asked Jim to get me some plain paper and some glue.

By the time he returned I had cleaned up the cell. I had swept the boulders and rubble under the bed, shaken the dust from the blankets and put them back on the bed, and dusted the windows, shelves and walls with a damp rag. The only evidence that remained was a fair-sized hole in the ceiling. I cut the paper to size, but before gluing it over the hole I stuffed some newspapers in so that a dark patch wouldn't show through the paper. The paper blended in perfectly with the lumpy white plaster – no one would have known there was a hole above it. The only tell-tale sign was that the glue on the white paper had a shiny appearance, unlike the rest of the ceiling, so I squirted some Vim over it to make it lose its sheen.

The only other problem was that there was no way we could get all the boulders and rubble out of the cell that night – and if we left it there Checker was sure to find it and panic. I felt I had to tell him. There was no recreation for the next two nights, so it would be Thursday before I could get back in to work on the ceiling. It wouldn't be noticed by the warders so long as we got rid of the debris in the morning. On the top gallery there was a heap of granite and rubble which the works warders, who were fixing a pipe, had left for the pass-men to clean up, and I thought we'd put our rubble in with the rest.

I went to find Checker to bring him in and break the news to him. He froze when he saw us and there was a look of distrust in his eyes. I couldn't really blame him. I asked him to look at his ceiling and tell me if he noticed anything. He couldn't see anything wrong, so I stood him right underneath the hole and asked him to look again. Still he couldn't see anything. I stood on the bed and peeled back the glue-covered paper, and poor Checker had to sit down on the bed while I explained it to him. When I told him I wanted to come back the following Thursday, he agreed to help by pretending that nothing was wrong. I nearly laughed out loud when I asked him to look under his bed – Archie had to give him a drink of water to bring him round.

Next morning we got rid of the rubble, but on Thursday we were told Checker was in the punishment block for attempting to escape! The warders had got to know about it. We knew he wouldn't grass on us but we had a guilty conscience about him. Rather than see him in the cells, possibly losing remission for nothing, I thought that one of us should own up to it and get him out. We decided to draw straws and Jim drew the shortest. We made sure he had tobacco before he went. Jim walked down to the PO on the bottom floor and told him that they had the wrong man. I was sorry to see him go, but I was proud of him for not hesitating to take the rap for Checker.

Next morning Jim went in front of the governor, who said he admired Jim for not letting an innocent man suffer. Jim was locked in punishment for a week or two and all the charges against Checker were dropped.

T.C. and Shadow had been charged with aiding us in the escape and in October 1980 we appeared in court, handcuffed and with an armed guard, as witnesses for them.

The newspapers, radio and television carried the news of T.C. and Shadow going free. They had been found not proven. There was a large photo of them both standing smiling outside the High Court in Glasgow.

20

The Cages of Inverness

There was much tension in Peterhead, and after I'd found myself in more trouble a warder asked me how I felt about going to Carstairs state hospital for the mentally ill. I thought they were only trying to frighten me, but then I realised they were serious. I felt I'd rather die than go anywhere near such a place. I knew I was sane and I hated the thought of being tagged as a mental patient.

My cell door opened and a mob of warders beckoned me out. Once I was in reception they pounced on me. They handcuffed my hands behind my back and carried me off to a waiting transit van, which roared out of the gaol to be met by an armed police escort. When I asked where we were going the warders didn't answer, but then I heard one of them talking about the Cages of Inverness. I had heard a great deal about the Cages and the goings-on there. They were thought of by the prisoners as a miniature Carstairs for crazy prisoners, a place for degrading men the system couldn't control.

Six warders were waiting for me – the ratio per prisoner in the Cages. I was stripped of all my clothes and then taken inside a brilliantly lit 'cage'. It was a cell that had been divided into two with steel bars so as to make a cage.

I was the only prisoner in the Cages at that time, and I felt really lonely having no one to talk to. I paced up and down the floor, from one wall to the other. I could only take three paces either way, because they had cemented a huge concrete stool into the floor.

All I was allowed in the cage was a pisspot, a plastic mug and a book. Pens, pencils, soap, toothpaste and toothbrush were all forbidden – supposedly to protect the warders from being injured! Outside in the corridor was a lock which controlled the cage door: before the warders opened the cage they always came into the cell to make sure that I hadn't gone mad and wasn't about to attack them.

I couldn't eat my first meal – I couldn't even swallow the soup without taking a mouthful of water with it. I couldn't believe it when I was offered a choice of chicken or a chop! The chop looked good, but it was nearly all bone. I hid the bone: that night I began to work a brick out with it, but was discovered. From then the bones were taken out of my chops. I vomited all over the floor my first night there – I couldn't stand being in that small cage, like an animal.

Next morning I was taken to see the governor and informed of the rules. I was told I could expect to stay there for up to three months. I could write one letter a week, and as for wages I was to make fish nets for £1.20 a week. Needless to say, the governor said he knew my dad.

The warders never let me out of their sight when I was slopping or exercising.

A works warder spent a few minutes showing me how to make a fish net with a piece of S-shaped metal. He hadn't been out of the cage two minutes before I'd straightened it out till it was about ten inches long. I had to laugh – they wouldn't allow me a pencil, yet I'd been given a tool ten inches long. I bent it back to its S-shape again and sat all dinnertime wondering what to do with it. I felt so depressed that I began to think about murdering one of the warders because I couldn't take any more. I put the S-shaped piece of metal in my pocket and pressed the bell to go to the toilet. I had lost all fear of consequences, and felt no regard for human life. It was a strange feeling.

Once in the toilet, I pretended to be having a shit. I sat there with the weapon in my hand, picturing what might happen. The door on the toilet cubicle was only about two and a half feet high, enabling warders to see the prisoner's head, shoulders and legs. It was disgusting and degrading: they stood there looking on, and it was even worse when they all stood there in silence, listening. I kept telling myself to go out and stick the weapon into the heart of the nearest warder, but although I felt I had nothing to live for, I couldn't bring myself to kill anyone, or even attack someone with my weapon. I wanted to, but something held me back. I began to look on the warders as human beings, just like me. I had a thousand reasons for stabbing them, but I always found one reason not to. I had to do something, but escape seemed the only logical thing and it was easier to do than stab or kill one of the warders. Shaken, I went back to the cage with the concealed weapon and began to check the walls and the brickwork for weaknesses. I noticed that the beans on my dinner plate were almost the same colour as the pinkish paint on the walls, so when I started digging around one of the bricks I used the beans to cover up the hole. When I ran out of beans I had to stop digging. I put the debris into my chamber pot and emptied it. If I heard the slightest movement out in the corridor I pretended to be working. They found the hole one day when they came in to search the cage; they confiscated the tool and refused to let me work again.

The warders kept spying on me, so I threw my food at the spy-holes. They warned me that I could do my time the easy way or the hard way, and that hard cases like me soon gave in to them. I spat at them and they spat back.

I found a piece of pencil in the exercise yard and hid it among some shit in my pisspot so that the warders wouldn't find it. I started to write poems on pieces of toilet roll. I wrote and wrote, seldom tiring of it.

A priest, Father McDonald, visited me every Tuesday evening. He was good company and he laughed heartily when I told him stories about Ma and Maw. When I told him that Maw was blind and would like to visit me, he immediately offered to pick her up in his car and bring her to the Cages. He used to sit outside the cage with me inside, and there was no warder present. We never said a mass, but I'd whisper so that the warders couldn't hear me confessing to him. Before he left he always shook my hand and promised to pray for me.

After three miserable months in the Inverness Cages I was taken back to Peterhead and put in a cell in the punishment block until the governor had seen me.

The police who had arrested us when we were on the run came to see us. They wanted a statement about the warder in

Barlinnie who was supposed to have taken the bribe, but they left empty-handed and furious. We decided not to give them a statement or help them with their inquiries in any way, because we would get too much hassle. They also asked me for a statement for the Procurator concerning Lana and the other two lassies who had been arrested for harbouring us, but again they got nothing.

Some time in the late summer of 1981, I received a citation from the Crown to appear at the Glasgow High Court as a witness in the trial of Lana and her two friends. We picked up Archie, who had been transferred to Aberdeen, and from there we were taken to Barlinnie.

We were never called by the Crown to give evidence. We were told we weren't required, and although we demanded to be taken into court, we were refused. The lady who owned the house was found 'not proven', and Lana's pal was given a six-month deferred sentence and released there and then. Lana was sentenced to one year in prison for harbouring us, and her children were put into a foster home till she got out. I was heartbroken and cursed myself for getting Lana involved. I was now more determined than ever to escape.

I said goodbye to Archie at Aberdeen, and then I was taken away to Peterhead under armed escort. In Aberdeen a Highland prisoner made a snide remark about Lana. He was stabbed for it – and who should get the blame but Archie, who was moved back to Peterhead as a result.

21

Savage Strength

In October 1981 I tried to escape again, hoping to get out of this hell. I started cutting through my bars and got plenty of background music from my neighbour, Skylark, to drown out the noise of the cutting. My pal, 'Bald Eagle', wanted to come with me, as did a couple of other guys who had heard me sawing my bars. Each time I finished cutting a bar I filled it with wood filler and painted it over till it was unnoticeable. I never cut the bars completely through – I always left them on a thread, so that when the warders shook them or hit them with their truncheons they wouldn't fall off. I only cut them through completely at the very last minute.

Jim and Skylark advised me to hold off till the afternoon recreation period, as the warders were on their toes. The warder on my gallery was the one who was infamous for killing prisoners' pet pigeons, and on the afternoon that I was preparing to escape, I was told that the pigeon killer had been in my cell! I was talking to a pal at the time, and when I looked up at my cell on the gallery above I saw that the door had been locked. I wanted to lie down and die. I had spent night after night cutting the bars till my fingers were raw, blistered and bleeding and I felt furious with frustration. Big John, my pal, sensed this and tried to persuade me not to do anything crazy. I left his cell and walked upstairs towards my own. Everyone knew about my sawing through the bars, and they were all watching me. As I approached my cell I saw the pigeon killer coming up the other flight of stairs, staring at me with an evil grin on his rotten face. I wondered if that was how he looked at the pigeons . . .

I attacked him then and there, at the top of the stairs. I kicked him, butted him with my head, and punched him. I felt others grab me from behind. I remember them all on top of me; one of them had me in a stranglehold and was choking me, while the others held my arms and legs. Then Jim appeared with a pool cue in his hand, demanding that the warders let me go. I managed to get one of my hands free, so I grabbed the pigeon killer's balls and squeezed them. Instantly he let my neck go. As I looked in his eyes and saw the fear in them, I laughed in his face and asked him who was sorry now. But before he got the chance to answer Jim had crashed the pool cue over his head.

By now warders were appearing from everywhere. I'd had the shirt torn off me and I jumped on to the hotplate and started throwing steel trays and bowls at them. Two warders were on the floor with Jim, one of them the pigeon killer. I jumped off the hotplate with a tray in my hand and ran to help him. I brought the steel tray down hard on the pigeon killer's head, and he let Jim go and crawled away. I jumped back onto the hotplate. The riot bell was ringing, but I kept on throwing trays and bowls at the warders and screaming at them to fight me.

Some of the warders tried to calm me down, and Jim and the others urged me to surrender, but I couldn't stop: as far as I was concerned the Peterhead Mafia were getting a dose of their own medicine. And there was nothing to surrender for, except to go back to the punishment block.

Warders were lying on the floor, groaning, and dozens more were coming up the stairs – but they couldn't get near me. When I came to my senses and saw the pigeon killer, with blood on his face, holding his balls, and the other warders pleading with me to surrender, I suddenly felt sorry for them. I had caught a glimpse of what lay beneath their uniforms and realised that they were no different from me.

One of the POs said, 'I'll take you down, Johnnyboy, and make sure nothing happens to you.' I knew him from being locked up in solitary, where he was quite sympathetic towards me – he had passed me tobacco from Jim when I shouldn't have been getting any – and I decided to give myself up.

When I reached the double doors of the cells some warders came towards me as if they were going to beat me up, but the

PO told them to leave me alone. They didn't seem too pleased at that. I was stripped of my trousers and pants and shoes, and thrown into a cell. Burnsy and Tam had also attacked the warders to help me. I could hear thumps, and Burnsy and Big Tam screaming. I kicked at the door with my bare feet and shouted at them to leave them alone. It's horrible to be in a cell listening to guys being beaten up and screaming. I was so furious that when the warders opened my cell door I ran out with two bits of shit in my hands.

I refused to take in my bedding and threw out everything in the cell, including the pisspot. A warder brought it back and told me I would need it during the night, but I told him that from now on they could clean up my shit and piss. When they came next they removed a pile of shit I had stored in a corner, and when I realised what they were doing I made a dive for it and tried to throw it at them. I refused to wear my clothes. I was sick of wearing drab grey clothing that didn't fit me and made me look even skinnier than I was. I put on a pair of large pyjama trousers, the old-fashioned type that tie at the waist with a piece of cord. I ripped them at the knees and I wore nothing else. However uncomfortable I was, I enjoyed knowing that the bastards wouldn't have the pleasure of telling me to put my clothes outside the cell door each night. Nor could they take my mattress from me in the early morning; it went too. If I had nothing, there wasn't anything they could take from me, in a material sense. I knew the one thing they wanted was my spirit.

Next day I was taken to the governor's orderly room, where he told me that I was to be remanded in the punishment block for assaulting warders and attempting to escape. Jim, Burnsy and Big Tam were also locked up and charged with assault. The governor was worried that I wouldn't stop fighting the system. I informed him that it was my sanity I was fighting for – not that he was interested. He seemed more concerned that I hadn't put on my clothes when appearing before him as a sign of respect. For me there was only one way out: my sentence was getting ever longer; it was up to 15 years – and I was becoming more desperate.

A few days later I was taken away to the Cages again, still

wearing my torn-off pyjama trousers. I was filthy black and stinking, and the warders argued about who was going to be handcuffed to me in the van.

Back at the Cages, I wouldn't wear gaol clothes and kept my pyjama trousers on. On the wall outside the cage, facing the bars, was a small square mirror, and I could see myself looking out of the cage. I stared at my white face and kept going back for another look. I wondered why the mirror was there, and whether it was a two-way mirror through which they could watch me.

About this time my dad had a massive heart attack and couldn't do much for himself. I must confess I wasn't very upset when I learned of this. I couldn't really have cared if he died, but I was concerned for Ma, so I prayed that my dad wouldn't die too soon. He still wrote to me, trying to persuade me to be good. Ma came to visit me at the Cages with her friend, Mary Carroll, whom everyone mistook for her sister. As usual they complained about how thin and pale I was. I lied to Ma, telling her I felt fine and was eating my food. I had to keep repeating myself through the wire when talking to her – she had bad hearing, and it seemed to be getting worse. She told me that Maw was still going strong and that she kept talking about me and missed me and cried over the thought that she'd never be with me again. News like this had me crying inside.

At night I'd get the urge to write some verse, and having no pen or pencil I used my excreta to write on the walls, just as one would write on a blackboard. By the morning I had written dozens of poems, and when it was time to write my weekly letter I could copy the poems on the walls into a book or onto a piece of toilet roll. The shit was horrible to handle, but I had got used to it by now: I had been living for so long like a caveman with nothing but raw intelligence to get me through each day. Verses were flowing out of me, and when the authorities realised that writing was keeping me quiet, I was allowed a piece of lead from a pencil and some paper.

Father McDonald continued to visit me every week, and sometimes I'd recite to him verse which I had written. I became very friendly with this wee gentleman. I told him that if I ever got out of gaol and was getting married, I'd like him to do the service. I even used to clean up my cage for his visits.

I was charged with assault and taken to Peterhead Sheriff Court. I pleaded guilty, and a further four months was added to my sentence.

I spent another Christmas and New Year in the Cages. The warders told me that they'd be glad to see me back at Peterhead because I caused them nothing but trouble. There was one warder there whom I hated in particular. As he walked, both his arms swung to and fro at the same time and it made him look like he had a humph, so that was the nickname he was given: 'Humphy'! Every time I saw him I'd say, 'Hi, Humphy!'

No sooner was I back in Peterhead than I was looking for a way out again.

When I was very young and my dad was drunk he would say, 'When I die, son, I want you to make sure that I'm buried in the garden in front of our house.' But even though he was in such ill health, I couldn't imagine him dying. He couldn't walk more than a few yards without his walking-stick, and he had to get permission to be driven into the gaol in Mary's car when he came to visit us; but he still looked as smart as ever, and even more like Lee Marvin. I was sorry to see him so frail. He asked me to behave myself and not put my Ma into an early grave by causing her worry. I found myself praying for my dad that night in my cell. I never saw him again. He died in March 1982, a few days before my twenty-sixth birthday. Jim and I were shattered and depressed, and I wondered how Ma would be able to cope on her own with Maw now that Brenda had married.

The governor told us that Ma wanted us out to attend the funeral, but that he couldn't get any warders to take us! It seemed the bastards were pleased to hear that my dad was dead. Some of them told me they were very sorry, but I thought otherwise. Eventually the governor told us that he had managed to find six warders, none of whom had had any trouble with us, to take us to dad's funeral, and he promised us that they – the warders – would wear plain clothes at the funeral. He told us they knew what sort of people would be at the funeral – meaning that there would be many gangsters there from all over the country – and he warned us not to try to escape as there would be armed police present.

I had never been to a funeral, and I didn't know how I would react. Dad was to be cremated, and his last wish was that his ashes be scattered over the East End of Glasgow. There were hundreds of people there to attend the mass. Ma was helped in by Brenda and Lana – she was all dressed in black and sobbing her heart out – but Maw had to stay at home; she was too old and frail to come out. All my uncles and aunts and some cousins were there, and many people whom I hadn't seen for years. As the priest said mass I saw the casket containing my father slowly disappearing under the floor. I whispered goodbye to him, to the father I hardly got to know.

We managed to speak to Ma in the back of the transit van for about 15 minutes. We tried to comfort her and she begged me to stop fighting the system and get out before she too was in her grave.

When I got back to A Hall, and went upstairs to my cell, who should be on the gallery but the pigeon killer, staring at me. I went into my cell and put my belongings into the cupboard. The door opened and the pigeon killer came in. He warned me that he hadn't forgotten about my attacking him. Just then another prisoner, Bill, came into my cell. He had been a friend of my dad's, and he was the biggest con in the gaol – about six foot four, with the weight to go with it. The pigeon killer turned white when Bill walked straight up to him, never taking his eyes off him, and asked me if everything was okay. I said I was fine, gave him a wink of approval and told the pigeon killer to get out. There was an atmosphere in the hall.

The new governor told me any time I felt like cracking up or was having difficulty doing my time, I was to let him know and he would lock me up in solitary! The idea of this, he said, was to save me from getting myself into further trouble. It hurt me to hear his solution to my problems, and getting up to leave I told him to fuck off. 'You're missing the point!' he called after me, and I answered: 'So are you!'

My dad's sister Mags came to visit me. I couldn't remember her as I'd only been a wee laddie when I last saw her. She showed me some photos, including one of her babysitter, Margaret. She told me that Margaret had been with my dad when he died, and had tried to revive him and given him the kiss of life. Mags and Ma had been on holiday in Spain at the time – he died the day before they arrived home. Poor Ma had stepped off the plane clutching the presents she had bought for my dad.

I asked Aunt Mags if she would ask her good-looking babysitter to be my pen-pal. Mags said she couldn't wait till she got back home to tell her, and for the rest of the visit she boasted about how lovely her babysitter was. Margaret wrote and asked if she could visit me. She came with Mags and she was indeed lovely looking, with beautiful green eyes. I could see she was shy, and must have felt awkward sitting across from me and having to put up with my staring at her. I felt shy and awkward too, but I wanted to make an impression on her, so I said some funny things which had her laughing. Jim was there as well: he told Aunt Mags that the babysitter and I were in love already, which had Margaret laughing shyly.

In May 1982, I was cited to appear at the Inverness Court to give evidence on behalf of a friend; so were Burnsy and two other pals of mine. We were told that we would be kept overnight in the Inverness gaol – not in the Cages, but in the main gaol. The warders there weren't too pleased to see us: they expected trouble, so they kept us locked in our cells. I'd smuggled in two steel rods and I passed one to Burnsy. We'd dug a hole in the wall big enough to put our hands through by the time the warders caught us. They took the rods and removed everything, but left us in the cells. On the cell floors at Inverness gaol there is lino, which I was surprised to see, for there's certainly none at Peterhead or the Cages. I lifted it up to see if anyone might have hidden a knife under it which could help us to tunnel through, but there was nothing. The lino, I noticed, had a kind of canvas material stuck to the bottom of it. I had an idea which seemed ridiculous: I broke a length of the lino off. It was about six feet long and four or five inches wide, just like a plank of wood. The cell walls were made of red house-bricks with half an inch of mortar between each one of them. I gave Burnsy one end of the lino through into his cell and, resting it on the mortar between the bricks, we started sawing – and it was doing the trick, though every little while we had to replace the lino with a new bit because it was wearing away with the friction. I had to stop because I couldn't keep from laughing at our luck. Suddenly, on the other side of the spy-hole, we saw a warder who was shouting: 'I don't believe this!' I had managed to squeeze through in beside Burnsy where both of us, in our excitement and knowing we had fucked them, were doing a Highland jig around the cell. We agreed to take the rest of the wall down, so I went back into my own cell and put the lino through and sawed away . . . They came in and dragged us both to different cells. I lost another 14 days remission and got a £50 fine. The Inverness warders were glad to see the back of us and I was told I'd never be allowed back into Inverness gaol again, for any reason.

One day we heard rumours that Big Tam had been badly beaten up after falling into a trap laid for him by one of the warders. My heart went out to Big Tam, but when I told the warder in charge, he just laughed and said that if Big Tam was being beaten up by the staff he must have deserved it. We rioted, chasing the warders off the third and fourth galleries, smashing what we could and throwing beds over the galleries onto the warders below. At the top of the stairs we made a barricade of toilet seats, sinks and beds to stop the warders rushing us in their protective riot gear. The governor came in while I was taking off a cell door and asked me what it was all about. I told him that Big Tam had been badly beaten and that we wanted an inquiry into brutality in the punishment block. It was hard for him to hear what I was saying because the cons were still busy wrecking the gallery. He told me I should petition the Secretary of State if I had any complaints about brutality, and that there'd be no retaliation if we surrendered – which, in the end, we did.

We went quietly, one at a time, to the punishment block,

where we were stripped of our clothes. They came round later and beat us up for rioting and assaulting the warders.

So there I was, back in my pyjama trousers and without any bedding. I covered the cell in my own shit, and I would run out the door covered in shit and throw handfuls of it at the warders' desk. Every day the warders had to clean up the shit which had been thrown at them. It was a good weapon, and one the warders feared.

I appeared before the visiting committee in May 1982. For my part in the rioting and assaults I lost 365 days' remission. I had hardly any remission left on my twelve-year sentence, so they took it from my three-year sentence. When I pointed out that they couldn't take remission from a sentence I hadn't even started, the governor said that the Secretary of State had accumulated all my sentences for the purpose of depriving me of my remission if necessary. I was fined £25 and given 28 days solitary confinement.

'I hope this will be a bloody lesson to you, Steele, once and for all,' one of them said as I was being taken away to my cell. It would be almost a year before I got out of the punishment block – but it wasn't a lesson, it was just another punishment, and nothing more.

I destroyed every cell they moved me to, and I was destroying them faster than the works warders could repair them. They put in a new type of Perspex, unbreakable window-pane but I removed the first one to have a look at it while the warder was installing the second. They were right – it was solid and unbreakable, and I began to use it to dig out a brick from around the window. It was better that some of the best tools that I had ever managed to get hold of. I was taking the brick out of the wall when they came in and dragged me to another cell.

Margaret continued to write and to visit me. I began to call her 'Honeybugs'; soon we were talking love – which was crazy, because we couldn't possibly have a future together as I had years to serve. When Honeybugs and Aunt Mags visited me, I was usually in solitary confinement or the Cages. I didn't tell them about the conditions I was in, but pretended everything was fine. Even though I had taken a shower and put on clean clothes before the visit, Honeybugs always said there was a funny smell – I told her it must be off 'them', pointing at the warders. I was in love with her, and I guess my Aunt Mags knew this, for she would say things like 'I think yous would make a lovely couple', and we would laugh. I'd sit and stare at Honeybugs while she blushed and lowered her eyes, and after each visit I gave her a long kiss. I could feel my love for her growing stronger, which made doing my time seem even worse. I had to get away from love somehow: I knew that sooner or later we would both end up being hurt.

Because there was no heating in the cells I had to light fires to keep me warm, with matches smuggled in by the pass-men. I always lit them immediately below my window so that the smoke would go up and out, but sometimes the wind blew it into the cell.

There were hundreds of flies in my cell because of the shit and stench, and they were breeding. They swarmed all over my food; when it was dark, I could hear nothing except the flies buzzing around. I would spend hours killing them and throwing the maggots I found amongst the food slops in my cell out of the window. My food was always cold and insufficient, and they wouldn't give me plastic utensils because they said I could tunnel through walls with them. One of the cells I was moved to was crawling with lice and had to be fumigated and left for 24 hours before anyone was put into it. The lice were everywhere. They seemed to come out from under the paintwork. To stop the lice from crawling on me I set fire to a piece of towel and let it burn out: then I took the burnt black material and rubbed it all over my naked body. I stayed like this until they fumigated my cell and rid it of the lice.

A warder from the surgery came to see me one day and warned me that if I didn't stop they would have to give me some injections for my own good. I knew the sort of injections he meant: the brain-numbing kind. It frightened me to know they were serious.

'What else can we do?' he said when he saw the expression on my face.

I felt fear of a kind I hadn't known before, and I told them that I would kill if anyone attempted to come near me with a needle. It was either kill or be killed. After they had left me alone I gave much thought to my life – what it was all about and where it was taking me: I had cousins and aunts and uncles out there in the decent world whom I didn't know. I had hardly known my own family – my dad especially. I hadn't even lived. I had been running most of my life and couldn't stop. I promised myself I would make an extra effort to comply with prison rules and get the fuck out of this hell-hole. But no sooner had I thought of trying to settle down when the panic came over me at the thought of trying to get through fifteen years and four months. I didn't have it in me to serve that length of time: for me to settle down was merely wishful thinking.

In the mornings, when the warders came to take me to the governor's room to be punished, I refused to walk – which meant they had to carry me, wearing surgical gloves to protect them from the shit on my body. They'd dump me on the floor of the orderly room while the report was read out.

One day a warder threw me a canvas bag to sleep in. I tied this up to my window and jumped into it. When they came to take me away to the orderly room, I refused to get out of it, because at the bottom of the bag I had some bits of metal which I had taken off a steel grille on the outside of the window. I curled down at the bottom of the sleeping bag, clutching the tools – which I wrapped in a piece of towel to stop them rattling. The warders turned the bag upside down and shook it, but I had jammed myself tight inside it. In the end they had to drag me down the stairs and into the orderly room in the bag, which they placed in front of the governor's desk in an upright position, and I heard the governor ask them if they were sure I was in the bag. After he'd read out the report I heard once again, 'Have you anything to say to the charge?' and of course, once again they heard, 'Fuck you, and your charge, you bastards.' I was dragged away in the bag.

They stopped putting me on report for a while even though

I was still rebelling: the punishment block was out of commission because I had damaged all the cells in it.

They would make us go for exercise in the 'pens', come hail, rain or snow. I was in the third pen one day, and I heard Frank screaming. I told the warder on the catwalk to let me in, but he ignored me. I stripped off the pyjama shorts I was wearing and threw them over the wire at the top of the 16-foot wall and onto the corridor roof. I knew that the only way to get through the razor wire was to go naked so as not to get one's clothes tangled in it. The warder on the catwalk was at the first pen and had his back to me. Putting one hand on one wall and one hand on the other, I crawled up the wall through the razor wire and onto the corridor roof, where I put my pyjama trousers back on.

The riot bell was ringing as I climbed onto the roof of the punishment block. I threw down slates and smashed some 30 windows. When I looked inside I could see warders running for shelter from the falling sheets of glass. The cons in the exercise yard and on the football field cheered me on. The warders were furious that I had got out of the pen – no one had ever done so before. They put it around that I was mad, and that only a madman would do such a thing. Eventually I came down of my own accord because, for the first time on a roof, I felt dizzy and frightened that I was going to fall off.

On the way to the surgery I felt like fainting, but I had to fight it. I couldn't pass out now: I was terrified that the surgery warders would give me an injection when I was unconscious. They had begun cleaning the cuts on my body with antiseptic when I saw the needles. They told me not to panic as it was penicillin. I could hear the high-pitched noise in my head and ears, the warning sign that I was about to black out. Still dizzy, I pushed the surgery warders away, saying I didn't want any injections. They took me back to the punishment block. I was charged by the police for assaulting three warders whilst on the roof. After this I was handcuffed to a warder whenever I was allowed out to exercise.

Whenever I went to the orderly room and started screaming abuse, they would put on a tape-recorder and hold the microphone to my mouth! A warder then told me that the tape-recordings were being analysed by psychiatrists, but that didn't stop me either. I knew the warders were having a lot of meetings about me, and wondering what they could do with me. It was even suggested that I should be left in the exercise pen all day with a huge lump of granite and a hammer and chisel.

One day, when I was coming back from the exercise pen, I saw some works warders smashing the window-panes out of three cells near the warders' desk. Three of us were moved into these cells, from which everything had been removed, including the paper plates and pisspots. Not even a sheet of paper was allowed in. The absence of window-panes didn't bother me at first, but one night I almost froze. I wasn't allowed a blanket at any time, night or day – all I had on was my pyjama shorts and a pair of slippers. I sat below the window so as to keep the bitter North Sea wind off me: if I sat down and put my bare back to the wall, it was like being touched by an ice cube. I tried walking to keep my blood circulating, but then the wind got at me.

I cowered back into the corner below the window like a frightened animal, fearing the worst. I took off my slippers and sat on them to stop the cold concrete getting into me, and I tried to rub my feet with my numb hands. Too weak to kick the door for help, I shouted for the warders through the broken spy-hole. When they eventually came to see what I wanted, I asked for a blanket, but they refused, on orders. I tried pulling my head down into my shoulders and rocking to and fro, but that didn't help. Again I called on the warders and asked them for something to keep me warm, even a sheet of newspaper – but no. I was in agony again from the pain in my belly, and they agreed to get a surgery warder. By now I was shivering violently, and the wind was howling in through the window. Then I had another idea. I squatted and leaned right back till my head was almost on the ground and my body arched; then I urinated over my belly and chest so that it ran warmly down to my shoulders and neck. The heat felt great – but it didn't last long, and before long the urine had frozen.

The surgery warder was a decent type. He told the warders to give me my bed – but they said they had been left strict instructions to give me nothing, not even a sheet of newspaper to wrap around me. The surgery warder then went away, and came back with a huge tin in his hand. In the tin was a deep-heat rub ointment, which he rubbed all over my body. He warned me that I would feel as though I was burning, and he was right. It felt as if I was coming back from the dead, and I could have cried with joy.

About a month after I had been charged with assaulting three warders while on the roof, I was again charged with assault. The incident happened in August 1982. There had been five or six warders on duty, and they were known throughout the gaol as the 'dog squad', because they acted like dogs and treated us like dogs.

I had walked up to Frank's door and looked through his spy-hole to see if he was still there, as he had been very quiet. I saw him on the floor, cuffed by his legs and arms; he was gagged around the mouth and it looked as though he couldn't breathe properly. I went berserk and attacked the warders. I managed to get away from them and I ran into the toilet cubicle, where I jumped onto the seat and started kicking them. I managed to rip out the ballcock from the cistern and used it as a club, raining it down on their heads. The toilet cubicle was pretty small, making it difficult for them to get at me, so they used a mop to try to throw me off balance. They had all lost their hats as they fought with me. But before long they got me, and I could feel the blows from their truncheons as they dragged me back to my cell. Blood was pouring from a head wound and running down my face, but I couldn't feel any pain – and then I fell unconscious.

The three of us were moved from the windowless cells to cells that were almost pitch black. Once my eyes had got used to the dark I saw that a huge steel sheet covered the entire window, blocking out the daylight. I felt around the cell. There was a mattress and bedding on the floor, a cardboard table and chair, and a pisspot. In a hole above the door there hung a dim light bulb which lit up part of the ceiling. In front of the light bulb was a sheet of unbreakable Perspex to stop me from getting at the bulb, or climbing through the hole. The heating had been fixed and hot air was coming in through the ventilator high on the wall: a huge sheet of Perspex outside the window prevented a breeze from getting into the cell, which was boiling.

Some tiny holes had been drilled in the steel grille, but I covered them with food slops and shit till no light got in at all; and with a match I had been given I set fire to the sheet of Perspex, which melted easily enough, so that I could reach through and break the bulb. The cell was now in complete darkness. I ripped my foam mattress into thousands of small chunks and the table got torn up as well.

When the warders opened my door next morning they couldn't see a thing. They came back with a flashlight and shone it round, but they couldn't see me lying under all the bits of torn-up foam. They prodded it with a mop handle to find where I was.

I seldom emerged from my 'cave', though I had to read my letters in the exercise pen. The governor told the warders to leave me alone, and they did. I was in one helluva mess, and in my 'cave' I could shed tears without fear of being seen. Sometimes crying helped, and sometimes not, but singing always did, and I went through most of Jim Reeves' songs as I lay in the darkness of the cave.

The pass-man told me that they were using the darkened cell as an experiment – and that they were livid because it had backfired, and they didn't know what to do with me any more.

I don't know how many weeks I was kept in the dark, but they soon tired of not being able to see me, and put me back in an ordinary cell before my case came up at the Peterhead Sheriff Court. The governor had often told me to get myself a lawyer, but I knew if I did I wouldn't convey the full story to the court. He said I wasn't capable of presenting my own case, but that if I pleaded guilty, he would write a plea of mitigation to give the judge. I told him he was also cited for attempting to pervert the course of justice by trying to influence me into pleading guilty. He was raging at me when he got a citation to appear as a witness at my trial.

At Peterhead court I was approached by a lawyer who said he had been appointed by the court to defend me. I told him to fuck off – I didn't need him or anybody else.

On 18 January 1983 the jury were sworn in. During the trial

I had to stand handcuffed in the dock while defending myself and taking mental notes of what was being said by the warders who were taking the oath and lying my life away. One warder in particular told lie after lie to get me convicted. I stood there helplessly, raging at this bastard who hated me. When my turn came to cross-examine him, I simply told the judge and jury that he was an out-and-out liar and that I had no intention of cross-examining him. I told him to get out of the witness box – 'You've been telling lies all your life,' I shouted.

After about half a dozen of the warders had given their evidence they sat behind me in the courtroom to watch the rest of the trial. Whenever I stood up to cross-examine a witness I could hear them laughing and sniggering behind my back. I could only imagine they were trying to make me look a fool in the eyes of the jury. I turned round and said, 'Hey! You're not in your fucking governor's orderly room now, ya turnkey bastards!' The Advocate Deputy then stood up and looked at the warders: he told the judge that there were too many warders in the courtroom and asked if they could be removed. When the judge told them to leave they were livid – still more so when I turned round and smiled at them.

The lassie who was taking down the proceedings in shorthand sent the court clerk over to ask if I could speak more slowly. It must have been nerves on my part: I tried to do so, but whenever I looked across to her she waved a clenched fist at me. She had a smile on her face as she did so, and I fell in love with her! We used to say hello and goodbye every day. Normally I hated anyone to do with courts, thinking they were all bastards with no human feelings, yet there I was in love with this girl because she smiled at me and seemed friendly. As I was getting dressed up in my civilian suit to appear in court I would try to look tidy for the jury, but soon I started dressing for her benefit. I'd try my hair in different styles, wondering which one she would like best.

I think it was on the second day of the trial that Jim sent word down to me that a newspaper had carried an article about my assaulting the warders in which I was referred to as a 'killer' and a 'murderer'. In court I reported this to the judge, saying I feared it would influence the jury against me. Next day the reporter responsible for writing the article found himself sitting alongside me in the dock. I asked him where he had got his information from and he replied that some warders had told him – but he told the court that he had had a brainstorm and was fined £500.

One warder accused me of punching him to the ground and hitting him on the head with a bolt. He had tried to jump over the wire to get at me on a flat part of the roof across from the punishment block. I asked him not to as I had no intention of surrendering to him, but he wouldn't listen – his feet caught in the wire and he fell on all fours in front of me. I told him I didn't want to fight with him as he had taken me to my dad's funeral, but when he got up he began to circle me in a threatening manner with his truncheon in his hand. He took a few swipes at me and I ducked, but then I caught him on the side of the head with my fist – after which I turned and walked away.

The lies he told in the witness box about my assaulting him when he was on all fours made me wish I'd jumped on his head, and I cursed myself for being too soft with such ruthless bastards.

I had cited Jim, Checker, Dez and Frank as witnesses. I felt sorry for Frank when he was giving evidence. Like me, he had been locked up for so long he didn't know what was what.

So the war of hate between warders and prisoners went on in the courtroom. When warders gave evidence in the governor's orderly room, they were never cross-examined and their word was taken for granted, but here they had to mend their ways. The warders lied to get me convicted and my witnesses lied to stop this happening.

On the fourth day of the trial, when all the witnesses had been heard, the Advocate Deputy started his summing-up to the jury, asking them to bring in a verdict of guilty on each charge against me.

When my turn came to sum up, I had barely got four words out when the judge stopped me and said he couldn't hear a word I was saying and he didn't think the jury could either. I thought this was a tactic to put me off my speech and make me feel nervous. I told the judge I had a cold sore in the corner of my lips which made it difficult for me to speak. 'Do you mind if I come out of the dock and stand directly in front of the jury so that they may hear me more clearly?' I said. He seemed confused at my request, but then said, 'Oh, very well then!' I walked right up to the jury with the warder handcuffed to me, and I began my summing-up to them, looking them all in the eye as I contradicted the evidence the warders gave. One of the warders admitted that he had hit me on the head with a truncheon to subdue me. They admitted the cells had no sinks or toilets for us to slop out, and that we were on a dirty protest. I admitted to punching one of them as they ran forward to manhandle me.

With the trial at its end, I felt I was going to miss all the members of the jury, whatever their verdicts. I had got to know some of their habits: and at least they had listened to me. This was the first time in my life I had spoken to an audience for so long – and with so much to say.

The judge then summed up after I had finished. He told the jury that even though I hadn't been represented by a lawyer, I had presented my case very well indeed. The jury then left, and when they returned to give their verdict the court was hushed. I was found not proven for assaulting the warder on the flat roof, and for hitting another two warders on the leg with a slate I was found not guilty. On the two charges of fighting with the warders in the toilet and assaulting them with the ballcock, I was found guilty.

I was happy with the verdicts. I noticed one wee woman in the jury was crying, and the shorthand girl laughed and waved to me as though I was her long-lost brother. Even the judge showed his approval by giving me a wink and a nod, after which he lowered his head and continued to write.

The judge asked me to stand while he passed sentence. I prayed he would let me off lightly – and he did, sentencing me to four months consecutive. I thanked the jury and waved my pal the shorthand girl goodbye. I was driven back to Peterhead under armed escort and locked up in the punishment block. The warders were furious at the verdicts, but when I told the guys in the punishment block they started cheering.

I'm not sure if it was before my trial or just after that the governor told me that he was going to rescind all punishments, except loss of remission. That meant that I was to be given a wage for tobacco, and he allowed a radio, a mattress and bedding, a cardboard table and chair, and books in my cell. I couldn't believe it and thought he was up to something devious. He said it was the only way he could see of stopping me from getting into further trouble now that they had tried everything else.

It was great to have everything back. It seemed like a decade since I last had such luxuries, and I began to think the governor was a decent enough guy. But before long I couldn't accept it. It meant lying down and accepting solitary confinement, and I wanted out. The governor came into my clean cell with a smile on his face, but he wasn't smiling for long as I demanded all my punishments back, and then told them all to get the fuck out of the cell. I threw away the bedding and radio and started smashing up the cell.

They refused to give me back my punishments – they wouldn't even put me on report for digging at the walls or cursing them. 'Just leave him,' they said. I was told that there was no way they would risk letting me back into circulation, and that the Secretary of State for Scotland had ordered them to keep me in solitary confinement until further notice. I was an embarrassment, the most disruptive prisoner in Scottish gaols and I had more punishments and reports than any prisoner in the penal history of Scotland. I was 26 years old. I had served three and a half years of my sentence and had twelve still to serve.

About a week after the end of my trial they took me away to the Inverness Cages once again, and I remained there for three months. The warders at the Cages had heard about my 'caves' at Peterhead and they reckoned I would be glad to be in a cage rather than a cave, but it didn't make me feel any better.

I arrived back at Peterhead in April or May 1983 and went into A Hall. Franco gave me two little pigeons, only weeks old, and I had to mouth-feed them. Every day when I came in from work the wee birds were still there. They'd come running over to me flapping their tiny wings, and I often shared my food with them. One day I was emptying my basin of water when Franco told me I was being followed. I looked behind me and there were the two wee birds. When they were old enough to fly I let them out of my cell window to roam, and I found myself worrying about them if they stayed out too long.

One Saturday evening I was sitting in my cell, which wasn't unusual. What was unusual was that I had with me two crowbars, a ladder, a tool-kit of spanners and screwdrivers of all sizes, a hacksaw blade and a civilian suit. I was still on strict security because of my continuous attempts to escape, but although my cell was searched every day they had failed to discover my escape equipment. The wood I needed for a ladder had been provided by the authorities – the hardwood frame of two poster boards, three wooden lockers and the framing underneath the table top. That evening I put the ladder together with over 50 nuts and bolts that a pal had stolen for me from his work shed. I drilled all the holes with a huge screwdriver. It was hard work and I was soaked in sweat. I'd covered my spy-holes with paper – had the warder come to my door I would have told him I was having a shit. The ladder was up against the wall with the spy-holes in it.

My door had two steel bolts on the outside as an extra security measure. I broke off the two end prongs of a steel fork I had stolen and slipped it into the tiny gap in the door so that it was touching one of the bolts. I then pressed a fork onto the bolt, spreading the two prongs till they had a firm grip on it; after which I turned the bolt towards me, freeing it from its safety bar, and shoved it to the left till it was clear of the hole. I then did the same with the other bolt. After that I took one of the thick crowbars and worked on the cell door. There was a sheet of metal on the cell door to stop anyone digging their way into the lock, and another sheet of steel on the door frame. I wedged the crowbar into the gap and began forcing the door open. Wood was splitting and snapping, so I stopped to listen for the warder before I continued.

I removed the steel plate from the door frame and dug my way through the wood behind it; but behind the wood was a steel bar, and behind that I could see the 'sprung' tongue of the lock. Before I could get the door open I would have to get the steel bar off – and I couldn't do that because it was part of a steel frame bolted into the side of the door frame. I tried sawing through the bar with my hacksaw blade but had to give up because of the screeching noise it made, which echoed through the hall. I had nothing to worry about from the guys in the other cells since I knew they wouldn't grass. They knew what I was up to, and while I was working on my door they played loud music to drown the noise.

Once again I wedged the crowbar into the gap between the door and the wooden frame, working it up and down and making the gap wider. At one point the bottom half of the cell door had bent and buckled inward, but the lock and the bar still held. I could see out into the gallery and to the cells across the way from me. I worked non-stop, heaving and forcing with the crowbar – and then, as if someone had put a key in the lock and turned it, it opened! I had ripped the whole jamming device out of the door frame.

I crawled out onto the gallery on my belly, making sure no warders were on the 'third', where I was; looking over, I could see them in their office on the bottom floor, by the hall entrance. I pulled my cell door closed and drove the bolts home. The damage couldn't be seen from outside, and with the two bolts holding the door shut the warders could walk up to my door and shove it – and they always did – to make sure it was locked.

Then I crawled along the gallery on my belly to my pal the Bald Eagle's cell door. I rapped three times to let him know it was me. He had taken the steel plate off his door frame and dug out the wood till he could see the steel bar holding the sprung tongue, which he had cut through with a hacksaw blade, but he couldn't get his bolts open – that was my job. I sat with my back to the door as hard as I could – and it gave. We spoke in whispers, congratulating each other. So far so good – but then someone pressed their bell, so we had to hide in one of the arches while the warder went to find out what the guy wanted. The Bald Eagle pushed his cell door to and shot home the two bolts. The warder passed our doors, gave them both a shove and moved on to check the other security prisoners before going back downstairs.

We both slipped upstairs to the top landing, but no sooner had we got started with a jack on the bars of the huge window at the end of the hall than someone else pressed their bell a few feet from where we stood. We removed the jack from the bars and slipped quietly past the cell doors and into the arch, where we waited while the warder came to see what the guy wanted. In the arch were toilets, showers and sinks, and two slop-out sinks. The arch was, in fact, two cells knocked into one; there was no door or grille to it, so there was no need for a warder to go there. It seemed an age that we waited there in the darkness.

I knew Big Shug, the guy who had pressed his bell. When the warder reached his door they argued for quite some time. As soon as the warder had left we began to make our way back to the big window – and then Shug pressed his bell again. Once again we slipped back to the archway and waited. I felt like asking Shug to leave off pressing his bell, at least until we had got away, but it was too risky. The warder came back to the cell door and spoke to Big Shug once again, and then some surgery warders came upstairs to his cell. I wondered what was wrong with him. Time was getting on and we couldn't afford to hang about much longer. We had never thought to tell the guys on the top floor not to press their bells if they could help it.

Once the warders had left Big Shug's cell, we continued back along the gallery only to hear one of the warders coming upstairs on his rounds. Yet again we got into the arch. He was at my cell door and I heard him call my name. I was almost above him in the arch. I had butterflies in my belly and an ache in my heart.

'If you don't take the paper down from your spy-hole, you're going to the cells!' I heard him say. I could have killed myself for forgetting to clear my spy-hole before I left my cell. 'Are you listening to me in there?' he was shouting through my door.

We tried to figure out what we should do next. It was obvious we were caught, so I took the hacksaw blade out of my pocket and hid it inside my underpants – if they found it, too bad, but if they didn't I could use it on the bars in the punishment block. We could hear other warders coming upstairs and heading for my door. A warder pulled back my bolts and was about to put the key into the lock when he discovered it wasn't locked. They quickly pulled the door shut and fastened the bolts again. One of them then ran round all the security cells, turning out the lights, never bothering to look in the cells. They didn't want to alert anyone to trouble in the hall. They thought I was still in my cell, even though they knew the lock had been burst open, because the bolts were still in; once they were in my cell they searched for me under the bed and in the tiny cupboards. We could hear them calling me, asking where I was. I looked through a small window into the gallery, where I saw a worried-looking warder holding a flashlamp and gazing at the skylights on the roof high above him. He came into the arch, shining his lamp – and when he saw me with the crowbar in my hands, laughing at him, he dropped his lamp and ran away, shouting for help. The Bald Eagle came out of the arch, warning him not to come near. They panicked again, not knowing he was out of his cell – or how many of us were out.

I told one of the warders that we were surrendering and would come downstairs with him as long as the others stayed away. They couldn't have been nicer, and it was Johnnyboy this and Johnnyboy that and 'You're doing the right thing in giving yourself up, Johnnyboy'.

When I reached the double doors of the punishment block I froze, frightened of what lay behind them. I was shoved into a cell and they closed the door on me, telling me to calm down. I took the hacksaw blade out of my underpants and hid it outside the window. Then they asked me to take off my clothing so they could search me. They came back in and told me there'd be no brutality since none had been used on them, and one of them asked me if I had any tobacco. When I said I had none he took out some of his cigarettes and threw them on the floor, asking me to keep quiet and not smash the cell up. That night I started cutting my cell bars with the hacksaw blade, singing loudly to drown the noise. Alex had put his radio up at his window to help cover up the sound of what I was doing. This was the second time Alex had offered to aid me in escaping.

The next day I was taken to see the governor and charged with attempted escape. He was very embarrassed at my having broken out of a security cell, and having so much equipment. When he asked me where I got the crowbars and tool–kit from, and what the ladder was to be used for, I laughed in his face. And so I was taken before the visiting committee for the sixth time. They sentenced me to 28 days solitary; I forfeited 30 days remission and was ordered to pay a fine of £25.

The warders were so embarrassed at my breaking out of the cell that they locked up Big Shug in the punishment block and charged him with aiding us in the escape! They claimed that he had deliberately rung his bell to cause a diversion. I told them over and over again that Big Shug had nothing to do with it, and that if it hadn't been for Shug ringing his bell we might have got away.

Honeybugs had written me a letter with the hint of a proposal in it. I read it over and over and thought so much about its contents that it brought a tear to my eye. She didn't know the mess I was in and I didn't tell her. I knew she was good for me, but I knew I'd be no good to her because I couldn't stop doing what I was doing.

22

Dying Within

A fight broke out on the ground floor of A Hall over a
game of pool. I was cutting through another bar when I
heard the commotion; some warders ran over to break up the
fight, and they were being a bit rough on the guys. Dez and
a few others, including Micky and Frank, ran downstairs to
stop the warders. When I saw what was happening, I left the
guy in the cell with the hacksaw blade and went downstairs.
Dustbins and billiard balls and brushes were flying
everywhere, and the riot bell was ringing throughout the
gaol. I didn't want to get involved, but I couldn't stand there
and watch Frank being dragged about the warders' office. As
I moved to pull Frank clear, someone hit a warder with a
pool cue and Frank got away. Someone else said the riot
squad were coming and there was a panic.

I had no option but to get out of the way, because if they
saw me they would automatically assume I was involved. We
all moved up to the top gallery, and everyone started
smashing sinks and toilets and windows. I stood by and
watched them. I was shattered to be caught up in this
situation: my mind was on the bars I'd been cutting.

That night a mob of warders rushed into my cell, dragged
me down to reception, handcuffed me and threw me into a
van; and once more, for the fourth time, I was taken away to
the Cages, as were Micky and Dez. I was told I was to be
remanded for assaulting a warder with a pool cue, but I kept
thinking about the half-cut bars.

In Inverness once again, I paced up and down my cage till
I was exhausted and fell asleep. The newspapers had made a
big deal out of it and there was a hue and cry about our being
put in cages. The Cages were unpopular with the media, and

the National Council for Civil Liberties had been trying to get them closed forever on the grounds that they were inhumane.

I felt sleepy all the time I was at the Cages and Micky and Dez said they felt the same. I wasn't there long before I had a visitor, and when I walked into the visiting room Auntie Mary let out a scream: she had her hand to her mouth and stared wide-eyed at me as though she was seeing a ghost. She kept saying: 'What have you done to my boy?'

I asked her what was wrong, but this only seemed to make her worse, and she started bawling that I had been drugged and that my speech was slurred. I didn't feel as though I had been drugged, but I didn't feel right. The warders denied I had been drugged, but Mary wouldn't believe them. I began to fear that the bastards had put drugs in my food. Auntie Mary said she was going to the National Council for Civil Liberties – and she did. Its Scottish general secretary, David Godwin, told the story to the newspapers and asked for a public inquiry into conditions in the Cages.

After that, I was careful what I ate, as were Micky and Dez. We started throwing our food and shit at the warders. Humphy was there, causing trouble as usual – he was a master at persecuting prisoners. Some of the warders had told him to ease off and not bother us, but he wouldn't.

'I hope you enjoy your food now – don't be thinking that any of us nice warders would put anything in it,' he'd say, with an evil grin on his face.

They wouldn't let us out of our cages, so our food was slipped under the bars. Somebody had urinated in our food. I even found some shit on my plate, and when I reported it to Humphy he asked me how I knew it was shit. I told him I'd tasted it, at which he grinned and slammed the door.

One day I asked to be let out of the cage, promising not to attack anyone. I told them – especially Humphy – that I'd had all I could take and wanted to settle down. The grin crept up his face and he ordered a warder to open my cage. They were dressed in riot gear and carrying baseball-type riot sticks, and they warned me not to do anything. I promised again I wouldn't. I stood by the sink brushing my teeth and

179

looking in the mirror. I could see Humphy behind me in the corridor. I squirted an entire tube of toothpaste into my mouth and turned to face Humphy, holding the toothbrush and empty tube out to him. With a grin on his face, Humphy reached out to take the brush and tube, not knowing what I had in my mouth. My lips almost touched his as I spewed the toothpaste into his eyes and mouth. I remember laughing and then being knocked to the ground by the riot sticks. But it was worth it to see him running about, holding his eyes and screaming.

They beat me all the way into the cage and left me there on the floor. Humphy appeared, holding a wet handkerchief to his eyes; he looked as though he was satisfied that I had got what I deserved. I couldn't get up – my knees and shins were aching from where they had hit me – so I crawled over to the cage bars and, just to get back at Humphy, asked him to let me out of the cage and promised not to cause trouble. He stared right through me, humming the same nonsensical tune he always hummed, and then he left, slamming the cell door with considerable force. I knew this was to annoy me, so I told him he hadn't slammed the door hard enough. He opened it and slammed it again. 'That's more like it,' I called after him.

David Godwin arranged with the Prison Department to come and see me and the others. He seemed a nice guy, and not just because he wanted to close the Cages. He had worked hard over the years in dealing with prisoners' complaints about brutality and ill treatment. While I was talking to him through the wire, the chief warder came in and asked him if he wanted a cup of tea or coffee. I told him not to in case they put something in it.

Back at the Peterhead punishment block conditions got worse, the dirty protest got worse, and the punishments got worse. Once again the warders took away our pisspots so that we had nothing to throw the shit in. But it didn't deter me. I made the shit into balls about the size of tennis balls and threw them onto the walls outside the cell. Others started to do the same. Each time the shit made contact with the granite walls everyone in the punishment block would cheer. It kept our spirits up, but it didn't do the morale of the warders any good as they constantly tried to clean the shit from the walls.

In the end even the warders rebelled against conditions in the punishment block; for three days they refused to clean up the shit that had been thrown everywhere – especially the stairs, since the governors had to walk up them. I burned the Perspex above my door and kicked out the steel sheet so I could see out into the gallery. Soon most of us had removed the Perspex and steel sheeting. Apart from talking to each other through the hole, we could lie in wait for the governors.

A warder came into my cell to try to persuade me to stop my rebellion. He said I was only degrading myself living this way. He stood in my cell among all the shit: he didn't even bother to use the stepping-stones I had made from some granite bricks I'd removed from the wall. He was crying as he told me that when he went home he had to change his clothes in the garage, and that his family could smell the shit, which humiliated him. I cried as well, not because of what he'd told me, but because I saw him for a brief moment as a fellow human being, and I began to feel as if I had taken a liberty with him. Every day I looked forward to getting out of my cell, if only to go to the governor's orderly room. I started carrying my shit bombs with me because the warders were stealing them from me when I left them in the cell. Sometimes my door would open and there'd be no one there. It was a strange feeling – and a good one – to step out into a gallery and not have warders follow my every move. I would strut up and down in my loincloth and home-made blanket shoes, picking targets to aim at. The warders would hide till I had thrown my last, then they'd come out.

The governors stopped me taking my letters into my cell – I had to read them in front of the warders because I was always lighting fires – and keeping warm wasn't a good enough reason for the fires. I wasn't allowed a book – not even a bible – or any paper whatsoever.

I came off exercise one day and instead of being put back in my own cell I was taken to another, clean cell. I refused to go in, saying I wanted to go back to my own cell, but they dragged me into the empty and newly washed cell and left. I was furious – and frightened, because the cell was so clean after my own, with its yellow-painted walls and a door painted blood-red on the inside. The bare, clean cell brought one back to the reality of it all, and somehow I had to get away from it.

I shouted to my pals and told them that I had no shit to put on the walls or throw at the warders. I was so angry that I asked the others if I could borrow some shit from them. They thought I was joking at first, but when they realised I was serious they lowered some down to me. One guy said if he gave me one of his shit bombs he wanted two in return! God knows it was horrible to do what I was doing, but I was determined to fight back with everything and anything short of physically harming the bastards. Within an hour of being in the new cell I had covered all four walls in shit, and whenever I vomited violently I smeared that on as well. At one point I was on the verge of pressing the bell to get out of the cell and away from the smell and thought of other people's shit, but I fought against it. I kept some aside for throwing into the warders' area. Eventually I did press my bell, and when the warders came to see what I wanted they found the cell walls completely covered in filth, and me with shit in my hands. They forgot to close the door in their panic to get away, and I threw some shit at them. I could hear them whispering outside my door. I thought they were going to beat me up when the door opened, but instead they stood there with shit in their hands, which they then threw at me. Far from ducking and diving out of its way, I grabbed it and threw it back at them.

Early in May I was out in the exercise yard in the same pen I had climbed out of before – only they had cemented the corners to stop me from climbing out that way again, and had put roll upon roll of razor wire at the top. The warder on the catwalk hadn't been all that long in the gaol. He was an ex-marine and was recognised as a decent guy who never bothered anyone, and for this reason no one threw shit at him.

He must have sensed something was wrong with me as I paced back and forth in the pen in my underpants. It was a beautiful day, too good to go back to the punishment block. Everywhere was covered in filth: it was driving me crazy. By being sent to Peterhead I had been classed as a hard case, yet they were the ones who had made me into a hard case, after which they tried to break me and use me as an example to others.

I told the warder I was going to get out of the pen because I couldn't face going back to the punishment block. I told him I wouldn't do him any harm. He pleaded with me not to try it as I would rip myself to pieces on the wire. I was afraid that what he said was true and that I wouldn't get out: I began to panic and could feel the madness creeping up on me again. I felt trapped like an animal, with nothing to live for but to be punished again and again: I felt my belly turning and I wanted to scream out for help – a jag, shock treatment, anything to get me away from the reality of this bare existence. I could have asked for medication, but when I thought of myself being locked up in a mental hospital and living a life prescribed by psychiatrists I decided I would do better to be torn apart by razor wire than by doctors.

I took a run from one end of the exercise pen, clambered up the wall, and pulled myself through the razor wire. I became caught up in it, and I could hear Toe and Dez calling me from their windows, pleading with me not to struggle or I would bleed to death. I saw the warder on the catwalk run and press the riot bell, but I was out of reach of any warders who might try to pull me down. I was wrapped in wire and it was worse than being in a cage or cave: everywhere I turned I could feel the needles sticking into me.

'Don't move!' the warder on the catwalk called, but others were cheering and saying they hoped I would bleed to death. What also frightened me was that I was covered in shit, and if I cut myself I might poison my bloodstream. But somehow I managed to get through and I ran onto the roof of the punishment block.

The chief warder was shouting at everyone to go back to their halls. I ran up and down the roof to make sure the warders weren't trying to sneak up on me. Some slates came loose, almost making me lose my footing and fall off, and again I felt dizzy at being so high up. I saw Jim in the crowd below staring up at me: I wanted to ask him for help, but I couldn't bring myself to do it – he had been out of trouble for some time.

Jim walked over and stood below me and I could see he was upset by the state I was in. He asked me if any of the warders had beaten me up, but how could I possibly have said yes? If Jim attacked the warders, it would have meant his losing all he had: a half-decent job and the training hall.

The chief warder shouted at me not to cause any problems for my brother and the others who were still in the yard – he was well aware of the tension there.

Jim said Ma would have a nervous breakdown if I did anything crazy. Standing there with open arms, looking up at me pleadingly, he told me he was getting home leave to see Ma because Maw wasn't well. I was shattered. I couldn't see Jim getting home leave if there wasn't something seriously wrong. I dreaded hearing this sort of news.

Wee Smiddy came towards me, and when a warder tried to stop him he shoved him away. He winked, said, 'Here, pal', and threw me a tobacco tin and a cigarette lighter. I was grateful to Wee Smiddy and the others, not just for the tobacco, but for risking punishment by going on strike and remaining in the yard against orders.

Fearful that I would fall off, I started crawling on all fours. I felt as if I was swaying to and fro and was about to black out. I lay down on the roof, holding on tightly. Toe warned me that some warders were coming up for me and that they had a rope. I warned them not to come near me or I would dive off and take one of them with me. I turned to the guys standing in the yard and asked them to go back to their halls, and we waved and said our cheerios. I assured Jim that I would be all right and that I would come down without hurting myself or any of the warders – but I really wanted to scream, 'Jim, help me! Don't leave me to die!'

I crawled to the other side of the roof and lay out of sight, crying for Maw and remembering how she walked about with her arms outstretched, feeling her way about the house. Then I crawled onto the roof of the archway, where I could see the guys in the punishment block looking out at me from their windows a few feet away, unrecognisable, covered in their own shit. I was choked with tears to hear a big friendly country guy say, 'Could you spare a couple of those cigarettes for your big pal?' – and to see that when his arm came out of the window it too was covered in shit. I reached out and gave him a handful of tobacco and I heard him singing away to himself.

The warders said they were coming up to get me, but they didn't have to. There was no fight left in me. They took me to the surgery and cleaned my cuts – again I refused the penicillin injection – after which I was taken back to the punishment block. I expected them to beat me up, but they didn't. The chief warder sent for me and thanked me for not smashing the roof and windows or assaulting his staff. He told me I could keep the tobacco as long as I didn't start any fires.

An MP came to Peterhead as part of an all-party penal affairs group, and he asked to see me. He asked me humorously if I was the Johnnyboy Steele who had been causing so many problems. I didn't find it funny and told him so. He told me that Mick and Aunt Mary had often written to him, complaining about my health and the conditions I was being kept in. I didn't like his attitude – and still less so when he claimed that the authorities were trying their best to help me. I thought he was only saying this to please the warders, and so I accused him of taking sides without even listening to my case. He stood up, grabbed his briefcase and said in a high-pitched voice, 'I'm not talking to you – you've accused me of taking sides!'

As he headed for the door I called after him, 'You're running away because you're afraid of the truth, you old bastard!' He sat down again while I told him about the governor fighting with the prisoner and the brutality of the

Cages. I could see he was getting nervous and was ready to leave in a hurry. He was up again with his briefcase and kept repeating, 'I'm not sitting here listening to this – you've accused me of taking sides!'

'I bet the bastard governors never told you about the fucking caves they had me in when they were telling you about all the trouble I was causing them!' I shouted. He looked at me as if he couldn't believe what he had heard.

'Caves? What caves?' he asked with a worried look on his face.

I had no sooner started telling him than he jumped up again and said he had no intention of listening any more. I was screaming at him as he left the visiting room: the warders jumped on me, but they couldn't restrain my anger and I cursed and spat at the MP. Next day the governor told me to give in, since the outside world couldn't give a damn for me or any other prisoner.

That June one of the prisoners from A Hall told me something that made me fall back from my window onto the filth and urine on the floor: Joseph, my younger brother, had been arrested and charged with six murders. T.C. and Shadow had also been charged, along with three others. A fire had been lit outside a house door in Ruchazie and the fumes had killed six members of a family. I wasn't worried by the warders shouting at me that Joseph was a mad dog like me – I was too hurt thinking about Joseph and Ma, who I knew must be going crazy. I lay there thinking about my little brother: I could clearly remember the day he was born, and the silver I had pressed into his tiny hand to bring him good fortune in the life ahead of him . . .

Ma came to see Jim and me not long after Joseph's arrest. She was helped in by one of my aunts and I could see the tears in her eyes and the mark the shock had left on her face. I fought back my own tears for her sake – I wanted to grab her and hold her tightly, and I've no doubt she was thinking the same. She couldn't compose herself, but she eventually got some words out: 'My wee Joseph was in his bed when that fire was lit.' I could hear the high-pitched noise in my ears again. Mental and physical exhaustion was making me black out, but fear of every kind had me fight it. Jim told Ma that Joseph wouldn't be taken to court for the murders because the only evidence against him was police verbal, but I reminded him that my dad had had explosives planted on him in our house by the police. It wasn't easy for me to say, but I told Ma to expect the worst in Joseph's case.

Jim disagreed and told me not to tell Ma such things and make her feel worse. Ma was more inclined to believe what Jim said – that Joseph wouldn't get done. I felt bad about arguing with Jim during the visit, for I knew he was shattered too, and like me was holding back the tears: I knew he was right in his way to tell Ma that Joe couldn't get done, but I also knew I was right in telling her to prepare herself for the worst, because I knew too many men in gaol serving long sentences – including life – for crimes they hadn't committed.

It was the worst trial I ever experienced. Some time later I received a letter from Ma in which she said she was worried about me, having heard from someone about the conditions I was living in and my ill-health. Whoever had been talking to Ma told her about the brutality in the punishment block, and she knew I had worn no clothes for months. I cursed whoever had told her, as it only had her worrying more than she could handle. I decided to write back and tell her that I wasn't that badly off and that I had no clothes because the fat rat governor had removed them.

The following day I was told that the governor wanted to see me. He was sitting behind the desk when I walked in in my underpants, covered in filth. I noticed he was turning a letter over in his hand and looking at me all the while. I hated this man, this subhuman who thought *me* an animal – we hated each other, and when we met we screamed abuse at each other. Holding it up, he told me he had read my letter to Ma and that even though there was truth in it I shouldn't send it. He said that Ma was being attacked by her neighbours because of Joseph being arrested. I was numbed by the shock as I stood there, helpless, imagining Ma being beaten up by people she'd been friendly with. I took in every detail of the governor's room for the first time: a golden sunbeam that ran along the wall and across the desk till it reached the governor, the bare walls that seemed coated with intimidation and fear. I had to lean on the desk to stop myself from swaying, and that high-pitched sound was back again.

I asked the governor where he had got his information from and he said, 'Steele, as governor it is my duty to know what goes on in prisoners' families.' He held up my letter again and asked if I still wanted to send it. For some reason I said I did.

I don't remember going back to my cell. Perhaps I dreamt that Toe Elliot leaned over me and cradled my head on his lap. His face was covered in hair from his thick black beard; he was smeared with filth and he was crying. I remember him saying, 'Don't believe the bastards, Johnnyboy!' but I hadn't been dreaming, it had really happened. The guys in the punishment block told me later that I had broken down when they told them about Ma. Toe had asked if he could go into my cell to comfort me.

I wrote to Mick and asked him if there was any truth in what the governor had told me, and he wrote back to say that it was a load of rubbish. Ma then wrote to say that the governor was simply trying to get me to crack up.

Jim was granted his home leave. When he got back I went to see him in the governor's orderly room. He showed me some photos he had taken, including one of Maw lying on what looked like her deathbed – but then I noticed that in one hand she had a small glass of whisky and in the other a cigarette, as if to say she was going out of this world in a blaze of glory. I had to smile.

The orderly room door opened and the governor came in with a mob of warders.

'I have some bad news for you,' he said. 'Your grandmother, Mrs Elizabeth Padden, died yesterday.'

I looked at him, hoping to see something in his face that would tell me he was lying again: I looked to Jim, but he turned away from me; and then I broke down completely in front of them all. I wanted to die, but I was too weak even to will myself to die in this fucked-up world. Warders were holding me up, but I pushed them away. I couldn't contain my tears, and I didn't want to. The governor said that since Maw was like a second mother to us we would be allowed to attend her funeral. He asked me if I would like to go, and I said I would – but then I declined, because I wasn't sure if I could trust myself, and I didn't want to cause a scene at her funeral by running away.

Next day the governor said he would like to see me again. He stared at me for a moment and then he said, to no one in particular, that they had finally broken my spirit. I didn't answer, but did ask if I could go down to Barlinnie so that I could see Ma and comfort her. He asked me if I was ready to stop fighting the system, and I said I was. He told me he hadn't come across anyone quite like me and wanted to know what made me tick. I couldn't answer him. He said I had broken all penal records and caused them terrible embarrassment and trouble. The chief warder, who was also there, told me I had matured ten years over the last few days.

Back in my cell I could hear the guys talking about me. Andy Mac was telling the others – warders included – that it wasn't the warders that had broken me, but nature itself. I was touched by their sympathy. 'Slop out, Steele!' – and I walked out with my pisspot, emptied it down the slop-out sink and went back to my clean cell. 'Stand up for the governor's visit, Steele!' – and I stood up when he came in. 'Morning, Steele, how are you today?' I told him I was fine and said I wanted to apologise for all the abuse I'd given him through the years. He smiled and thanked me.

At Barlinnie I was allowed into the halls with some other guys: the first time I'd been in circulation for nearly a year. I was put into B Hall, third gallery. The news that I was back was all over the hall within minutes of my arrival.

I saw Ma, Auntie Mags, Aunt Mary and many other relatives and friends. Honeybugs had written me a note to say how sorry she was about Maw and asking if she could visit me. It was good to see her again – she was a mother now, with a baby daughter. She asked me how I was keeping and I told her lie after lie, pretending not to be as hurt as I was.

Joseph's trial began, and every day the newspapers carried horror stories of how the family, including a baby, had died. Ma and the others were convinced that Joseph would be found not guilty because they didn't believe he could have committed such a crime, and the police themselves said they believed that whoever set fire to the cellar outside the house had meant to do no more than frighten the family.

Maw's death had taken its toll on Ma. She looked very pale and was ageing fast. She and Brenda were in the little cubicle with its armour-plated glass and wire: she turned her back to me and leaned backwards, resting her head on the little shelf, her eyes closed. I stood up, wondering what was wrong with her, and Brenda peered down at Ma with a frightened look on her face. When I asked her how she was feeling, she said she was simply resting her head.

Brenda told me about Maw's last days and how she kept demanding whisky and cigarettes. She said Maw was always talking about me, and that the family had to read my letters to her over and over again. When she began to lose her senses she would call out, 'Where's my wee Johnnyboy?' thinking I was there. Whenever I thought about this, it hurt me terribly to think that I had wasted so many years in and out of homes and gaols, being away from Maw and the family for so long. I began to think about God and His heaven, and wondered if Maw was there . . .

I was due back at Peterhead before Joseph's trial ended, but I needed to have more time with Ma since I sensed from the headlines that Joseph would need to be Jesus Christ to be found not guilty. I asked the governor if I could spend a bit longer at Barlinnie so as to be with Ma. It was embarrassing to have to ask him – after all, I had put the police onto him only months earlier.

'Why should I do you any fucking favours after what you've done to me?' he shouted, calling me a grass for sending the police to investigate the slashing of the prisoner. I could hardly believe my ears. He leaned over his desk, cursing me. I didn't back off but leaned over the desk too, arguing back, and the chief warder had to keep the two of us apart. The governor asked me why I'd decided to get in touch with the police after so long; I told him it was because I was being tortured by his pals at Peterhead. He denied they were his pals, adding that they didn't know how to run a gaol – I had to agree with him on that. Before I knew it I had told him to forget about my request for an extension, but as I was walking away he called out, 'You can have the extension, but only because your ma needs a shoulder to cry on.' I thanked him under my breath and left.

While the jury was out, Ma was at home preparing a meal for Joseph, his girlfriend Dolly and his solicitor – she was that sure he'd be found not guilty. Dolly had taken the radio into the toilet and was listening for a news-flash of the verdict. There were quite a few people in the house at the time – which was just as well, because when Dolly ran in, shouting that Joseph had been found guilty and sentenced to life, Ma went berserk. She had to be held down and have a bread knife taken away from her after she had threatened to go to the Easterhouse police station and stab the police for manufacturing evidence against Joseph.

An appeal was lodged immediately. The newspapers and television were full of it. Some papers carried stories about how Jim and I were serving long gaol sentences, and how our dad had been a well-known Glasgow gangster who had connections with the Kray twins – painting as black a picture as they could, as if to justify Joseph's sentence.

Joseph was sent to Barlinnie and put in the same hall as me, on the second gallery, so I got to talk to him each day at work and at nights in his cell. He was shattered and couldn't stop crying. He said he had nothing to do with the deaths of any of the fire victims and vowed that he would fight the case for the rest of his life if necessary.

I was in my Barlinnie cell one evening in November when I heard smashing of windows and screams for help coming from one of the other halls. Shortly afterwards, while I was washing and shaving for a visit from Ma and my sister Brenda, I was told that someone had died in a fire during the lock-up period in C Hall. On the way down to see Ma, I stopped at Joseph's cell. He had been put into solitary confinement for punching and kicking a warder who had called him a murderer; he had been charged by the police and was waiting to go to court. As I passed C Hall I saw a blackened cell window and could still smell the smoke.

I spoke to Ma and my sister and promised to stay out of trouble. They knew about Joseph assaulting the warder. Ma said she was writing to the Queen about his being sentenced to life for murders he hadn't committed, and my sister said she was going to write to the Pope and ask him to intervene.

On my way back I was approached by a guy named Alex Fullerton, an old pal from St Joseph's and St Andrew's. He had a strange look on his face, and told me he was very sorry.

'Sorry about what?' I asked.

'Didn't the bastards tell you that your Uncle Atty was the man who just died in the C Hall fire?' he blurted out.

I collapsed on the floor. I wasn't unconscious, I just couldn't stand up any more. Alex helped me to my feet and leaned me against a sink. I kept thinking of Ma and how it would affect her. I even began to wish she was dead so that she wouldn't have to suffer any more, and I could kill whoever I wanted to without torturing her. If Ma had been dead I would have slaughtered a warder – any warder; governors, chiefs, I hated them all. They knew Ma had been seeing me yet they never informed her of her brother's death, never even told me or Joseph.

Either they were playing psychological games or Alex had been mistaken. I asked him who had told him that Atty had died in the fire – I hadn't even known he was in Barlinnie. Alex told me he had heard the warders talking about it.

All that night I paced my cell, thinking, crying and praying for Atty. In a sense I was happy that he had died, but sorry about the way it had happened. For most of his life he had been in a mental hospital, and I knew it had tortured him and that he always wanted out.

Next morning everyone was talking about Atty's death. It seemed that Uncle Atty had been arrested for a breach of the peace and remanded in Barlinnie. He was receiving medication and should have been in the hospital wing – but Barlinnie is full of guys who should be in hospital.

On the Monday night I had a visit from Ma and Brenda.

I couldn't bear to look at Ma – I felt too emotional and upset. She told me they had learned of Atty's death from the television. Brenda warned me that Ma had to be watched carefully in case she tried to commit suicide and begged me not to do anything crazy.

Control Units

M y extension over, I was taken back to Peterhead. In the shower room I was searched and one of the warders said he had found a hacksaw blade in my shoe. I told the bastard he must have put it there. I was taken back to the punishment block and shoved into a cell. The first things I noticed were the silence and that there was no smell of filth. I wondered what was happening. I was determined not to fight back now: I just wanted to get back into circulation as soon as possible and settle down if I could.

An hour or so later my cell door opened and I was told to follow some warders through the double doors, down the corridor and into B Hall. For months B Hall had been empty, with the noise of hammering and drilling coming from it all day long. The bottom landing had been renovated, new steel doors had been put on each cell and all the walls had been reinforced to stop us digging through them. Looking up through the safety net, I could see that the other galleries were empty. It looked like a condemned building up there, with paint peeling from the walls, but down here it was brightly lit and the walls had been newly painted.

I was stripped and given new gaol clothes, and then locked in a cell. Each cell had three sets of bars and a steel grille on the window; a steel bed which had been bolted to the floor, and cardboard tables and chairs. I spoke to Toe and the others, who told me that B Hall was the new psychological control unit. We were to be kept away from the other prisoners in the mainstream of the prison and kept locked up alone for 23 hours a day under Rule 36. We were divided up into twos or threes and let out in groups to work during the day and to walk about or watch the black and white TV in the evening. There were no games, and the only hobby we were allowed was a jigsaw puzzle. The authorities had kept the regime of the control unit a secret and a hospital screen covered the double doors to stop anyone seeing into the hall. At night some of our pals would shout to us from A Hall and ask what they were doing to us and when we were getting out. We sat at our windows till morning, talking quietly: all we had was each other for company.

I was taken to the governor and charged with having a hacksaw blade. When he asked me how I pleaded to the charge, I merely smiled at the stupidity of such witless persecution. I told the chief warder that I had had enough of punishment and only wanted a chance to settle down, and would he please get me out of the control unit and back into circulation. He patted my shoulder as I sat there with tears in my eyes. He said I had caused so much trouble that no one thought I was capable of settling down and accepting prison life; if I started talking about settling down it would only make the staff more suspicious of me. I was trapped again: they were keeping me locked up indefinitely because they believed me to be incorrigible.

Jim was allowed to see me before he was transferred to Perth prison. We cuddled and cried together; he told me I was showing real strength of character by not reacting to the brutal regime, and that he was glad about this because he'd been afraid I would end up getting myself killed by the warders or being sent to the nuthouse. With Jim gone from Peterhead I was glad for him, but I missed him very much.

Alone in my cell, I told myself they would never give in tormenting, and brutalizing and degrading me, and that I was a fucking sucker for allowing myself even to think about settling down. I was at times so confused. We were exercised in a new cage at the back of the control unit; some of the passing warders seemed to think it funny and would make a barking noise like a dog, so I started barking back at them.

I spent another Christmas and New Year locked up in punishment. I started kicking my door and shouting at them to get me out of there. I stripped off my clothes and covered my body and my cell in shit. I smashed everything I could. A warder told me I was on governor's report: I told him I couldn't give a fuck for the governor or his reports, and that I wanted back all the punishments that the fuckers had rescinded.

Next morning I heard the others being given their breakfast, but no one came near me. I managed to smash the spy-hole and push shit through it into the corridor. They rushed in and some of them grabbed me, while others kicked into me. I couldn't feel any pain, only fear.

I didn't know what was happening, or where I was going. They took me to the punishment block and dragged me into the silent cell. It was as dark as ever in there, and the window on the roof was covered in bird shit. I was glad to be there, away from the gaol and all that went on in it. Singing helped, and I sang every day, often composing my own songs. I didn't want to go on living in that hell-hole of cages, punishment blocks and psychological control units. They kept me there for three or four days. I didn't know what punishment the governor had given me, or even what the charge was – I kept my fingers in my ears and whistled whenever he tried to talk to me.

The Bear, who had slept through the riot in 1979, was back in the punishment block. He'd been told he would stay there unless he volunteered for the B Hall control unit. He told me that he wasn't going to any control unit, whether on a voluntary basis or under orders. 'Dae ye think that because I've been in Carstairs I'm an idiot?' he used to shout at the governor and warders.

He was right when he said he wouldn't go into a control unit, for he took his own life down in Barlinnie, where he'd gone on visits. They found him hanging behind his cell door.

The governor came into my cell soon after I had heard of the Bear's death, and he said, 'All right, Steele?' I lay on the floor, looking at him and wondering what made him tick.

'Yes, I'm all right,' I told him – and just as he turned to leave I added, 'But you're fucking sick!'

I cut one of my bars, but the warders heard me digging with it. I barricaded the cell door by jamming the bar between the door and the bottom of the concrete bed, and laughed at them as they tried to get in, and couldn't. The warders on the catwalk were unaware that I had removed the outside bar, since I had made a dummy to replace it. I knew they could have burst down the door with a jack, but they didn't – their idea was to leave me there, and if I didn't want to be fed or exercised that was fine with them.

My pal, Joe, who was in the cell next door, asked if he could have my breakfast. They were only too glad to give it to him, hoping this would torment me. As soon as the warders had gone, Joe threw me a line out of the window and passed over my breakfast in a plastic bag that he had kept hidden. He did the same for dinner – he had only the one bag, so as soon as I had finished with it I gave it back so that we could refill it.

In the end they forced my door open with a jack. They searched me for the hacksaw blade with which I'd cut the bar; one of them told me to bend over so that he could look up my arse. I refused and was ready for them to attack me, but they didn't. I was taken away to the silent cell again.

I had spent about five weeks in the punishment block since my removal from the ten-man toilet. One day I was slopping out and brushing my teeth when two warders started talking to me. I was told that I wouldn't be allowed into circulation unless I agreed to go into the ten-man toilet for a spell, and that I'd be guaranteed a year's remission if I did. The ten-man toilet was a brand new punishment block built near the Burma Road. I wrote to the governor – it was easier than looking at his face – and he summoned me and confirmed that I would continue in solitary confinement if I declined to go to the TMT. I turned my back on him and walked away, saying that if I had to stay in the punishment block I would rather be in the silent cell, away from them all. And so it was the silent cell again.

One day I was reading my book – I had been given a copy of *Les Miserables* by Victor Hugo – when I heard a voice say, 'Are you going to hide away in here for the rest of your life, Johnnyboy?' I looked up and saw one of the governors standing in the doorway. I hadn't even heard the door open. He asked if he could come in. I had never heard him be so friendly or polite before. He said things were different now in the TMT: only Toe and Alex were there and I would be allowed out with them every day for exercise, work and recreation. I could work in the garden too, and get plenty of fresh air. Again I was told I wouldn't be kept there too long. I asked him where the logic was in giving me better conditions for no more than three months and then putting me back into circulation under worse conditions. Instead of answering, he told me he was throwing me a lifeline by taking me to the TMT, of which he was the governor. I gave in and went to the TMT.

As soon as I arrived, Alex and Toe were allowed into my cell to make sure that I was all right. They confirmed that the TMT had changed and that the warders didn't seem to bother with them. In fact, some of the best warders in the gaol were there.

The three of us used to sit in the garden during the day, and sometimes we'd dig it for something to do. The warders were growing vegetables and using the silent cell as a hothouse!

At night Toe and I used to sit at our windows, talking into the wee small hours. From him I learned more about my dad than I'd ever known. Toe said he was one of the best guys he'd ever known. When I told him about the punishments he gave me as a kid, Toe laughed and said his father had done the same – all the older mob believed in beating their sons to keep them in line. He said how my dad often worried that I would follow in his footsteps and spend my life in and out of prison. Toe told me things that made me think twice about my dad and the hatred I felt for him. I couldn't make sense of it, so I started to write about my childhood experiences, putting down all I could remember, trying to analyse myself and catching only glimpses of the gentleman Toe referred to when speaking about my dad. All I could remember was a man I feared, hated and hardly knew, who was not only forever punishing me and saying it was for my own good, but on many occasions told me I wasn't even his child.

'If, as you say, my dad always boasted that I was his favourite, why all the witless beatings and punishment?' I asked. Toe said it was obvious that my dad was doing it to try and stop me from doing wrong, no matter how trivial. Why, then, had Jim never been hit for the trivial things he did as a kid? Toe had no answer. I reckoned that Jim was his favourite son, and that – as my dad always said – I wasn't his. I couldn't find any other reason for what he did to me. I let Toe read the hundred-odd pages of self-analysis. He sent it back to me with a note saying that I should turn all my sufferings and misery into something constructive by writing my life story, which could be very beneficial to society and save other kids from being brutalised. Because of my song-writing and verses Toe reckoned, as others did, that I was quite a talented writer, and tried to encourage me. When it dawned on me that perhaps I had a hidden talent I felt a sense of pride. Toe often said he knew I wasn't evil, but that if I didn't do something positive with my life the authorities would turn me into a killing machine sooner or later. He was right – I wasn't evil, but I did wonder how long it would be before I used a knife on one of the governors or warders.

The ten-man toilet allowed me more breathing space. On sunny days I worked in the grounds stripped to the waist. We saved our wages to buy tomatoes, cucumbers, tinned pilchards and pickles. We got potatoes from the cookhouse and I stole the odd lettuce from the garden – the warders looked on, telling me to hurry in case I was seen by anyone else. Alex made up a salad each night, and the warders let us use their cooker and pots. I told the governors that I would sooner stay in the TMT than go back to the mainstream of the gaol where I wouldn't survive long. They said they had noted my progress.

After about five weeks, I was told to pack my kit since I was going back to A Hall. I asked about the year's remission I had been promised and was told I would have to earn it by long periods of good behaviour. I was also told I would be working in the mailbag party.

I told the governor that I wasn't going back there to be persecuted. I went back to my cell, and when they came for me I wouldn't let them in. Toe and Alex put up a fight on my behalf, but I told them it was okay and that I would just have to go back and make the most of it. I shook hands with them and left.

I didn't know many of the prisoners in A Hall. That afternoon I was taken to work with the mailbag party in a cold and dirty shed. When I was given some filthy mailbags to mend, I refused and threw them on the ground at the warder's feet. Everyone stopped working. He threatened to put me back into the punishment block if I didn't get down to work. Eventually it was decided that I would get no wages for refusing to work.

My first day back in circulation hurt me just as much as my first day in gaol – nothing had changed, it was still as ugly to look at and to be trapped in. The warders wouldn't let me out of their sight, and there were many new warders whom I'd never seen before.

I was about to take my clothes off and put them outside my cell door that night when one of the cons told me that he had overheard the warders talking about my being taken back to the punishment block. I put my clothes on again and walked downstairs to the double doors and out into the damp and empty corridor. I was taken to the silent cell in the punishment block at my own request. It was peaceful there in the darkness and I could relax. With no windows to sit at, and cut off from everyone else, I took to thinking about my life.

Early next morning one of the chiefs came to see me. He said that they weren't going to allow me to lock myself away from the world, and that it was time I got a grip of myself. He added that they didn't want to see me being punished any more, and that they would all go out of their way to help me. I took this with a pinch of salt and reckoned they must be furious about my walking into the punishment block, which was supposed to be so frightening. Again I was asked if I would like to see the prison psychiatrist, and again I refused. I agreed to go back to the hall that afternoon and try to fit into the regime once again. But the witless persecution started again and I was put on governor's report for having my hands in my pockets in the exercise yard, and locked up in the punishment block for three days. I talked to T.C. in the punishment block. He was fighting his case and studying law. He had no option but to be there, because the authorities were persecuting him and making it difficult for him to fight his case. He had been on hunger strikes and was so thin I hardly recognised him.

When they put me back in circulation once again I decided to get away from it all by trying to escape. A guy called

Midnight offered to help, after failing to talk me out of it. I knew that there was a huge ball of twine which was used for mending the mailbags: it was very strong and could be used to make a rope. In the mailbag party was an old lifer called Pat, who was in for murder. I asked him if he could smuggle out the twine, since he wasn't searched as thoroughly as the rest of us. He knew right away what the twine was for and asked me if he could come too, but I said he was too old to climb. He went off in a huff for a few moments, but then he gave me a bear-hug and said he would help.

Midnight and I cut lengths of twine, which Pat then rolled into small balls and hid under the cap he always wore. At night Midnight made the rope in his cell. I managed to get some iron bars off some sewing machines with which to make grappling hooks: these were smuggled out in a tea-can, which was collected every morning and taken back to the cookhouse. They were then passed to Wee Smiddy, who was a pass-man in A Hall, and he hid them till I got in from work. Rather than risk sawing my bars, I decided to dig through the ceiling of a cell on the top gallery, and I managed to get hold of a five-foot crowbar for tunnelling through with.

The gaol was full of new warders, which gave me the idea of dressing up as one of them in order to get across the exercise yard and round to the back of C Hall. We made a warder's hat, and Midnight stole one of their plastic raincoats. I also made, with Midnight's help, a minister's vest with dog-collar attached, and someone made me an imitation fur jacket, with a hat to match. I had found a small hole behind a steel plate inside the showers, where some pipes went up into the loft, and stashed the rope up there.

Joe the Meek was one of the pass-men in A Hall, and over a few mugs of tea at night we reminisced about my family. He told me about Ma as a schoolgirl, and how some of them called her the wee innocent lassie of the Gorbals. I told him about how my dad used to tell me that I wasn't his son, and how Ma and Maw would argue with him and shout at home that I was his flesh and blood. I stopped to look at Joe's face – a hard-looking face like a boxer's – and the tears were streaming down his cheeks. He asked me if I knew that my Ma had been married before she met my dad! I was shocked to hear this, since it seemed to confirm all my suspicions. 'No, Johnnyboy,' Joe said, his arm round my shoulder like he was supporting me. 'You are his son – it's Jim who isn't.'

For days and nights I thought about what Joe the Meek had told me. I tried to analyse my life as I paced up and down my cell and it started to make sense. I had been wrong about my dad all my life, hating him for being so cruel, for the beatings and for sending me to bed. I remembered how Maw had told me that one day I would understand my dad and how much he loved me. As for the escape plan, I couldn't stop now. I was still doing what I had always done when faced with hardship – running.

While we were preparing for the escape, some guys in the punishment block got out. A dummy gun was used and a hostage taken, but they gave up. A few days later T.C. was rushed to hospital with a broken spleen that he got from a beating.

I managed to get into the top gallery cell and started to tunnel through the ceiling with the crowbar, making a hole big enough to get my head through. I was stripped to my shorts, and there was dust and debris everywhere. As soon as I had finished for the night I gave a couple of knocks on the pipe and Midnight and some others came in with mops and pails and paint and paint-brushes to cover up the hole. But the guy whose cell I was grafting told the warders about the hole in his roof. He didn't grass any names, though he knew I was responsible. He told me that it was too heavy for him to get involved in, as he had only six months of his sentence left. He was right – it was heavy for him. They put him on protection over in the surgery where no one could get at him, but no one wanted to get at him.

The next day, two guys who were supposed to be involved with me were locked up for subversive activities, and soon I was taken away to the B Hall control unit to await a governor's report for having forbidden articles in my cell. I told the governor that I had never had any forbidden articles in my cell, but he said that he knew I'd been heavily involved in the escape plot, and I was given 14 days solitary.

T.C. was in the cellblock. He couldn't hold his food down since the operation. He looked like a corpse. He was still fighting his case.

When I got back to A Hall I went to see the governor about T.C.'s health and about him being moved to hospital for proper treatment. I was told to mind my own business. Soon after, my work shed went on strike to protest against the brutality being used on T.C. in the punishment block, and to have him transferred to hospital where he could be looked after properly. I was the last to be called to see the governor about it. I had barely walked in when he got half out of his seat. He was leaning on his desk, his face almost scarlet. In a fit of rage he screamed: 'You, Steele! Get into B Hall control unit!' There were more warders around me than normal, and they formed a circle to stop me from getting to the governor. I told him my reasons for striking, but was cut off by him screaming: 'Get him out of here!' I tried to hold onto the framework around the door and screamed back at the governor that he was an animal and worse than any of the craziest prisoners in the fucking gaol. The warders hauled me away and over to B Hall control unit.

24

A Hope in Hell

In February 1986 I was sent yet again to the Cages: it was the sixth time I had been there. I sat down naked and buried my face in my hands, wondering what my life was all about. It was 1986 – the year I should have been going home. I didn't know where the years had gone. I never thought I'd live to see 1986 when I was first sentenced back in 1978. But I still had almost another eight years to serve. I felt I'd never get through them. I didn't want to, it was too frightening. I couldn't stay out of trouble, and I couldn't settle down. My sanity couldn't hold on that long, and I'm not sure if I wanted it to. The authorities thought me a nutter, but in my heart I knew different.

Next morning the governor came to see me after I had refused to go and see him. 'Welcome home, Steele,' he mocked me. I couldn't even look at him: I just lay down on the floor shouting 'Fuck off!' till he left.

I managed to cut off one of the bars in my cage. My pal Bill, an Australian, had done the same, and we jammed them back on so that the warders wouldn't notice. We decided to tunnel our way through our wall outside the cage. It must have been about ten o'clock one evening when I removed the bar from my cage and crawled through. I began digging at the wall which led to the outside yard, removing the cement from around the brickwork as quietly as I could. A guy called Ben listened out for the warders: when I heard him singing a certain line in a song I knew the warders were coming, so I brushed the bits of cement behind the cell door so that they couldn't see them, crawled back into the darkened cage, jammed on the cut-off bar and pretended to be asleep. The warder came to my spy-hole and put on the light, but when he saw me there he went away again. Then I heard him ask Bill what he was up to – he'd noticed that Bill's wall was damaged. The warder ran away to get some help, so I grabbed the bar and went mad on the wall with it. I could hear Bill doing the same. There were dozens of bricks all round me, and I was choking on the dust, but I kept on smashing down the wall. It was a mad dash for freedom. I could hear dozens of warders running down the corridor and the blare of their walkie-talkies. Soon they were at my spy-hole, shouting at me to stop. I was crying with rage and frustration. They shouted that the perimeter wall was surrounded by police with dogs, but I kept on smashing till I collapsed exhausted on a heap of rubble and bricks. The door burst open and they rushed in in full riot gear and grabbed me. A surgery warder handcuffed my arms behind my back.

They carried me along the corridor to a punishment cell. As soon as they had closed the cell door I took the handcuffs off and started digging a hole in the wall. They came in, snatched the handcuffs from me and dragged me off to another cage, where they handcuffed me spread-eagled to the bars and left me standing in the dark.

My eyes soon grew accustomed to the dark and I could just see my reflection in the mirror on the wall outside the cage. I kept looking at myself and thinking about what I saw there. With my boyish face I looked much the same as ever: but I didn't feel like a boy, I felt old. I laughed and cried and cursed and screamed: I prayed to God, then I cursed him, then I prayed again. I imagined doing all the things I had never done with my dad – camping and fishing and laughing all the while, just like fathers and sons should do.

In the morning they took me down from the bars. My hands and wrists hurt badly; as I moved them slowly to my sides the pain went shooting through my arms. In the daylight I could see I was filthy. They passed me my breakfast but I kicked it out again; I was sorry I did for I was starving, which was unusual for me. After the warders had left I put one of my legs through the bars and pulled in a slice of bread.

I noticed there was a foul smell in my cage. It smelled of shit, but I wasn't on a dirty protest at the time. I assumed that the cage hadn't been properly washed and thought no more about it. That night, as I lay on the floor, I heard a noise.

Remains of food were splattered all over the outside of the cage, and eventually I made out what looked like a rat with a slice of white bread. I threw something at it and it scurried away down the hole which led to the exercise yard from the outside of the cage. In the morning I put my hand into the hole and discovered an open pipe that smelled of the sewers. I was furious and demanded the doctor. I explained to him about the open sewer and the rat, and he promised to investigate. Some of the warders said it was only to be expected that rats would come up the sewer and into the cage as long as I left food slops lying around.

I wrote a petition to the Secretary of State. I got hold of one of my encyclopaedias and discovered that it was illegal to have an open sewer in an inhabited building. I quoted this to the governors and doctors. About a week later the warders came in and blocked up the hole.

One of the assistant governors asked me which gaol I wanted to go to, but I said I wanted to go home. The chief warder then told me that the governor of Peterhead didn't want me back – nobody wanted me, and certainly not them. The only places left were Carstairs or the Special Unit at Barlinnie.

'Is there any difference?' I asked.

It took them 19 days to decide where I was to be sent. They had to inform the Special Unit community and get its views. They had to decide if they could trust me not to smash the place up or escape. After that, a recommendation would be sent to the Secretary of State.

On the 19th day the warder in charge came into my cage, stood looking at me for a while, then said, 'There's a team coming from Barlinnie in a couple of hours to collect you.'

I still had a one-inch piece of hacksaw blade hidden up my arse in a small sheath to stop it from cutting me; it was the only comfort I had, and wherever the bastards were taking me it was coming with me.

The cage door opened and I saw one of the warders from the Barlinnie Special Unit plus a couple of others. I was handcuffed to one of them in the back seat of a car.

I was really glad to be leaving the Cages, leaving what

seemed to be the worst behind. They kept talking to me but all I really wanted to do was lie down and rest.

'What the fuck is the matter with me?' I wondered. The warder leaned over and took off the handcuffs.

'Relax, Johnnyboy,' he told me.

Suddenly I felt naked and vulnerable to be away from my cage and punishment. I felt abnormal sitting here as close to humanity as I was and my emotions were in turmoil.

The words came back to haunt me: 'You'll never learn, Steele!'

'You'll end up in an asylum, Steele.'

Fear gripped me tightly as I struggled to hold on to my life and what was left of it. Somehow that journey, which took hours, ended when I saw the big gates of Barlinnie prison come into view and I knew only then that I wasn't going to an asylum. Once through the gate I heard the usual: 'One on the numbers!'

I could see some of the warders stare in at me and I knew what they were thinking. The big guy next to me told me not to let them bother me, that I'd soon be out of their lives and that they would look after me at the Special Unit.

I was quickly taken to what seemed to be a separate building secluded by a large wall topped with razor wire. As the door locked behind me I stood there in my three-piece suit looking around, waiting on the unexpected – whatever that may be. I was told to come inside the building to meet the others.

As I stepped through the door, four warders came towards me each taking his turn to introduce himself and shake my hand. One in particular reached out to me but I quickly drew away – I remembered him from Peterhead. I could never forget his stony-faced look and I hated the bastard.

Someone called a special meeting to announce my arrival at the Unit and soon I saw some other faces I knew from Peterhead, guys who had been there with me in the punishment block: Big John, Cokey, Adja – the guy I helped break out of the punishment block – Bob, the guy who'd been fighting with the governor in the cell block. They were all wearing plain clothes and looked somewhat healthier since I last saw them.

I could sense no animosity from anyone. But my animal instincts brought me back to reality and the concrete jungle, which I had become accustomed to. Cokey, my old pal from Peterhead, reassured me that all was well at the unit and that all the warders there weren't the same guys we once thought them to be. How could they be any different, I thought to myself?

Once the meeting was called everyone took turns to introduce themselves. Prisoners and warders told me they wished my stay at the Special Unit would be a happy and pleasant one and that all would help whenever they could. All I had to do was trust them with my life. Imagine that! Me trusting my life with warders? I couldn't comprehend that, for somewhere deep inside me was an instinct that told me never to trust them and to escape the first chance I got.

I knew I had to overcome certain weaknesses and face certain strengths. The only thing was I didn't, at times, know which was which.

The Unit housed only seven prisoners but there was a buzz of excitement as we exchanged stories about where I came from and what was going on there.

There were civilians walking about the place with no warders standing guard over them: men, women and children who were related in some way to the prisoners at the Unit. People came and introduced themselves to me wishing me a pleasant stay. It somehow reminded me of the old tenement buildings at Carntyne, where there was a friendly atmosphere. A stranger came and offered me a bowl of homemade soup, saying I needed fattening up! I found out later it was Cokey's cousin who had been visiting him. Some other visitors came to talk to me; they seemed so humane towards me . . . this thing that had just been taken from a cage.

I hurried myself to the toilets and sat there in a cubicle crying. Something inside me awoke, shattered me and brought me back to the reality I so often tried to escape from. It wasn't that everyone was being too humane, no, they were acting normal – something I had long since forgotten to do.

Everyone at the Unit had their families up to visit them and seemed so happy, relaxed and dignified. They didn't seem to resemble themselves, as I knew them back in the old gaol. I felt out of place being amongst ordinary people and found it hard to converse, so I sought sanctuary in the pottery room. Adja found me there and told me he felt the same when he first arrived there.

It was a comfort to know I wasn't alone in my experiences and feelings and I was thankful to this guy who only a few years ago was at the mercy of warders who were trying to kill him, and I know he was thankful to me for saving him back then. It was strange for us to meet under such different circumstances.

I had a visit from Mick and Mary who had so often looked after me. I was really happy to see them and they me. They told me Ma was in hospital for an operation but not to worry and that she'd be home to see me soon.

I was allowed to decorate my cell and furnish it like I would at home: a TV, a carpet, divan bed, fridge, even wallpaper. This was to help us feel more comfortable. But it was still a gaol; it only lacked the gaol regime and that made one hell of a difference.

The stony-faced warder came to speak to me. I found it hard to communicate with him for obvious reasons. He was part of the Peterhead Mafia who hid behind a cloak of responsibility and as far as I was concerned was knee deep in it along with the others. Cokey sat with me while he told me that in all the years he was a guard in Peterhead he had never placed any prisoner on a charge nor had he ever assaulted a prisoner but had in fact fought with other warders because of the difference in their beliefs. He said he wasn't part of the Peterhead Mafia and for this reason didn't get on with any of his former colleagues.

I was shocked to hear this statement come from the lips of the stony-faced man and watched his eyes well up.

He was right, I had never known him to put anyone on a charge nor assault a prisoner in all his years in the service. The only thing that stood between this man and me was the way he looked – stony-faced, uncaring and a hard-looking bastard who seemed like an animal.

Cokey turned to me and said, 'Johnny, I used to think the

same about him . . . but he really is a gentleman and a humanitarian'.

I could see I had somewhat hurt this guy's feelings . . . if only he knew what it had done to mine.

He was trying to reach out to help me and probably would have back in Peterhead, but the old gaol regime doesn't encourage such behaviour. It left us to get on with it and behave like animals, not caring who or what it damaged in its wake. This guy told me that he too was damaged by the prison system in that he too was degraded and humiliated whilst working for a regime that did more harm than good.

Sometimes we have to examine ourselves – our inner selves – and there's nothing more hurtful than the truth. I would at times rather face the wrath of the prison system than face the awful truth of learning that my once worst enemy was just a friend I did not know. I felt my own eyes begin to well up and headed for the toilet cubicle for sanctuary. It was some time before I realised the stony-faced guy was there smiling with his hand outstretched.

Six weeks later it was decided that I come off supervised visits at the front area of the Unit and be allowed to have visits in my cell with my family and friends. Each prisoner on arrival would get visits in the front area for six weeks; this was a square and everyone had to pass through it. This was to allow everyone to see what was happening and what kind of visitors would be visiting you and to be sure there was no abuse taking place, like drinking or taking drugs. Everyone went out of their way to help new arrivals and get to know them and for us to get to know them and their visitors – we were after all a community and functioned as such. No one man was bigger than the Unit but the actions of one man could affect everyone's life here. So it was in everyone's best interests that we looked out for each other. Prison staff were all called by their first names and each would introduce himself to a newcomer and his visitors, telling them they were here to help all they could. To many it was hard to believe because of past experiences. It was much like trying to convince someone to clap a dog that had so often bitten one in the past. It wasn't an easy task.

We were told that the psychiatrist, Dr Peter Whatmore, would be there should we ever need him or even the psychologist David Cooke. Everyone was ready to make himself available to help anyone at anytime; it couldn't have worked any differently.

Every Tuesday there was a community meeting attended by the psychiatrists, all members of staff and all prisoners. This is what held us together, for everyone had a chance to raise any points, faults or grievances at the meetings. And here we could keep track of an individual's progress at the Unit. We also had members of the community who were civilian workers: the priests, the ministers, the social worker and George Sharkey, who specialised in the care of ex-offenders. He was an ex-SAS soldier in days gone but whose only goal was now to help those less fortunate than himself. It was a great set-up and a sensible one at that.

For instance if a prisoner was being abusive to another con or member of staff he would be brought to task and had to explain his actions. No matter who he was, everyone had to justify his mistakes or wrongdoings. Here brutality would not be tolerated – and whoever was responsible would be put out of the Unit. So we, the cons, had an obligation to look out for each other and if one should fall by the wayside then we'd pull together to help.

The names of cons who the main gaol wanted to recommend for the Unit were raised at the meetings and each and every one of us had a say as to whether we thought he was suitable for our regime or not. And it was in everyone's best interest that the truth be told.

Every day prisoners were walking about with their visitors and families. Some were sunbathing; others playing tennis in the small yard; I'd never witnessed such scenes before. Sometimes the warders' and prisoners' families were playing tennis and other sports in the yard – the amazing thing was that some years ago these cons and warders were arch–enemies assaulting and abusing each other.

My old friends came to visit me, including Tony Tamburrini, my co-accused. I felt sorry for him as he had become a heroin junkie and was losing the plot rapidly. It was sad to see. He, on the other hand, was astonished to see the transformation in me, telling me that he thought I'd never make it through my 16-year sentence.

Eventually the drugs killed Tony. He was a long-term pal who could have had a lot going for him. As a kid he was so talented at all sports, especially at football, and those who knew him knew he could have made it with the right guidance. Instead he became a thief and was swallowed up in the system. I cried at his demise.

Big Gak also came to visit me. He had never changed in looks and appearance but sadly he too was hooked on heroin and would steal anything to feed his habit. I couldn't help but feel sorry for Gak. He would at times be so funny, especially when we were stressed out and on the run. But it seemed that I had lost another pal in one way or another.

Two guys gone and my fondest memories of them were when we were delinquent children starting off in an unworthy life of crime and escaping from miniature prisons known as approved schools and remand homes.

Often people asked us if we were having conjugal visits at the Unit and it was the prisoners' policy to refute such allegations, fearing reprisals from the prison bosses. Of course there was sex. Every prisoner there had built up a relationship with a female, whether it was his wife or girlfriend. One new governor said he had heard of such goings on at the Unit and demanded to know if it were true. We all denied it. But what all the fuss was about I don't understand because in most Third-World countries conjugal visits are common and humane.

No one advertised it at the Unit that they were having sex, the subject was taboo. You couldn't see if it was happening behind closed cell doors. Nor was it a case of a bunch of cons having their leg over every minute of the day. Everyone had sensible relationships, which also helped to stabilise him and keep him sane.

One day at a meeting the governor read out a letter from Gartloch Mental Hospital. Staff there wanted to visit the Special Unit to talk to the inmates and staff and share their experiences. It was agreed they could come. I went around to meet them on their arrival. Most of them seemed young but there were some older. I asked if anyone there had ever come across my Uncle Atty whilst there. I was quite taken aback when a few of them acknowledged they had. I told them about my experience way back then and Atty running away because he was being abused, given electric shock treatment and being used as a guinea pig with drugs. I mentioned about the brutality on Atty who was, after all, a voluntary patient. I informed them that Atty died in a fire in Barlinnie C Hall when he should have been at the hospital.

I could see I had hurt a few feelings. One young student said she was sorry for my loss but that I must accept that abuse and brutality no longer existed at the hospital nor did electric shock treatment and that those days were long gone.

One day another letter came from the Strathclyde Police who informed us that some police officers wanted to visit us at the Unit. There were wide condemnations and 'no ways' but in the end common sense prevailed and we let them in. The topic was police brutality and fit-ups and officers being 'economic' with the truth in court. One of the coppers said as he was leaving that he had orders to shoot me on sight when we had escaped from Barlinnie.

A new prison warder from Peterhead had applied for a job at the Unit. We all knew him and had some dealings with him. We listened to what he had to say to us and why he thought he would benefit from a stay at the Unit. With careful consideration we discussed his comments and decided that he was entitled to a chance to show that he could help and gain experiences from all, and also to get away from the pressures of the old system which was turning him into a sub-human. We felt sorry for him for he was young and had obviously been thrown into the deep end and was being used and abused at Peterhead.

He was there only a few weeks when he called a special meeting and informed us all that he wanted out of the Unit to return to the old system. He seemed to be psychologically drained and mentally exhausted. He said he couldn't cope with such a regime where all concerned acted humanely, considerately and sensibly. He thought it would be easier for him to go back to the old system.

I for one could identify and sympathise with him. But like us cons who knew nothing but brutality and inhumanity, he too was a victim of a regime geared to torment and destroy and humiliate one and all; a system devoid of humanity, care or any real notion of rehabilitation.

In the mornings I was up early and jogging around the small yard, then went to the gym to do a workout. It was good to hear the sound of children running around the Unit. At times the other cons would entertain the kids by playing football or pool.

As the months wore on Ma came to see me with my sisters. Brenda, who was the youngest, now had two kids. It was a great feeling to have them share my cell and sentence with me. It's a true saying that a boy's best friend is his mother. Poor Ma was so frail and pale and much older looking now; but all she was concerned about was me, Jim and Joe who were scattered in gaols across Scotland. It may have been easier for Ma if my dad was still alive, or even Maw Padden. But they were gone and it must have been a great loss for her to have her three sons away from her, especially Joe, who was innocent of the murders he'd been sent down for, and I know it was hard for Ma to accept this. I can only imagine how Joe felt. I felt helpless being unable to support either him or Ma under the circumstances and I guess Jim thought much the same.

We, as a family, knew that we were up against the whole judiciary system and police force who were determined that Joe would remain in gaol guilty or not. We made a promise that we would do all we could to help Joe, who was framed by notorious members of the Serious Crime Squad.

From time to time Jim, Joe and I were allowed family visits at the Special Unit. There were forty visitors present in the cell area. Cokey and some others had to entertain some of our visitors as we were running out of space and seats.

Ma's oldest brother Alec was there playing his guitar and singing just for us as he did back in Carntyne. Dad's sisters were there with cousins I'd never seen before. The cell block had transformed into a tenement building. Ma was making soup in the kitchen with my sisters and cooking roast and making salad. The sound of Uncle Alex's voice filled the cell block. I looked over at the stony-faced guy who was merrily tapping his feet to the sound of music. My young cousin, who then was a hairdresser, chatted away to me as she cut my hair. Behind me sat two or three cons waiting to have their hair cut too.

I was amazed I was allowed to have as many visitors, but the staff had told me to make the most of it as they wanted to try to undo the damage the gaol had inflicted upon me. I couldn't remember a reunion like this even when I was out of gaol; it brought back so many fond memories, and strangely enough for those members of my family who had died there seemed to be a number of new replacements; nephews and nieces and cousins.

All the bitterness and hatred seemed to have abandoned me; the instinct for revenge, which so often flared up in me, had extinguished. This was all I needed to get out of life, this friendly, loving feeling, this human feeling that had been gone from my life for so long.

Uncle Alec had smuggled in a half bottle of brandy and told me to drink it when they left. Jim and Joe were handcuffed and taken back to their own gaols. When all had left the staff and cons from the Unit had gathered around me to see how I enjoyed my family reunion. I was speechless and somewhat weakened emotionally.

That night as I lay in my bunk in my prison cell, a thousand fancy thoughts waltzed me around my cell, just me and my half bottle of brandy and my music playing. Then a horrible thought struck me as I caught sight of myself in the mirror on the wall. Has this really happened? Have I gone mad? Where am I? Am I in a 'cage' imagining all this goodness in my life? Is my mind playing tricks on me? Have the warders drugged me?

I remember sitting up at the window staring out at the skies. An urge came over me to smash the cell up; to attack the warder; to escape.

I heard the cons all shouting out of their windows asking what was wrong with me. The warders were at my door, worried about my state of mind. They must have thought I'd gone mad for they went away and got another con to come in and help calm me down. He had been a very good friend of my dad's and I knew I could trust him so I told him I thought I was going mad. I questioned him about the day's events, about the family visit. I was relieved when he verified everything for me.

This guy was serving life for a gaol murder and had already served 20 years. He told me that he too had felt this way when he first arrived at the Unit. He said it was because we had become institutionalised and had become accustomed to the brutal prison regime so that anything that was normal seemed to be abnormal. Having spent 20 years in a cell, he was speaking from experience. So there we were in the wee small hours of the morning reminiscing and drinking the remainder of my brandy, which was of course unknown to the staff on night shift.

As the months went into years the Special Unit went through some changes. Cons, governors and warders who came to the Unit to work found it hard to adjust from the old prison system. Some made it; some didn't.

One day a letter was read out by the governor. It seemed Glasgow and Strathclyde Universities had joined forces and wanted to hold a debate at the Special Unit. The debate was on a 'hang them, flog them or rehabilitate them' theme. They wanted to challenge the community at the Special Unit, a community that they and so many others had heard about.

At the community meeting the governor, who was new to the Unit, asked for volunteers. We were all trying to avoid the issue as none wanted to face a university challenge situation. These students were the holders of the Observer's Mace, which seemed to intimidate us. All the prison warders and cons didn't want to know – me included.

The governor volunteered to go, hoping others would follow, and David Cooke, the psychologist, put his name forward, followed by George Sharkey. Now they were looking for a prisoner and the cons wanted me to represent them, because they thought I was able to deal with them. Toe Elliot, who had also come to the Unit, encouraged me to take part. I refused point blank but finally I gave in.

On the night of the debate I wore my tuxedo, bow tie and

Italian shoes. I was at least trying to look smart! All my family and friends were seated in the hall, which was packed with other visitors and many students from the University. The challengers were piped in, looking really smart in their kilts while the Scottish music in the background was rather haunting and nostalgic. I felt so out of place in my tuxedo but then I always felt out of place somewhere along the line.

The governor and I sat side–by–side and he offered me some chewing gum.

The strange thing for me was that the first time I came in contact with this governor was in 1972 when I was a borstal boy, aged just sixteen, and he had me locked up in solitary confinement for stealing a slice of cake. Now here we sat together ready to challenge the brains of Glasgow and Strathclyde Universities.

At one point I went to the cubicle at the toilets and was only rescued when George Sharkey came looking for me. He knew I was nervous and so held out his hands to show me he was shaking. I thought it strange that an ex–SAS soldier was shaking like a leaf at the thought of facing the students.

When the debate started there was an intimidating silence, especially for me as I was next to stand and state my case in front of one and all with only so long to do so. At no time in the history of the Scottish prison service had there been a debate like it, this was a first. When the first guy was finished there was much cheering and clapping from the students who seemed to be much in favour of the hang 'em, flog 'em idea. When my name was called I walked into the middle of the floor feeling panic clawing at my throat when I saw everyone stare at me. I started the debate with a piece of verse that I had written when I was at the Cages.

> There stands a gaol by the sea
> You say reeking bad with sin
> And although there are men who don't get out
> There are men who don't get in
>
> Some say it was the devil's den
> That erupted out of hell

And there's some who say, in their philosophical way
'It serves its purpose well'...

But I'd like to tell a story
And facts I promise too
That these gaols are full of decent men –
But I leave that up to you

And if you find my judgement sound
Then I guess it says a lot
For the worst of men who lay in here
For any good in them to rot.

Then I went on to inform the audience that hang them and flog
them situations never served a purpose to anyone in society or
indeed in prison. I said the taxpayers' money was being wasted
on a prison regime which caused more harm and damage and
that surely a more humane prison regime would benefit
everyone. Our prison system and regime had been put together
hundreds of years ago and was still in effect to the present day.
Nothing much had changed. Rehabilitation was non-existent,
humanity and kindness rarities. The one thing that was
guaranteed was institutionalisation and the re-offending of
many who had become victims of a brutal regime that had no
check or balance on its human livestock. Worse still there was
no one to question it, but many to enforce it. I told them as
taxpayers they were robbed.

I spoke about the regime at the Special Unit, which was
geared to help those of us who had been brutalised and
degraded by the old regime to rebuild our lives and confront
and deal with our problems rather than sweep them under the
carpet. On and on I spoke. To my complete surprise, when I
concluded my speech, there was a thunderous roar and
applause. It was a great feeling being the centre of attraction
for all the right reasons. The governor, who was next to speak,
nervously asked me how it felt to be standing up there. I knew
he was feeling insecure – as I had been – but I told him to calm
down and take a deep breath.

When George Sharkey and Dr David Cooke were finished a

vote was put to the audience. There was great roaring and cheering and celebrations when it was announced that the jury had found that we, the community of the Special Unit, had won the debate unanimously.

Everyone was congratulating me. I chatted away to the students and they gave me their phone numbers so we could keep in touch. These were training to become lawyers, doctors, surgeons and professors and here I was among them being hailed as the con who taught them a thing or two as far as crime and punishment was concerned.

Everyone I spoke to suggested I became a probation officer to help others. That would have been a great challenge but I was still plotting and planning as to how I could help my younger brother Joe.

Ma was beginning to perk up and I knew she was happy and relieved to know I was settling down at the Special Unit and in no more trouble. The Unit had offered me sanctuary and a life; had given me back my family and dignity.

Everyone had high hopes for me when I got out. Everyone except me that is. I wasn't one for resting till I challenged the system that had sent my brother down for a hideous crime he didn't commit. I knew I would have to face the whole police force and challenge their wrong, and the frightening thing for me was I feared that it would cause me to be sent right back into the heart of the old prison system that would surely destroy me.

Jim and I had already spoken to Joe and discussed what plans to draw up. Our main problem was that everyone who knew of us knew too that when we were released something was bound to happen. All my family and friends were united in the fight to help my younger brother. Even Joe was determined to put his case back into the public eye and show there had been a miscarriage of justice and that police officers had fabricated evidence to help convict him.

All crimes are ugly and no one deserves to be a victim – but it's worse when one is framed by the police who are there supposedly to protect us. At the time, the Ice Cream Wars murders were the worst crime of the century in Scotland. Six members of one family were killed in what was described as an arson attack.

Two men – Joe and Tommy 'T.C.' Campbell – were convicted and sentenced to life in gaol. Police officers of certain ranks were hailed as heroes, knowing fine that they had been part of the worst miscarriage of justice that Scotland had ever witnessed.

It was hard for me to live with this monstrous atrocity that hung over our family's head and hell mend anyone who dared think they could get away with it without repercussions. So there were sparks of life within me, one being the would-be probation officer and the other the angry brother thirsting for justice. But I would have to bide my time.

Cons came and went back into the old system. It was hoped that all they learned here at the Special Unit would hold them in good stead and they would be wiser and stronger and able to cope better with life in the mainstream. We often argued against this policy of sending guys back to a regime that was responsible for putting them in the Special Unit in the first place. But that was the way the bosses at the Prison Department wanted it to be.

An old friend of my dad's came to visit me often. His name was Danny boy, he was a poacher and in some ways reminded me of my dad; regularly he would bring me pheasants, rabbit and venison. He brought his family on many occasions, so much so that his family and mine became one. On one occasion Danny built a barbecue outside my cell window and the smell of venison must have made its way throughout the whole gaol because the governor at mainstream Barlinnie phoned over enquiring about it.

Story has it that Danny and my dad were good friends and had met when they were young and serving sentences at Barlinnie. Both came from the Lanarkshire area and he was just like the dad I had never known and a gentleman.

There were times when I was depressed and emotionally disturbed yet I could turn to Danny boy. One day I decided to escape and so I asked if he would assist me.

'Sure,' he said, 'but tell me why?'

I told him I felt depressed and needed to get out of the Special Unit.

'And go back to what? A life on the run? To finish up in the Cages? To throw all this good away?'

He seemed baffled at my outburst. 'Sure I will help you,' he said, 'but not to escape or do anything to jeopardise yourself, your future or the Special Unit and everyone else who has done more than their share to help you.'

Danny boy gave me my first CB radio and mobile phone so that I could keep in touch with him whenever I felt down. I found out later that he had asked a couple of warders whom he got on with to keep an eye on me in case I had a relapse.

Soon everyone at the Unit got to know him and respect him as a sensible and regular visitor. It may not seem too smart for him to smuggle me in a phone and CB but it was a life-saver and that's as far as he would go, and as far as he was concerned that was bad enough.

My life was blossoming at the Special Unit, then one day Joe got a home leave from Perth Prison. The authorities had decided to let him home for a few hours because Ma was unwell and unfit to travel. At this time, Jim had already been released from gaol. It was time now to do something about the case.

Joe, Jim, Danny boy, Lana and I had arranged that Joe escape from the home leave and flee onto the roof of Ma's house to protest his innocence in our own housing scheme, Garthamlock. Joe was very fortunate in that he had many old friends who believed him to be innocent and were willing to help him in any way. One guy was Mick McLaughlin, an old pal of Joe's and a new pal of mine. As a kid Mick was a champion runner and held the record for years at the detention camp centre for every race. The sad thing about it was that the authorities knew they had a champ in their custody and did nothing about it, so instead of being a gold medallist for Scotland he became a statistic in the crime figures. But he was there for his pal Joe Steele. And so too were half of Garthamlock when he scaled from Ma's house onto the roof. Immediately the Scottish news bulletins and newspapers had him in their headlines. Even the cops who framed Joe were on the roof trying to convince him to hand himself in to the authorities.

The governor sent for me, telling me police and prison

bosses were hoping there was something I could do to help them get Joe down from the roof. What a cheek these coppers and prison bosses had asking me to get Joe down! This was the first of its kind as far as protests were concerned and they couldn't cope with the solidarity. They'd never seen anything like it. Hundreds of people turned up to support Joe Steele and the coppers were raging. I was surprised to find that Joe's solicitor was at the skylight on the roof trying to persuade him to come down. From time to time his head would appear then disappear then a copper's head would pop up. But what surprised me more when all was said and done was that Joe's lawyer had a chance to state his case to the waiting press but declined. I was upset when I heard this. The thought did occur to me that perhaps the lawyer had been put under pressure by the police for there is no other explanation as to why he kept silent when he knew my brother was up there fighting for his life and freedom that evening. I wrote to Joseph advising him to get a new solicitor to act on his behalf.

I fell in love with Margaret, my pen pal from Peterhead Cages, and our relationship grew strong. I got permission from the community to get engaged to her at the Special Unit.

I had permission to go out under escort to a jeweller's shop in the East End of Glasgow to buy a ring. I know this must seem like a life of luxury but I can promise it wasn't. For one to get a home leave after so long in gaol is a terrible culture shock; my first leave I wanted to turn back to the gaol. It was really strange walking down the street with everyone going about their business; I wasn't used to seeing the world like this. I somehow felt insecure and vulnerable and began to panic, then that old feeling came over me again and once again I began to doubt my sanity.

I had a disc jockey entertain us at the engagement party; some of my pals brought presents, others brought in alcohol and so out of sight in my cell we secretly celebrated. As always the life and soul of the party was Uncle Alec with his guitar. Ma seemed much happier than I ever could remember.

The newspapers got wind of it all and approached Margaret at her home asking her for a scandalous story on sex, drugs and rock 'n' roll. She sent them away with their ears roasted.

One popular visitor was a special kind of cop. His name was Mark McManus, otherwise known to millions of TV viewers around the world as 'Taggart'. He was a sentimental guy and it was said he liked a good drink, being especially fond of malt whisky. On his many visits to us this guy would actually cry, especially when leaving. We had many discussions during our visits and of course the occasional malt passing hands behind closed doors. He'd often tell me of the deep love he had for his wife, who had died of cancer. His eyes showed sadness and his craggy face softened as he spoke of his loss and often he'd recite the poem 'Bonnie Jean'. He was a kind and decent man and it was with great sadness I heard of his death a short time later.

One day one of the staff came to do a parole report on me. By now I'd been in the gaol 11 years. He informed me that the Prison Department had accumulated my sentences and had made them into one. This meant that instead of serving 12 years + 3 years + 4 months + 4 months + 60 days one after the other I was now serving one total sentence, and that the 4 years' remission I lost on the 12 year sentence would be added to my last sentence of 60 days!

Four years' remission on a 60 day sentence doesn't add up, I told him. In fact it got worse because the year's remission that was forfeited from my 3 years' sentence was also added to my last sentence of 60 days. Then it turned out that my 12 years must have expired in 1986 and that my three year sentence started on expiry of my 12 year sentence. This being the case they couldn't take remission (4 years) from a 12 year sentence, which had long since expired and add it to a sentence of 60 days.

At my High Court Trial for the Barlinnie escape the Judge sentenced me to three years consecutive to run on expiry of my present 12 years sentence and therefore the Prison Department had no powers as such to accumulate my sentences. I called a special meeting and explained to one and all about my predicament.

There was much confusion and no answers from the governor who looked rather pale and agitated when I told them that by law I should be released as of now. Some staff agreed, taking into consideration that I was being detained under separate warrants and that all the sentences were served by different judges in different courts up and down the country.

They knew my forfeited four years remission from the twelve year sentence should have commenced in 1986 – this would have seen me through till 1990 (considering no remission was returned), then I would work my way through the three remaining lesser sentences and on to my last sentence of sixty days. Soon everyone agreed with me that the Department had made an error. I demanded my immediate departure from gaol. The prison bosses denied me this, stating that they were within their rights to accumulate my sentences. They could show me in writing how this was possible. My family and friends became involved in various protests at the Prison Department Headquarters.

At five o'clock in the morning Danny boy led a couple of dozen of my friends on a protest outside Barlinnie Prison. From my cell I could hear someone calling my name from a loudspeaker, 'Johnny Steele is being unlawfully detained!'

There was a commotion outside my cell door and a voice shouted through, 'What the hell is going on outside my gaol, Steele?'

I didn't recognise the voice but he obviously seemed upset. I could hear all the other cons from the mainstream of the gaol cheering and shouting and banging their cell bars.

On the outside, my fiancée Margaret had superglued both her hands under the runners of the electric steel gate in a daring and frightening protest. The warders at the main gatehouse (who could see what was going on outside) were in a panic because they thought it was IRA soldiers storming the prison. The visitors' gate was only a few yards from the sliding gate and to my amazement one of my friends had stripped himself to his waist and superglued himself to the door and to the wall so no one could open the door without ripping his skin off. The warders were told by Danny boy what was happening and that no one should attempt to open either of the two doors. The warders were shocked and had already contacted the police, who had responded immediately, some armed. They decided that no one could get in or out of the gaol as it would endanger the protesters, so the fire brigade and paramedics were called out to assist. Meanwhile, hundreds of warders were gathered outside the gaol waiting to start their shift and those inside were waiting to get out.

There was pandemonium. I was worried about Margaret who risked her life just to help me and I was grateful for such loyalty. The fire brigade finally freed them both from the gates and after some treatment Margaret and my pal were taken away and questioned about the incident. The police told them they were both being released without charge because the bosses at the Prison Department wanted it swept under the carpet.

When the gates finally opened, the governor called a special meeting and officially informed the community what happened and that I may be getting removed from the Special Unit. Within half an hour about 12 of my family and friends were up to see me. They told the governor they would continue to protest and removing me to another gaol wouldn't solve anything. All we wanted was a straight answer in writing regarding the outcome of my sentences.

The new prisons minister came to visit us and said he had been given this post to help stabilise the unrest at Scotland's gaols. There had been many riots taking place and warders were being held hostage. The old system was up against a new generation of prisoners who were serving sentences much longer than ever before because politicians and the likes wanted to deter others from committing crimes. In a way many things had become Americanised and by now part of the American prison system had found it's way into the Scottish penal system. Suddenly new phrases were being used such as 'lock down' and 'time out'.

However, attitudes among the cons had also changed. Young prisoners, mostly troubled with drugs, were taking desperate measures – and hostages – for the sake of a tranquilliser or some other form of medicine. Gaols were rife with drugs such as heroin and many guys already in gaol became addicts.

And with the drugs came an increase in violence with stabbings and murders taking place regularly. Old-school warders were slowly but surely disappearing from the scene and being replaced by younger ex-soldier types with special training to help them cope with most situations. Control units were springing up in most gaols to help keep troublemakers at bay and away from other cons while the old-type punishment blocks were seldom in use. Some old guards quit their jobs because they couldn't fit in with the changes.

There was talk of Peterhead closing down but the Prison Officers Association were doing their best to keep it open for some strange reason. Shotts had opened at Glenochils, a new American-type gaol stuck out in the wilderness surrounded by a huge fence. They also had a Special Unit there, but nothing like the Barlinnie Unit.

The Prison Minister sat with us on general discussions about the state of his gaols and how things could be made better for all concerned. He told us that he had inherited a dinosaur system and was up against a hard core of prison authorities who, like most, didn't want to change, or see change for that matter. We listened to him intently and optimistically, believing that we might be talking to a man who could change the way our gaols ran for the better. One thing was for sure – he sent shockwaves of fear down the corridors of power; rumours had it that the 'old-school' governors would be getting replaced by a new breed trained in management and psychology.

I told the minister about the brutality in gaols hoping he would intervene. I also told him about the degrading 'slop outs' and conditions I thought he should look into as well as the attitude of the prison warders. He promised a radical shake-up of the entire system.

At a Tuesday meeting, the governor read out a letter which stated that Princess Anne would be coming to Barlinnie Gaol and also to the Special Unit. In the mainstream of the gaol painters and decorators were at every building trying to do the impossible – make the Victorian building look habitable. New gaol uniforms were being handed out to prisoners and the food started to improve. At about five o'clock in the morning my cell door opened and four men appeared with a sniffer dog. There was a scream from under my bed, then a yelp. I had befriended a feral cat and it had attacked the sniffer dog before shooting out of my cell window. The dog, instead of sniffing for explosives, ate my cat's food. The security men for Princess Anne searched every cell for guns or explosives before she arrived.

I was in my cell with Ma and a friend when Princess Anne came to my door. I brought her in to meet Ma. She seemed amused as to how I had so much furniture crammed into one little cell and asked how I was coping at the Special Unit. She seemed quite concerned and I knew from various newspaper reports that she had done much for charity and the underprivileged in the Third World countries and so was very much a humanitarian. She spoke to Ma who referred to her as 'hen'.

Throughout my years at the Unit I had been involved in charity work especially for the handicapped kids of Glasgow. Kids from Easterhouse and Garthamlock often came in and we would entertain them by putting on shows for them. They were very easygoing and a pleasure to work with and soon they knew everyone by name. A councillor told us they that they were trying to raise money to have a swimming pool built for them, and we promised to help. An article appeared in a Glasgow newspaper from some of us at the Unit asking for help regarding the pool for the kids. Lo and behold, someone responded and came to visit us at the Unit. His name was Jimmy, and it turned out he was a very close friend of my dad. Toe also knew him. He was a godsend, for what he had to offer would have changed the entire prison system and created a work force like none had ever seen. His proposal was that he would provide all the materials to build the swimming pool for the underprivileged and handicapped kids. Myself, Toe and Jimmy and a few others proposed that all the prisoners in the mainstream of Barlinnie play a part in the building of this swimming pool by using their skills and trades and general labour. Jimmy offered to transport all the materials into Barlinnie's massive work sheds before drawing up a plan. There was a real buzz of excitement but still we had one more hurdle to get over – would the Prison Department accept this most unusual and generous proposal? How could they refuse? Each meeting brought fresh hopes but still there was no definite answer.

Word filtered back to us that all the cons were more than eager to help. Others had by now also offered assistance; slaters, plasterers, painters, decorators, plumbers and electricians, each with their own business. At one of our meetings the councillor for the handicapped kids had suggested that Jimmy also build a house next to the pool for him and his family. Sadly this is where the negotiations began to fall apart. Jimmy said he would certainly build a pool for the kids who were much in need but there was no way he was building a house for the councillor. The councillor argued that the house would deter any vandals. But Jimmy was having none of it.

In the end it didn't matter. It seemed that the Department weren't keen on letting the prisoners out to do work on the pool fearing that the public would be up in arms and that trade unions would cause problems. This was a real blow to our morale and caused a split in the community. I accused the Department of bullshitting and using any excuse so as not to get the project off the ground. I reminded the community that when I was a borstal boy the Department was quick to use as many prisoners as they could to help build Cornton Vale (the women's gaol in Stirling) and that I was locked up for refusing to participate in it.

Margaret and I drifted apart and saw little of each other, more my fault than hers I guess; but we remained good friends.

Father McDonald from the Cages continued to visit me; he was an inspiration and another Godsend. I had been encouraged by some to write a book about my experiences in gaol in that it may well help others in our society and give a better understanding to those young kids who would surely be destined to a life of crime and punishment. Freddie Anderson, the Glasgow poet and eccentric, would come to visit me occasionally and have me tell him about my life. He was from Garthamlock and was himself a writer–novelist.

I began to feel that the Unit had served its purpose for me. I needed more space in my life, yet for all its comforts it was still a gaol – a small one at that – and sometimes it was a struggle to get through a new day and sometimes I felt I would gladly accept the old regime to get away from the reality of it all.

Five years at the Special Unit had taught me a lot but it seemed I had got all I could ever get from this safe haven. When I was offered the chance of transfer to an open prison, I decided to brave the storm and leave. But it wasn't that easy. The guys at the Unit were like one big family and part of me wanted to stay. I felt that old insecure feeling come to haunt me again, I felt a sorrow for the cons who I'd be leaving behind.

There was a governor at Noranside who was nicknamed God. The reason for this was that he laid down his own commandments that had to be obeyed strictly. The governor at the Special Unit thought it would be a bad idea that I go to his gaol, fearing his attitude would prove too difficult for me to cope with and set me back.

The governor God came to visit me at the Unit with his chief warder. Smartly dressed, he entered my cell, introduced himself and shook my hand. He explained he wanted to help me and promised to look after me. He went on to tell me that Noranside was a very strict regime, one strike and you're out is the policy. The place was kept spic and span, bed blocks made each morning. 'But this won't affect you,' he told me, 'and I can guarantee that.'

He said he'd held a meeting with his staff at Noranside (who threatened to strike should I arrive there) and told them that he was coming to interview me and should I decide to go nothing would stop it. I'd spend six weeks at the open gaol and then I'd qualify for a home leave – five days at Christmas with my family in total freedom. Each prisoner was assigned to a work party on arrival but this would not be the case with me. They had decided I could work alone with one warder only.

I told him I had been advised not to transfer to Noranside as it might be too strict for my liking. He nodded and said, 'I have to keep a strict regime as half the guys sent to me are young drug addicts who couldn't give a monkeys about anyone and so I send them back to a closed gaol if they step out of line.'

'Cleanliness is priority in my gaol' he said. 'We've found dirty needles in the laundry, found dirty needles in the lavatories.'

Then he was on his feet, angry all of a sudden. 'You're fucking right I keep a tight ship – hundreds of people have to live there!'

Then he calmed down and told me about the prison, of its own herd of cattle, of its vegetable crops and how every able-bodied prisoner was put to work potato picking. He told me every prisoner ate well and no food was wasted. After work prisoners were allowed to wear their own clothes and walk about the gaol grounds and forest. Finally, I said I was willing to transfer.

I called a special meeting and thanked everyone at the Unit for their help and kindness, promising to keep in touch with them about my progress. It was a great feeling when my one-man escort and I drove up to the main gate and I heard him call to the warder at the gatehouse window, 'One off the numbers'. As the big gate opened and we drove out into the wide open spaces I once again marvelled at it all, only this time I was part of it.

25

Noranside Gaol

As me and my guard, who was like a friend to me, sped through the streets and into the countryside I found myself wanting to turn back to the Special Unit and all I had left behind. I felt insecure not knowing what lay ahead for me in my new environment where some old prison enemies – the warders – lay in wait. As I found it hard to come to terms with this, I was told by the warder that he had lost the way to Noranside!

We were in the country going around in circles. I found myself asking folk in the street if they could direct me to Noranside Prison. I had to laugh to myself, one minute I'm wanting to go back to the Unit and the next I'm helping my prison escort find the gaol I'm going to.

Noranside used to be a TB hospital and is in a beautiful country location set among trees. As we drove into the grounds I could see all the cons working on the farm grounds, could smell the cattle from far off. It was like a chain gang in America. There were no fences or walls or cameras in sight, absolute freedom, and going back to the Unit quickly went out of my mind.

I could hear guys call my name, asking how I was doing and telling me they were glad to see me again. A pheasant shot by me, then a deer and rabbits everywhere. I saw some warders looking in my direction and waving. The whole gaol feeling somehow left me, and I felt a new lease of life surging through me. I was taken to see the governor James Cameron Stewart, otherwise known as God. He welcomed me and told me to take a few days to get acquainted with my surroundings and get to know most folks.

I said goodbye to my escort and I was sad to see him go.

Over the years we had come to know and respect each other and I was grateful for all the help he had given me. Only now when he was driving away did I truly realise just exactly what that strange place called the 'Special Unit' had done for me. My life had been restored to me in instalments whereas in other parts of the system our lives were taken away from us in one go.

In a way I felt that the Special Unit was like an island in the system and that we were left there to get on with it — abandoned like lepers and here I was somehow rescued and taken ashore whilst others were still stranded there waiting for a ship. I wished they had all been able to come with me. I felt sad for them.

The Noranside warders seemed to be giving me a wide berth and I guess they were as wary of me as I was of them. Some guys were telling me I might not last too long here as the place was far too strict, in as much as they had to keep their cells or rooms spotlessly clean and that some warders were more into bullying than guarding. I heard many rumours, good and bad, but when I looked around me I realised that these guys who were complaining had never known how fortunate they were. I told them I wasn't interested in anything or anybody but me. The solution was simple, if they didn't like it they could escape or go back to where they came from. I know others had seen me as a guy who would fight their battles for them and stand up against the system but here my ears were burning with complaints.

I went to see the governor and told him there were many cons with grievances that needed to be aired. He gave me permission to set up a prisoners' complaint committee. I was the chairman, and my friend, Big Gus, from Aberdeen, was my secretary. We started to take all the complaints down from the cons to be raised at the meeting in the dining hall when all would be present. As I started to raise the complaints on behalf of the cons I found that they wouldn't offer assistance or contribute at the meeting: instead most of them wanted me to pave the way.

I had been there one week when I came across an old enemy from the Cages — probably the tallest warder in

Scottish gaols. I had cut my finger and went to get a plaster from the warder's desk and who should be standing there but 'he' – the one who had attacked me with a baseball bat in the Cages. I could feel the hairs on the back of my neck stand as I relived the attack and I reacted angrily. Another con told me to calm down fearing I would be shipped out to another gaol. But I didn't care.

Another warder came on the scene trying to defuse the situation and in the end it was decided that we both go into a room out of earshot of others and get things ironed out between us. I listened to this big guy's story of his life in the Cages and how he came to be the animal I thought he was. He told me that when he first started the job he felt like a human being doing a job that would pay well and make him feel proud to be helping society by keeping the likes of me locked up. It was only as the years went by he lost that humane feeling after living with such violent prisoners for years. At the Cages he was looked upon as 'the man' because of his size and was used and abused in every way by his peers to terrorise and subdue us prisoners.

I knew he didn't want me at this gaol and that he was one of the warders who threatened to strike should I arrive because he thought that I was a mad dog who would attack him and others as well as incite others to riot. He went on to tell me he had heard many stories about me before he had even seen me and that when I was being transferred to the Cages he was led to believe from other warders that I was and should be shown immediately who was boss.

The strange thing was I'd been told the same thing about him before I went to the Cages. I could somehow identify with this big giant of a man and relate to him and his story of gaol brutality. And there we were exchanging horror stories of the guys we were seen to be way back then. With a new understanding passing between us, we promised to let bygones be bygones.

I settled in well at the open prison, was treated very well by the governor and members of staff, but would at times regress and swear 'revenge' on the warders who I had come accustomed to hating and swore that one day I would return to cause them pain. I was worried about my mood swings; at times I wished I could forget the past.

The night before my home leave I couldn't sleep; I paced the floor; sat at my window playing my guitar and singing. I remember feeling sorry for my friends at the Special Unit and brother Joe and all my other friends in other gaols and of course I wondered about Margaret; from out of God knows where my life had somehow taken a turn for the better and tomorrow would surely be one of the happiest days of my life.

The next morning, as we stepped on to the bus, the governor pulled me aside and told me he hoped my Christmas would be an experience I would never forget and that if for some reason I didn't feel up to returning from my home leave I should phone him. And with this, he placed a piece of paper into my hand which contained his telephone number.

I thought it was a strange feeling when I had my day trips to the towns, but it was even stranger to be travelling on a bus heading home to Garthamlock. I was like a kid again. The old tree that Katrina and I climbed as kids still stood there, taller and prouder, 999 Gartloch Road never seemed to change much except that the kids who I remembered way back then were now teenagers with kids – and habits! They were dressed like American kids, and I noticed that American phrases were in common use in our vocabulary such as 'motherfuckers' and 'bullshit'.

Ma was at the window waving as she saw me come round the corner. My nephews and nieces and aunts and uncles were there with my friends. I was aware that all the folk in Garthamlock knew I was home and aware also that I didn't know who many of them were. This had to be it – the ultimate buzz in life and I knew in my heart that as long as I felt like this I would never want to cause anyone pain or harm. I could hear Ma singing as she made a meal for one and all. Lana told me that when Jim had been released and Ma was preparing the meal she was singing away happily to herself. I felt sorry for Ma for I knew that we, her sons, had caused her so much pain and grief throughout the years and had robbed her of the happiness she deserved. Every prisoner knows this sorrow of breaking a mother's heart, and none better than me, and if I could I would do anything to undo the injustice I helped inflict upon her.

The house, though, seemed bare without Maw and my dad being present.

After our meal I walked around the streets taking it all in and treasuring every moment of it. I noticed that many of the houses were boarded up and ready to be demolished. Some streets were deserted, almost ghostly. This was the only root I had, my heritage, and it was fading. Many parts were now regarded as slums and unsafe. In one street a burnt-out car lay in a woman's garden. Kids were getting into empty houses and setting them on fire to entertain themselves by watching the fire brigade put them out. Others were stripping the old houses for copper wire, wood and slates, leaving the area looking like a war-torn Third World country. Many of the cast iron stanks in the streets had been stolen for scrap and sold to a dealer who'd smelt them down before anyone knew he had them.

But for all that it was, it was like heaven for me to be there, regardless of the circumstances and conditions. I guess I only noticed it more because I came into it with fresh eyes.

Gangs were still about these housing schemes and it seemed many members were constantly on drugs – most people smoked hash or ate it and so it was no surprise to see many young men and their girlfriends being stopped and searched by the police, American-style.

Many young men were driving about in fancy and expensive cars and seemed to be living a life of luxury. I soon learned they were trading in drugs. As sad as it may seem the drug culture, apart from causing misery, also gave a lot of poor people a chance to earn some money and many of them saw themselves no different from tobacco traders or sellers of alcohol.

Selling drugs gave some an opportunity to get away from poverty and the slums they were born into. But to me it seemed like the prohibition era all over again; murders were constantly happening in the streets of Glasgow and all over Scotland. The gun had replaced the steak knives and open razors of the '60s and '70s. The city was just like America now.

The police and the government declared war on the drug

dealers and takers. Longer sentences were introduced in the hope of stamping out the drug trade, but for every major player to be taken out by the courts another would take his place; for every drug taker who died of an overdose, another ten were born into the habit. Almost every crime committed was drug-related – in and out of the gaol.

Jim and I went for a pint together to our local bar, known as Bennigan's, where most of the guys went for a drink. There was a Christmas party there on 23 December 1990 and I was invited to it. As I was leaving Ma's house to go to the dance she warned me not to get into any trouble and come home afterwards and she'd make me something to eat.

Bennigan's was buzzing that night and I was introduced to many people I'd never known and others who were only kids when I was sent down in 1978.

Some of my old friends from gaol also came to see me. Danny boy was there and all those who helped protest for me. Never before had I felt surrounded by so many good people who were only interested in helping me.

I saw a redhead sitting across from me and thought to myself she looked pretty. My friend said I should ask her to dance but I lost my nerve and asked him to ask her to dance with me. I saw her look over at me as my pal asked her. She was with her sisters and friends who were all looking in my direction. I felt a bit awkward, but not for long, for she agreed to dance with me.

I didn't really know how to dance and when I started I regretted it for I felt like a Zulu on the warpath the way my arms and legs were swinging. Her name was Irene and we laughed and danced to a couple of songs, but then she went back to her table and I mine. Every now and then I peered over my shoulder to look at her and caught her looking back.

She looked beautiful with her long red hair, sweet face, blue eyes and an Irish smile. She looked to me like an angel and I bought her and her friends a drink. I was invited over and sat amongst them, listening to them talking. The atmosphere at Bennigan's was great for me – I even forgot I was still a prisoner out on loan!

It seemed there were many parties being held after the Christmas dance and if I was invited to one, I was invited to them all. I was aware everyone was looking in my direction from time to time, obviously knowing who I was. I reckon that everyone who spoke to me asked me how I felt to be home. I asked Irene if she would come to a party with me back at Ma's house and she promised to meet me there.

Back at Ma's house Jim, Danny boy and some other friends spoke about what could be done for Joe. There was, as far as I was concerned, only one thing that could be done and that was to put our wits together and break him out of gaol to help him publicise his case.

T.C. had been making the headlines quite regularly with his hunger strikes and calls for a new trial. But we knew this wouldn't be enough to get a new hearing and that the authorities would gladly see T.C. die of hunger or any other way for that matter.

I heard a knock at Ma's door and left the others to see who it was. The redhead was there and I took her in to meet Ma and the others. It wasn't policy to talk out of school in front of anyone not involved in the escape committee so the conversation ceased and the party started. I sat with Irene who quietly said her mother had told her she had to be home soon. Ma took a shine to Irene and soon they were in the kitchen talking to one another.

Irene and I stayed at Ma's till the party was ended, and even then we stayed on a while, talking in low tones and cuddling. I never slept a wink as I lay beside this newfound godsend.

I was glad for those five days, as it was a reminder to me that humanity still existed and life wasn't all doom and gloom.

I was late getting to the bus station where all the prisoners were waiting on me. As I got to the bus I heard the warder say into his phone, 'All present – including Johnnyboy!' Every prisoner returned to the gaol from the Christmas leave.

The governor told me he was glad I came back as many warders and others at the Department were taking bets I would abscond.

Time flew by for me whilst at Noranside. The parole board

had taken another interest in me. The governor had managed to help me get some remission rescinded, some eighteen months in total.

My relationship with Irene grew and I was phoning her each night from the gaol and getting visits from her each weekend. When I was on my home leaves I spent all of my time with her. I knew I was lucky to have her as a companion and lover. I met her Ma and Da on one of my home leaves. They were a poor family from Garthamlock and like many others living below the breadline. But they were great in nature and character and known to everyone in the housing scheme.

I was given six months' parole and six months' training for freedom. The six months training for freedom would mean that I would be allowed out to work whilst at the gaol. After that period I would then be allowed home on six months' parole. I would be released in March 1992, age 37, having served 14 and a half years inside.

Irene was pregnant and I was quite excited and concerned. I was beginning to feel uneasy at the gaol now and wanted to be freed immediately to be with Irene. By now I had been moved to another building which was like an outbuilding with no guards in it at night. We were locked in and all the windows were locked.

But I was so in love that I, with the help of Big Gus, unscrewed the windows and off I went into the pitch darkness to look for a telephone to phone Irene. It was about midnight when I went out the window and crawled through the grounds when suddenly the fields lit up with spotlights. I immediately hit the ground as gunfire erupted all around me. I lay there stunned and shocked and rock still, scarcely breathing. My first thought was to stand up with my hands in the air. Then the darkness fell again followed by silence. I must have moved like a polecat through the fields and into a single-track road behind the gaol. Again the place lit up where I once lay and again guns were blazing. I climbed a tree to see what was going on.

The warders were in the fields in a jeep with guns and spotlights and every now and then they'd turn them to blast the rabbits, foxes and deer. I hurried away down a long dark single-track road, shaking from my ordeal but quite relieved to be in one piece as I went in search of a phone box. There was no moon or stars to see by and I did think about heading back towards the gaol, but I was desperate to talk to my Irene.

I knew it was stupid of me to be doing this. If I was caught I could be sent back to a closed gaol and lose all I had going for me. But I was in love.

I even began to consider that she might not be home to take my phone call – she could be at the dancing! And if so, I wondered what she'd be wearing and if some other guy would see in her what I had seen in her. I began to feel a jealousy come over me as I searched for the phone box.

I found a phone box beside a small white cottage so I had to be quiet. Irene answered and told me she wasn't too happy to learn I had escaped from gaol to make a phone call that could have waited till morning.

I made my way back up the long winding road to the gaol and made it back inside without incident. That night's activities were fun – but there was sadness ahead for both Irene and me.

In June 1991, Irene told me she was being taken into hospital with a possible miscarriage. I was shocked.

The governor granted me 24 hours compassionate leave to visit her at the hospital. Irene was in a hospital bed, pale-faced and tired looking. I sat holding her hand, not knowing what to do or say. So I just clung to her, hoping for the best. I don't know how long I lay there but I remember a nurse telling me I had to leave as the visiting was over. I told the young nurse I was on a compassionate leave from gaol and the nurses agreed I could stay till Irene went into theatre.

I felt helpless. The nurses pulled a curtain around Irene's bed so that no one could see us, as we lay holding on to each other and crying. I had already planned what to name my baby when she was born – for I was sure it would be a girl. I cried with a great sadness as I lay there with Irene on a drip, praying to God that my baby would live. Irene was also heartbroken and cried with me.

I thought I was being punished by God for all the wrongs

I had done. I had been hurt many times in my life but nothing quite like this.

The nurses woke me in the morning at about five o'clock asking me to leave before the other shift came on, as I wasn't supposed to be here. I left with a heavy heart and thanked the nurses for their kindness and compassion.

Irene and I lost the unborn baby. We were both devastated by the loss but it also brought us closer together.

I told the governor I wanted to go to Perth Gaol to serve my training for freedom. He was shocked to hear this and was worried I'd fall by the wayside. But the real reason I wanted to go there was because I'd be closer to Irene, Perth being only a 40-minute drive from Glasgow.

Before I left his gaol, the governor called me to his office and gave me his phone number, telling me to call him should I need his help. I shook hands with the man I had come to respect and who had helped me in many ways. I remember putting his telephone number in my diary.

At Perth Gaol I was put to work on TFF at the sawmills along with civilians. My job was to dye 8x4 sheets of wood, or perhaps it was a preservative chemical. The first day there I was covered in brown dye. It was in my eyes, ears and mouth. I felt sick and told the governor at Perth but he said I would have to go back to work. It was decided I should be given another job. This time I was working in a bus garage filling buses up with diesel and water, and cleaning them inside and out. I was beginning to wish I had stayed at Noranside Gaol.

After a few days there I began to feel pains in my chest caused by the exhaust fumes. I told the gaol doctor who prescribed tablets. When the bus company realised I was on medication which was causing me drowsiness and dizziness they weren't amused. I was kept in the TFF Unit till they found me another job. After about a week they found me another job – this time in a home for retired brothers of the De La Salle order, monks and priests. This time I was a kitchen porter and was told that if I couldn't stick this job I would be taken back to the closed gaol at Perth.

Whilst there I spoke to an old man who knew most of the

brothers at St Joseph's. I sat in his room with him: it was like a gaol cell, dirty and untidy, barely furnished with paint peeling from the walls. He told me that the others who lived upstairs in the retirement home were living like kings and that he was on his way out of this world and therefore didn't care much for his uncomfortable conditions. I felt sorry for him and I often brought him in some tobacco.

My job was to keep the kitchen spotlessly clean. When food was prepared it was sent upstairs using a dumb waiter: I seldom saw anyone from up there, although I did notice most of their knives and forks were made of silver. After about a week, the gardener asked me how long a sentence I was serving. I told him 16 years. To my amazement he called me a liar.

'You're not serving a 16-year sentence!' he hollered out loud. I couldn't believe what I was hearing. 'How long have you been in gaol?' he demanded.

'Almost 14 years!' I shouted back in anger.

Before I knew what was happening he was up on his feet asking what age I was. I told him I was 36. Again he called me a liar. 'You can't be!' he shouted. 'You couldn't have done that long!' He was looking from me to the other workers as if seeking confirmation from someone.

'Who did you murder then?' the gardener demanded.

I looked at this troubled man and said, 'No one . . . I murdered no one!'

'You must have murdered someone to have been in gaol that long!'

I'd had enough of this by then. I walked over to where my jacket was hanging up, took it down and walked away from the job.

When the governor saw me he was white with shock. 'This is the third job in a few weeks you have left,' he said. They were talking about putting me back into lock down and I knew they would put me into solitary confinement. I couldn't face that, so I went home one Saturday and went away to London with Irene.

I couldn't believe it – I was on the run again. Perhaps I should have stayed at Noranside.

I was beginning to rant and rave and threaten revenge on the warders throughout the system. The madness was creeping back upon me and I had to do something about it, for Irene's sake as well as mine. After about 14 days I remembered I had the governor's telephone number and decided to phone him. He sounded excited and concerned when he heard my voice, asking me what happened and where I was. I told him I was in London and why.

'I told you to stay with me in my gaol!' he shouted down the phone. 'Those other bastards couldn't give a shit about you nor anyone else in their care!' He wanted to come down to London and bring me back but I told him I would ring him back in a day or two and let him know. He didn't know about the three jobs I tried to hold down and was left with the impression I had absconded for no reason.

When I phoned him back he told me that the Department wanted me back into Perth mainstream gaol and there they'd keep me till they decided what to do with me. I was guaranteed no brutality and that God, the governor, would take me back there himself to make sure. I made arrangements to meet him at a train station in Scotland and he picked me up with his chief warder. On the way to Perth he told me what was likely to happen to me: I'd lose one month parole, be kept at Perth Gaol for three to four months then sent back to Noranside to serve the remainder of my TFF.

It was late at night as we drove to Perth and I dreaded the thought of going back into the jungle. I thought about Irene and how I'd miss her and regretted messing up. In the Perth governor's office I heard God say I wasn't to be abused or assaulted whilst in his care and that came from a higher authority. I could sense the Perth governor's unease. I was told I would be kept in solitary for the time being in case I caused any problems, plus the authorities were worried that I would disrupt the system there; they told me they hoped to have me back at Noranside soon.

Dr Peter Whatmore came to see me from the Special Unit, wondering if there was anything he could do to help me, or perhaps I wanted to go back to the Unit. I told him what had happened to me whilst at Perth and regretted coming here. I told him also that I didn't want to go back to the Unit as I felt I had outlived it and there was nothing more I could gain. He seemed quite relieved that I didn't want to go back as he was also quite satisfied that it had served its purpose for me.

He told me about a 'new unit' at Perth which had been set up some time ago and could be doing with someone like me in there to try and help others (staff and cons) work a regime that could benefit everyone. In fact I had no choice as I was to be kept in solitary confinement till I left Perth – which could be as long as three to four months away. At the new Unit there were a few young guys there whose heads were damaged – so too were the heads of their guards. I tried and managed to get a decent regime up and running at the Unit even though the assistant governor there said he didn't want a Special Unit type regime nor did he want to get involved in any debates with me as he had heard all about me. Common sense prevailed. I had the warders on my side as well as the cons and the Special Unit type regime I had managed to incorporate into the Perth Unit was working.

Special meetings were called first and foremost in order to defuse situations within the Unit. The governor at first wasn't too happy, but in the end he saw it as a sensible solution to a problem that would normally end up in a blood bath. We had a student teacher that taught art come to teach us every two to three days. Her name was Julie, she was young and very much involved in her work in helping prisoners at the gaol and her presence brightened the atmosphere much.

Helping to build up a Unit made my time fly by and before I knew it I was being taken back to Noranside where I was given a TFF job at the handicap centre. It was a comfort to be back. I was glad, and so too was Irene for in a few month's time I would be a free man.

One of Joe's pals came to Noranside Gaol. His name was Gordy and he told me Joe often spoke about me and that when I got out I would do the unimaginable and help him get out of gaol to protest his innocence. In a sense most people who knew me were expecting me to break Joe out of gaol when I came out. This kind of frightened me because I was worried that the serious crime squad, who were responsible for putting my young brother behind bars, would get wind of this and fit me up. I had to be careful, for talk is dangerous.

26

A Desire for Justice

Early March 1992 I was released from gaol only to be supervised for the next six months. Fourteen and a half years of being locked up is a long time.

As I walked up Irene's street I could see a huge banner in her garden which read, 'Welcome home, Johnnyboy'. It was a wonderful feeling.

I planned to set up house with Irene and raise a family and in a contradictory sense I planned to get Joe out and bring the judiciary system to the ground.

Ma was overjoyed to have me home and kept feeding me homemade soup as though trying to fatten me up. My pals from here and there came to visit me.

Irene was looking as beautiful as ever, with her long red hair and Irish looks and a beautiful smile that could melt a thousand hearts. All that was missing was my Dad and Maw Padden, for they would have been proud of her and her bonnie looks. Thirty-seven years of age and my life was just starting to knit together, to blossom and take shape. Many of my old pals were married with teenage kids and in a way I resented them – but they in return resented me because I had somehow stagnated all those years and remained youthful with a sort of freedom not known to many guys my age.

In Glasgow, as well as Garthamlock, there were many willing to help in the fight for Joe in his bid for freedom and many knew that there was a great liberty taken when the coppers framed him.

I was approached by two senior officers and warned not to step on any toes or I'd be going back to gaol before I knew what was happening. I knew they were serious but I also knew that they were frightened and this much I was glad of for they had never really been challenged before, at least not where it hurt. Publicity was the one weapon they couldn't handle, especially when it was used against them.

There were many in Glasgow who knew what these coppers had done and were powerless to do anything about it. To frame someone was a common event in Glasgow and it was even rumoured that it was political. The system or police regime was corrupt and had been for many years.

I went around with family friends to get as much support and backing as possible. T.C. was on hunger strike and it was rumoured he was at death's door. His family, especially his sister Agnes, was a pillar of strength and continued to campaign on his behalf.

The case of the Glasgow Two, as I called them, was known throughout Scotland and had tongues wagging in every section of society. I couldn't really tell Irene about my plans, though I guess she must have known. All she wanted was for me to come home and settle down, as I had promised to do so long ago. I felt I was letting them all down, Ma included, and it hurt me so. Somehow I knew we had to take Joe's case to London to publicise it.

I went to visit Joe at the gaol and he seemed depressed and verging on the suicidal; he was talking about going on hunger strike. I felt helpless at that moment, and I was gutted to think of his dying this way. He was, after all, my young brother and I felt ashamed because we had never shared a life together on the outside world: either I was locked up or he was. We were like strangers, born into poverty and crime and raised in approved schools, borstals, young offenders' institutions and gaols across the country.

I encouraged him to hold on as Jim and I had come up with a plan to help highlight his case and to let the world know about his miscarriage of justice.

Ma was sitting next to me, unaware of our conversation as she had broken her hearing aid. But she had a tear in her eye that told me her heart was broken.

I knew most of the warders at the visiting room and made it quite clear that I wouldn't be too happy should anything happen to Joe or should he mysteriously fall down any stairs, as this would only result in repercussions from others outwith the gaol. But they said they wouldn't harm Joe and that every prison officer in the country believed Joe to be innocent.

And it was true that many believed Joe to be innocent, as by now the main prosecution witness who helped manufacture evidence against Joe had admitted that he had lied in court because senior Glasgow detectives had promised him immunity from various charges, including discharging a firearm at an ice cream van.

His name is Billy Love and on many occasions he retracted his evidence. But this in itself was not good enough to get back into an appeal court – not in Scotland – and so we had to take drastic measures to make sure this did happen, and that this man, Billy Love, also a known and convicted perjurer, be brought to justice along with corrupt officials.

So we had to break the law to show the country that the Scottish justice system was seriously flawed.

We knew that we were up against the whole judiciary system and police forces throughout the country and that they wouldn't take too kindly to our interfering and causing them embarrassment. We were alone in our fight. We couldn't get into a court to fight them – so we would fight in the streets.

Almost every newspaperman and woman in the country had an interest in Joe, for they were aware that something was going to happen and each for his or her own reasons wanted in on it. Jim and I went to London with a few friends to check out a few locations, which we had in mind for Joe when we helped him escape. One of the places we looked at was the Houses of Parliament. We contemplated how we could get him up there in full view of the nation.

We then went to Nelson's Column to see if it was possible to climb to the top of it with his banner calling for a re-trial. Then we went to the House of Lords and there we pondered many ideas. We spent days searching for locations which we could use for Joe. Someone thought we should superglue ourselves across the M1 motorway and block all the traffic to and from London, but we decided against this because it was too dangerous and could cause serious damage and accidents.

Then we found the perfect location. I went to a friend of

mine who had a nightclub and there we discussed how we should approach this particular location and what to do once we got there. With a simple plan in mind and ready to be put into practice we now had to concentrate on getting Joe out of the gaol.

Our next task took us to the gaol that held Joe and there in the dark of the night Jim, myself and some others looked for ways in. Every now and then the patrol would pass us, never knowing that we were in the shadows of their top security gaol.

We had knowledge of the layout of the gaol from the inside for all of us had at one time been prisoners there. The escape committee had much at its disposal: fast cars that were ringers, telescopic ladders, still saws, but most of all 100 per cent commitment. We even had an explosives expert who could come and blow a hole in the wall for us. We thanked him but declined his offer fearing someone could get killed or injured.

There were times when Jim and I would argue as to what should be done and what shouldn't be done. Nevertheless, two heads are better than one.

We had one other big problem and that was Ma. How would she handle this when it sparked off? I decided the best thing to do was to let her know what was going on – but to leave this to Joe. Ma was a nervous woman and I was worried that the shock of this would cause her health to suffer.

T.C. was still hunger striking and using the publicity to demand a re-trial.

We had the most powerful weapon we needed to fight the miscarriage – it was Billy Love himself, but the police knew this and had him locked safely away. We even contemplated breaking into the gaol to kidnap Billy Love and take him to a press conference to tell all. He managed to smuggle out a letter from his gaol saying he was willing to go on TV and retract his statement that had condemned Joe and T.C.

Ma looked worried for a time and asked me if I would tell her what was going on. I denied anything was taking place but I guess her motherly instincts told her otherwise.

Back we went to see Joe at the gaol and I told him what we had in mind. There was a sparkle in his eye after learning he could be out and about with his brothers and friends and fighting his case. He was worried for me because I wasn't that long out of gaol myself and he didn't want to see me land back there should anything go wrong. Joe went to see the governor and asked him for a home leave to visit Ma who was finding it hard to travel to the gaol.

It was about April 1993 when Joe arrived home with his gaol escort. Ma was all excited to have him home. This was the first time since the 1970s that Ma had her three sons in the house together. I could hear her singing away in the kitchen as she was preparing a huge meal for all of us. Lana and Brenda, Joe's wife Dolly, his son John Paul, and all our nephews and nieces were there, as were aunts and uncles and many friends. The last time so many of our family were together was when they visited me in the Special Unit.

Even though we could see police patrolling outside, there was a great atmosphere for us in the know for we knew that soon Joe would be in London and that the fight would begin to clear his name and shame those involved in this travesty of justice.

But Joe was worried the warder who had escorted him to Ma's house would get into trouble for allowing him to escape. He asked me to get him a pen and paper so that he could write a note exonerating him from any blame. In it he said he was sorry for escaping from custody, that he hoped the authorities wouldn't be too hard on the man because no matter who had taken him out that day he intended to escape in order to protest his innocence. He went on to wish the warder luck.

I kept the note in my pocket until Jim gave me the nod. After a few hours Ma's house was just beginning to quieten down and Joe took Ma, Lana and Brenda into the bedroom. I knew he was telling them what plans we had. When I walked into the room, all three were crying and cuddling and I heard Ma sobbing, 'Don't worry about me son, I'll stay strong to stand by you, for I know you're innocent.'

Ma and the girls went back into the sitting room where the warder was sitting oblivious to what was going on.

Jim gave me the nod and Joe kissed Dolly goodbye and left via the back window to a waiting car, which would take him to London. The prison warder asked to tell Joe that they'd be leaving in about ten minutes. I felt bad about doing this to the warder but all the same he knew my brother was innocent and had even said so himself.

I told him I'd go and get Joe for him, and as I walked into the room I called for Brenda to come. I then looked out of Ma's window and could still see a police car patrolling.

There were about ten young guys playing football in the street, so I called them over and asked them to start yelling when I gave the order and to say that Joe was up on Ma's roof protesting his innocence. I then took the letter out of my pocket which Joe had written for the warder and told Brenda to give it to him. As he was reading the letter, nearly in tears, I gave the nod to the guys in the street. Soon the street was full of people all staring up at Ma's roof and yelling, 'On ye go, Joe!'

I walked into the sitting room and informed everyone that Joe was on the roof protesting his innocence. The warder ran to the window and could see for himself the commotion and was convinced Joe was up there. He asked Ma if he could phone the Prison Department and within minutes most of the streets were full of police and CID and fire brigades, searching the rooftops. I was in the street and was approached by senior police officers who asked me if I had seen Joe on the roof and I told them that I had.

Seven fruitless hours later they decided to call off the search. TV and newspaper reporters were on the scene looking for a story. They spoke to my family and were told Joe was fighting to prove his innocence. They tried to talk to Joe's escort as they had all heard Joe had written him a letter apologising for any inconvenience he may have caused. Some reporters were desperate to get hold of the note Joe wrote, but the police had taken it from the warder who was standing in the street along with the crowds staring up at Ma's rooftop. Ma kept sending him down cups of coffee and sandwiches.

Joe was making headlines across the country. He had made contact with some newspaper and gave them his story as to why he had escaped and stated quite clearly that he was no mass murderer.

T.C. was in on the act as well by getting in touch with the

newspapers and getting their case heard across the nation.

Some of Joe's pals joined him in London and went on the loose in Soho. I took them to my friend's nightclub where they were wined and dined. To Joe it was a culture shock but he was obviously enjoying his few days of freedom before he would cause a major upset in the judiciary system and police forces throughout the country.

Our contacts back in Scotland had kept us aware of the police activity and the search for him at the houses and haunts of family and friends. Police approached some of them with deals for any information. Meanwhile, all over London Joe was giving stories to newspaper reporters at secret locations, then disappearing. He knew that though many reporters were showing sympathy there was that fear that one might turn out to be a Judas and let the police know of his whereabouts.

I showed Joe a Glasgow newspaper with the headline I'M NOT A MASS KILLER and a large photograph of him. This gave him a psychological boost to know he was making headlines for all the right reasons and not the usual gutter press reports, which referred to him as a mass murderer. After one such interview we managed to get Joe away just in time before armed police searched the premises.

I had a friend who owned a private estate outside London with a forest, a beautiful river and a cottage. It was the perfect setting for some peace and tranquillity and no need to worry about strangers. I went with Joe and some of his old school pals for some relaxation. At night we were all walking around the grounds and woods having a good laugh. As we were all crossing the river under the cloudy dark skies we were using the various stepping stones to get across without getting wet when I deliberately turned off the lamplight; everyone was yelling and laughing and falling into the water. We were like kids again. It was the first time we had all laughed since meeting.

Back at the cottage we all changed into dry clothes and prepared some food while Joe and I chopped up some logs for the fire. We sat around the fire singing and talking about the old days.

Tomorrow would be Joe's big day and that would be the last we'd see of him till the next time we got him out. I felt sorry for that. Joe said he wanted to postpone his demonstration for a few days as he was enjoying his freedom. I knew how he was feeling for I too wanted to spend more time with the wee brother I hardly knew. The others felt the same. We decided to put it off another day.

The next day we went to my friend's club in Soho to have a meal and toast for Joe before he surrendered himself to the authorities. It was a hard decision Joe was making and I saw a look of sadness in his eyes. I promised him that I would break him out of any prison the authorities sent him to. And I meant this sincerely for he had only me, Jim and a few friends who would deliver the goods.

He was satisfied with this; we embraced and cried and everyone wished Joe luck as we set off for our predetermined destination – Buckingham Palace.

At the Palace, Joe put his back to the centre of the huge iron gates and spread his arms like Christ on the cross. My pal quickly handcuffed each hand to the massive gate that dwarfed Joe, while another mate quickly superglued his fingers and hands to the metal. To further underline the belief that Joe was a martyr to a corrupt and unfair system, Joe was wearing a white T-shirt with a picture of Salvador Dali's *Crucifixion* emblazoned across the front of it.

A group of Japanese tourists were on the scene and immediately began taking photos. Then the police came when we started chanting, 'Joe Steele is innocent.' Some of the Japanese tourists were also singing. They later claimed they thought Joe was a pop star.

One copper came towards Joe to drag him away and was shocked to be confronted by the fact that Joe was handcuffed. Many more police turned up – and all the while we were chanting. The newspapers and TV crews had been contacted and they were everywhere, trying to get a story from Joe and ourselves. A copper turned up with a pair of bolt cutters and smartly cut through the chains and tried to pull Joe off the gates. Suddenly everyone rushed towards him pushing him away. Jim grabbed hold of him and told him Joe was superglued to railings. A closer inspection from a copper in charge confirmed this to be true.

Hundreds of people had gathered now and the paramedics and fire brigade were on their way to help free Joe Steele from the Palace gates. All around us cameras were flashing and reporters were thrusting tape-recorders towards Joe as he shouted, 'I'm innocent – I've been framed for six murders I didn't do!'

Someone pointed to a window inside the Palace gate and said the Queen was looking out to see what all the commotion was. We had no idea if this was true but we immediately started chanting up at the window whilst the police crowded in around Joe.

I noticed Joe was talking away to a sergeant all the while he was stuck to the gate. He told the English coppers that he had been framed by Glasgow's Serious Crime Squad and that he had escaped to seek justice and clear his name. People going by in their cars were tooting their horns. The atmosphere was electric.

They got Joe off the gate after a while and as they were putting him into a police vehicle we were chanting, 'Free the Glasgow Two.'

Although he was now back in custody he had left his mark for he was on the front pages of every newspaper, complete with the picture of him spread crucifixion-style across the Palace gates. His antics had made him a household name and he was beginning to shake the very core of Scottish justice and have people talking. One story said the big English copper at the gates thought Joe was as good as gold! Others reported that Joe would escape at every opportunity to protest his innocence.

Back home T.C. was also hitting the headlines, backing Joe in his fight for freedom and a re-trial. Jim and I went to visit Joe at a gaol in Scotland. He was fine and told us the authorities never beat him up, that all they did was lock him up.

The authorities were clearly embarrassed and were under pressure to make sure Joe didn't get away with it again. During the visit, the three of us planned his next escape only a few feet from a prison warder who was none the wiser.

On the way out I saw an old governor who I'd had many run-ins with and I told him that should anything happen to Joe in a brutality sense then he could expect repercussions from a couple of hundred protesters.

'Are you threatening me, Steele?' he asked.

'Sure I am,' I told him. 'We'll find out where you stay and camp out in your garden for as long as it takes.'

I was only trying to protect Joe from harm; he was at their mercy in there and I had a bad experience of gaol brutality in the past. I know that when a prisoner is fighting the system it's the loneliest and most unfair fight imaginable.

Joe had something going for him that others don't have – he was liked by almost everyone who knew him. Also, everyone believed him to be innocent – even the warders, who appreciated what Joe had done for their colleague at the home leave by writing him a letter apologising for any inconvenience he may cause him.

Some months later I, along with two other pals, went up to the gaol grounds late at night to check out the lay of the land. Joe had directed us to a blind spot in the gaol's fence where he thought we could cut through without being spotted by any of the cameras. Every now and then a patrol would pass as we lay in the long grass beside the fence. We could see all the cell windows lit up; it was quite unpleasant for me to see. There was, however, as Joe said, a blind spot on the football field.

The next day, around six o'clock on a summer's evening, I went to the gaol armed with bolt cutters and a pinch bar. I cut the fence and peeled it back; we had another guy who was on the main road in a cattle wagon waiting to pick Joe up. There was to be a football match that night and Joe was being allowed out to watch it. I watched through binoculars as he appeared and walked around the field.

Jim was back in Glasgow waiting for us to return. What we were doing was risky and it was decided that if I was caught it was better he was free to carry on the struggle. I wasn't proud of what I was doing, and it's not that I didn't care if I was caught. I had to do this for my brother, to stand by him and help clear his name. I guess many others would do the same if they were in my shoes. I had my alibi ready with something like 86 witnesses ready to say I was at a football game in a housing scheme next to Garthamlock when Joe escaped.

I saw many faces that I recognised walking around the prison field, many of them obviously aware of what was happening that evening. Suddenly my pal turned to me and told me that there were six police cars only a few hundred yards away from the gaol.

We went away to investigate, driving past a few times trying to see what was going on. The man in the cattle wagon stayed where he was, waiting on Joe coming. My pal wanted to go home, believing the coppers were there for us, lying in wait. But I didn't think so because the hole in the fence was still there and the prisoners were still milling around the field plus the football had started.

Back at the gaol I noticed the cattle wagon had left the spot we'd left it. I was worried about this. I watched again through the binoculars, scanning the gaol football fields looking for Joe.

Suddenly I saw five guys all crouching and heading toward the hole in the fence. I was puzzled at this and got up to leave and head back into our own car, which was parked in the street.

I saw two of the cons on the run and drove up to them and asked them if they knew where Joe was! One of them recognised me. 'Johnnyboy!' he said, excitedly. 'He left about half an hour ago'. They had let Joe escape first and gave him half an hour start before they made their bid for freedom. They were all soaked after crossing a stream beside the gaol and asked me for a lift home.

In the car they told us what happened. Apparently everyone knew Joe was going to escape through the fence – everyone except the warders – and some of them had decided to take advantage of it. Joe had got away half an hour earlier while me and my pal went to investigate the police presence which, it turned out, was due to a burglary at the prison warders' social club.

We dropped these guys off in Edinburgh, giving them what money we could, and headed back to the meeting place. I didn't see Joe, but Jim and his pals were there. Their first impression when they saw me without Joe was that we never got him. They couldn't believe it when I told them that five other cons had escaped and that we dropped them off all over Edinburgh.

Every newspaper told the story in their headlines, saying it was the biggest mass escape in modern times.

We found Joe at a pal's house and it was great to see him. He was phoning all the newspaper reporters and giving them his story. They were desperate to know what he planned next and wanted to be part of it. Some of the reporters were asking us to give them exclusives and tell no other papers. TV reporters had been in touch also desperate to interview Joe.

We knew heads would roll at the top security prison because of the escape. The coppers were demented and searching high and low for Joe, who was well out of the way in London and in good hands.

T.C. was also back in the headlines congratulating Joe. Scotland had seen nothing like it before and now that the Glasgow Two had taken centre stage in a blaze of publicity, the authorities were at a disadvantage for it was this weapon that they used to turn the public against Joe and T.C. many years before. They had used the press to turn them into monsters who had murdered six members of one family, and now that same weapon was aimed at them and demanding answers that weren't forthcoming.

Again I was approached by the senior officers of the Serious Crime Squad and threatened with a homemade conviction and a guaranteed gaol sentence if I didn't lay low. I could see they were worried and I was somehow glad, for they had every reason to be worried. Nothing was going to stop us fighting – and they knew this.

By this time Joe had changed lawyers. The new man was John Carroll, who was also T.C.'s lawyer and an ex-copper. He was dedicated to helping their case and most of the work this man has done has been unpaid.

Joe's name and photos were known throughout the land as the man who would escape to prove his innocence and cause embarrassment to the authorities. Infamous as he was, he was easily recognisable and so we had many disguises for him to manoeuvre around.

While Joe and I stayed at a friend's house, we gave a lot of thought as to what we would do next. I had a thought and that was to contact Father McDonald, my friend and priest from

Inverness Cages, and ask him if Joe could be offered sanctuary in the Catholic chapels anywhere in the country – including Ireland.

When I phoned his number at the parish at Inverness I discovered he had been moved to the top of Scotland. It was an Irish priest who answered my call. 'What'd you want wi' Father McDonald?' he asked as though half drunk. I told him I was a friend and needed to speak to him. He threatened to break my nose if I were telling him lies but finally gave me the number.

I was glad to hear my friend's voice again, for this gentleman had comforted me at the Cages in Inverness. I told him I had Joe with me and that he had escaped from gaol to protest his innocence, but he already knew and told me he was praying for us. 'How can I help you son?' he asked.

I asked him if there was any way Joe could be given sanctuary from the authorities who were hunting him down. He said he would need to speak to someone on high or perhaps check the library for such information and promised to get back to us. Joe spoke to him for a while thanking him for his help. When Joe was at the gaol in Edinburgh he had became friendly with a nun who would serve mass and visit the prisoners. He asked Father McDonald to get her phone number for him so that he could speak to her once again and thank her for her support and faith in him.

Father McDonald promised to phone back. As Joe and I were reminiscing about my dad and his old-fashioned ways, the phone rang. It was Father McDonald. He informed us that it was too late for Joe to get sanctuary as the government had closed all those loopholes. He had a telephone number for Joe and told him Sister Teresa was awaiting his call. Father McDonald offered us prayers and I quietly said mass. I had a tear in my eye for this gentleman who had only goodness and kindness in his heart. He promised to pray for Joe and me and our family, then he was gone.

As Joe spoke to Sister Teresa, I could hear she was crying for him and telling him that she and all the little sisters were praying for him each night hoping he would be a free man. Joe put me on the phone to this kindly soul who was full of praise for us. They had come to know him at the gaol and took a shine to him. I felt proud to have their praise and backing and blessings.

This nun was asking me when I was last at Chapel. I felt embarrassed to tell her, but I did and I asked her also to pray for my dad and Maw Padden on my behalf as I didn't have much time these days. 'That's no excuse!' she hollered down the line at me. She was right – it was no excuse, it was more a regret than anything else. I think she knew this for she told me she'd do it – but just this once, and then it was my turn . . . and no excuses. Then she was gone. Two angels in one night, this was surely a godsend. Out of all this misery came two people who seemed to make this unjust and unfair world seem worth living in for the time being.

I opened up the Chapel within my heart and prayed for Maw, Dad and my Ma and of course Joseph, asking for guidance and help.

T.C. was holding a press conference at the Special Unit in Barlinnie. Joe said he wanted to attend this and was going to disguise himself as a visitor to join T.C. But the authorities were on the lookout for him for they had photographs of Joe at the gatehouse and had been studying them. The next best thing was for me to interview Joe on video, which I did in a house by the canal in Paisley. On the tape, Joe talked about his case and when we were finished I went down to Barlinnie where the TV crews had gathered. One of them ran over to me asking if I knew if Joe was coming. I said, 'He is here', handed over Joe's taped interview then walked away.

That evening Joe was on the telly.

My brother phoned me up and said everyone knew it was my voice talking to Joe on the tape and that the coppers were looking for me. I went home to Irene and told her what had happened. She was upset but said she could understand and begged me not to get too involved. Even when angry she looked pretty.

In the early morning I heard the banging on my door and I knew it was them. I looked out my window and saw them in my garden all staring at me. I knew they were armed. I opened the window and demanded to see a search warrant; they said they wanted me and wanted to search the house for Joe. In they came, whilst others stayed around the house on the outside.

The CID were mostly from the Edinburgh area and I could see they were upset by the gaol escape. Before they took me away I gave Irene a kiss, not really knowing when I'd see her again. In the car on the way to the police station they cussed me and told me they knew I had broken all the cons out of gaol and dropped them off at their homes.

I told them my young brother was innocent and had been framed by the so-called Serious Crime Squad.

They said they sympathised with us but wanted to know my part in the breakout and how I came to be on a taped video with Joe. 'My brother has been framed by the Glasgow Serious Crime Squad!' I repeated.

They told me that I had caused major upsets in high places and that some people wanted me locked up at any cost, especially the Serious Crime Squad of Glasgow.

About five hours later they came for me in my cell, took me downstairs and let me go into the street. One of them shouted to me as I walked away, 'He needs to be innocent to go through all this!' I headed back home to Irene knowing I was being tailed.

Our friends had offered us safe houses here and abroad. Many of these people had suffered at the hands of authority, or their friends or family had.

One day, Joe and I were out in a friend's boat just roaming the waters off the west coast of Scotland when we came across an island. It was uninhabited, except for some sheep. So we named it Freedom Island. The scenery was amazing and Joe was amazed by it. A small monk's cell on the island was the only evidence that people had at one time lived there. We could look across the water and see other islands. We pitched our tent and made a barbecue, drank some beer and later we were joined by another guy, a friend of ours.

At least we felt safe here, for back home police were searching the streets for all the guys who had escaped. One newspaper had reported that the prisoners had fled into the Pentland Hills near Edinburgh like the Hole in the Wall gang.

Joe did some fishing and caught a sea trout. At night it was pitch black, but when the moon came out and the clouds cleared it was an amazing sight. I knew that I'd want to settle down somewhere like this.

Through a friend of mine I managed to get an interested party from BBC Television who would be willing to talk to Joe about his case with the possibility of re-examining all the evidence and the evidence of the convicted perjurer Billy Love. But the deal was that when they had completed their investigation Joe would have to give himself up to the authorities.

Joe agreed to this, and so began a long six weeks of investigating the evidence of the Ice Cream Wars.

One of the senior officers involved had since taken his own life by putting a hose onto the exhaust pipe of his car and the other end into his mouth. Jim, who was on the mainland, kept us up to date with what was happening and occasionally putting out false information of Joe's whereabouts.

Jim also met the crew from the BBC who were quite willing to charter a boat and come to the island to meet up with us, so we gave them the co-ordinates. We were watching the waters with our binoculars looking for potential dangers. We saw the boat circle our island and were quite satisfied that this was our men from the BBC.

I had to stay in the shadows whilst this documentary was taking place, as I knew the authorities would be on to me in a flash. The crew were suspicious at first but they soon relaxed and enjoyed the barbecue we had made. They spoke to Joe at length about his case and the police who framed him after Joe had said, 'It wasn't me who lit the match.' This was meant to be a self-confession on Joe's part. But it was just police stitching him up.

The other important piece of the Crown's evidence was that Billy Love told police he had overheard Joe and others bragging in a pub about what they did to the family of the Doyle's that night. However, the prosecution had evidence that Billy Love was a liar and on the night he swore he overheard the conversation take place in the pub he had previously said he was elsewhere. Besides, Billy Love had now signed a sworn affidavit in front of professional witnesses and told how senior police got him to lie and help manufacture evidence against Joe and T.C.

There was also a book written about their case by Douglas Skelton and Lisa Brownlie called *Frightener* and it tells of the corruption of witnesses and wrongdoing by police and court officials.

The guy from the BBC said he reckoned that it would probably take about six to eight weeks to investigate what Joe and others in the case had told him. But he too was sure something was rotten at the core of the evidence.

We spent many days on Freedom Island, fishing and discussing our next move. I went for a swim in the water but Joe stayed put saying it would just be his luck to drown. Whilst walking about the island Joe found a bottle with a message inside. It was a simple message – 'Whoever finds this bottle please write to . . .' Joe replied and later received a letter from the person whilst he was in gaol.

We left the island after a while. On the way back to Glasgow we stopped at Inverary prison museum. I bought a T-shirt for Joe, which read: 'On the run from Inverary Gaol'. We took a photograph of Joe wearing the T-shirt right in front of the gaol and sent them to different newspapers which printed the story and photograph. This only made the officials furious but had many others laughing.

Back in London Joe was enjoying more space and freedom and was being looked after by many who sympathised with his plight. I took Joe to see Ma at a secret location and it was quite an emotional scene.

At this time, I had got word from a couple of well-known guys in gaol who were serving long sentences asking me to help break them out of gaol for a large amount of money. But I declined for it was only my brother Joe who I was willing to help. I knew, as many others did, he shouldn't be there in the first place.

But such was the reputation my family had, for all three of us had escaped from top security prisons, and so people got the impression that we were Houdini-type characters. But Joe was our main and only priority.

People all over the country were beginning to wonder and

speculate as to where on earth Joe would turn up on his next demonstration. Documentaries and newspaper articles on his antics were widespread, while political figures were demanding action and answers to the questions surrounding the case.

But the police refused to comment.

Petitions were being signed by thousands of people demanding a re-trial for the Glasgow Two.

Joe came up with the idea that he wanted to break into the gaol which he had escaped from, and walk back into the hands of the authorities.

Meanwhile the BBC crew was interviewing all the witnesses involved in the case, except for the police who refused to take part in it. Billy Love was interviewed again and retracted the story about how he perjured himself with the help of the police. They interviewed Ma and she told of how Joe was at home with her on the night of the fatal fire.

They also went to St Monans in Fife to interview another guy who had been approached by the Crime Squad whilst he was serving a sentence at Barlinnie Gaol. His name was Mally McAllister and he had an outstanding charge of serious assault to go up for at the Glasgow High Court. Mally used to stay in Garthamlock and he and his family grew up with my own. He was an alcoholic and whilst at Barlinnie was attending AA meetings regularly. The police had come to interview him, but instead of doing so in Barlinnie's visiting room they got him dressed in his own clothes and took him out of the gaol and to a quiet pub outside Glasgow. They tried to buy him alcohol, but he refused. They then told him that they could help him get his High Court outstanding conviction dropped as long as he testified against Joe by saying that he was involved in the Doyle's murders and that he heard Joe talking about it.

Mally declined to get involved and told them so. Again they offered him drink and again Mally refused before demanding to be taken back to gaol. Later Mally made a complaint to Joe's lawyer.

Joe wasn't feeling well and was going to hand himself up to the authorities by cutting through the huge steel fence which I had previously cut. It turned out his kidneys were badly infected and we wanted to take him to hospital for treatment. He declined to go there and instead said he would take the campaign back to Barlinnie Gaol and climb up a huge pylon that had a security camera at the top of it. He was sure he could get there even though he was in agony.

But beforehand, he met Ma and the rest of the family at a secret location in Glasgow's East End. Once again, Joe Steele was saying goodbye to the people he loved.

We managed to get the crew from the BBC to come to the location so that Joe and all of us could thank them for all they had done. It was an emotional departure as Joe was clinging to my Ma, trying to comfort her. When I saw them crying my own eyes melted along with almost everyone else. I could see Jim was upset at the thought of Joe going back. And I guess like me, he too was worried for Joe when he would be taken back into custody.

I decided to leave with Joe and we both hailed a taxi. 'Where to, lads?' the driver asked politely.

'Barlinnie,' I replied.

It was horrible to be sitting in the taxi along with my brother for it seemed like a prison vehicle and I was saddened to lose him after all we'd been through in the past six weeks: all the trauma, all the excitement, all the adventure.

The driver was trying to make conversation with us and asked where in Barlinnie we were visiting. Joe told him that it was the mainstream of the gaol and I looked out of the back window of the cab where I could see Jim and a convoy following not too far behind.

The cab driver told us that his cousin used to be in the Barlinnie Special Unit, and before he told us who his cousin was I could see he resembled Jimmy Boyle. He went on to ask me and Joe if we had heard anything about Joe Steele, who escaped from gaol and was causing major problems for the authorities. He told us he had just come back from holiday the day before and was wondering if Joe had been caught.

'I don't know, pal,' I said. I could see a slight smile on Joe's face.

About 30 yards from the main gate I asked the driver to stop and let me out, but Joe told him to drive him up to the pylon and drop him off. I said goodbye to Joe and reminded him that we'd be there for him.

Beside the pylon Joe gave the taxi driver 20 pounds for the fare and told him to keep the change, then told him that he was Joe Steele.

As Joe started climbing the pylon, me, Jim and everyone else moved in to support him. Within minutes TV men and newspaper reporters, who had all been tipped off, had gathered around the pylon.

Joe could be heard shouting down to the reporters that he was innocent and wanted a fair trial and that he would never rest till he got those responsible for fitting him up with false witnesses and police lies. Everyone was cheering, even the taxi driver was tooting his horn and waving.

The police were soon on the scene in force and trying to talk Joe down from the pylon.

The BBC crew were there and quite pleased that Joe had surrendered himself as he said he would once they had completed their enquiries into the miscarriage of justice.

I went home to my Irene somewhat exhausted and mentally drained. I felt I had somehow neglected her after promising never to get into trouble again when I got released from gaol. I had other responsibilities too; I had a son and daughter to think about, and of course my beautiful redhead who was obviously worried that I may not return to her. As we sat by a warm coal fire, I told her about Joe's plight and how we, as a family, had to stand by him and do whatever it took to help him clear his name. I was glad she could understand this.

Many police officers throughout the country do a good and decent job and would never get involved in such malpractices that involve manufacturing evidence to help clear up a crime nor would they knowingly help send a fellow human being to gaol for a crime that person didn't commit. But unfortunately there is that small evil hard core who call the shots, and the only way it's ever going to stop is to make the shots backfire on them.

Today it is Joe Steele and T.C. Campbell who rot in prison,

wrongly convicted of the biggest Scottish mass murder in modern times, and that's a tragedy to say the least. Society in general – and the Doyle family in particular – have been robbed of justice. Tomorrow it could be someone else.

But no matter who it may be I would be willing to offer any assistance that I could by way of advice on how to tackle such a problem.

John Carroll, who is still acting on behalf of Joe and T.C., has done a tremendous amount of work to help clear the Glasgow Two. His diligence and dedication into fighting this injustice cannot be undervalued. I would like to pay tribute to him for his honesty, integrity and steadfastness – but mostly for just being a good lawyer. And also a special thanks to all of you involved in helping to win justice for my family, especially to Douglas Skelton and Lisa Brownlee.

I have my own life to live, but something keeps drawing me back to the old ways. It's hard to break away and make a clean break for there is an attraction somewhere along the line, or perhaps it's just me losing the plot.

I want to go straight and live a good and decent life and grow old gracefully with my kids.

I believe it would torment me to think that my own kids could end up like I did or any other kid for that matter and this is what I strive to prevent.

I hope that by writing these few words I can get my message across to others and that they can learn from my experiences that there are no heroes in crime. There is nothing attractive about it or anything to be gained by it; nothing but misery and a waste of life.

I feel I am at my best when helping others; it sort of soothes my soul.

I hold no one personally responsible for my life of injustice, for I am just one of many.

I had choices and I often took the wrong one. I hurt many people in my time and was hurt in return.

There is one thing I do regret and that is that I never got to know that grumpy old bastard dad of mine and that he never got to know me or his grandchildren and that my family spent all those wasted years in gaol.

I have tried to help others and will continue to do so for I believe in the old saying that 'no man is an island'!

I have set up a website to help deal with troubled kids and adults who may want to seek advice, guidance and help.

I'll be happy to put something back into the community from which others can benefit.

27

Epilogue

The BBC showed the documentary about Joe and uncovered a catalogue of horrors. The makers of the programme *Trial and Error* also made a hard-hitting documentary about Joe and T.C. It was the opinion of almost everyone that a miscarriage of justice had taken place. The Crown Office and the police were now under the spotlight and promised to investigate the evidence, which convicted Joe Steele and T.C. Campbell. But who was doing the investigating? Why – the police, of course!

The protests continued frequently for Joe and T.C. A campaign was set up to help free the Glasgow Two and from all over Britain calls were made for a re-trial. It was obvious to one and all that this problem wasn't going to go away, and in 1997 they were released on bail pending an appeal. It was great to have Joe out – legally this time. Everybody was happy and we danced and drank well into the night. Newspaper reporters and TV crews were wanting to interview Joe while coppers were raging as the past was again being brought up and questions were being asked.

Just over a year later they appeared back at the court.

There was pandemonium in the court and streets of Glasgow as their appeal was rejected and they were sent back to gaol by Scotland's top judges.

The country was shocked at yet another miscarriage of justice. Many people were horrified to learn that the judges had refused to take into consideration that Billy Love had retracted his original statement.

The authorities had locked all the spectators in the court and fled fearing the worst. Jim and his friends showed their anger outside the court.

I was over 100 miles away in my cottage with Irene and my kids when I heard the result on the news, and Jim in a rage telling the cameraman that this was a travesty and that they'd break Joe out of gaol.

I could understand his anger but I was worried about repercussions. Sure enough, that night I was picked up off the street 100 miles away in a small village called Tarbert in Loch Fyne and told I was under arrest for driving a vehicle whilst being disqualified. I was taken into custody and held for a day or two; I knew the authorities were worried about me so they had me arrested on a false charge.

One copper in the police station told me that it was rumoured that I was going to help to break Joe out of gaol.

Later Joe tried to escape by dressing up as a prison warder having made a copy of a master key he got from a sympathetic warder who was a member of his 'Free the Glasgow Two' campaign. But he was caught halfway across the exercise yard just seconds from freedom and locked up in solitary confinement for the time being.

The warders were frightened to have him back in circulation in case he escaped again and their heads would roll. I eventually moved away to the west coast of Scotland to try a new life for me and my family. It was a beautiful part of the country and an ideal place to raise a family. But I knew the police were aware of my presence and were suspicious of me. Soon everyone was talking about me being in the area and rumour even had it that I was the one who had been involved in the so-called Ice Cream War murders.

I later learned that it was the police who had been telling the townsfolk these lies. One day Irene and I went into a shop when suddenly I was approached by a local man, a respectable figure. He seemed to be nervous when he asked me if he could speak to me alone. My first thought was that he was going to tell me that I wasn't welcome in the area. But no, it was much worse than that. He told me that he had waited some time to meet someone like me. It turned out he was involved in a business deal and that there was some skullduggery and a Machiavellian plot in which he lost out on the deal. This almost led to a nervous breakdown and he was a very bitter man, hell-bent on seeking revenge. He asked how much money it would cost him to have this other man seen to. He didn't care what happened to him, he told me, and said that money was no object, and that he would be glad if I could get this matter sorted for him. He gave me a description of the guy and an address, along with the registration numbers of two vehicles he owned. I began to get suspicious, believing that he may be trying to set me up. I couldn't understand why he chose me to do this dirty deed. However I asked a pal to go and check out the location that I was given along with the car registration numbers. He got back to me verifying that the information was correct. I got back to the man, only this time I had a dictaphone on me to record him plotting the demise of another man, for I was sure he was trying to set me up. He told me that he also wanted to see the man's cars petrol-bombed and blown up while they were parked directly beneath the windows of his house. He didn't care who was in the house when it happened. He just wanted revenge, he said.

I told Irene what he had said to me and wanted me to do. She was shocked and advised that I should keep away from him. I too was shocked to hear this 'respectable' man trying to entice me into an evil plot. I could see he was disturbed and it somehow reminded me of myself when I thought about exacting revenge on certain prison warders who had, as I believed, done me a terrible wrong. I told the councillor that I wasn't interested and wanted nothing to do with his revenge attacks, and that the best thing he could was get himself some serious psychiatric help. And there was me thinking that I had left all the madness back in Glasgow!

Meanwhile, an independent review board was set up to deal with miscarriages of justice. The committee could re-examine witnesses in depth and even look at fresh evidence. And so when they looked at the case of the Glasgow Two they referred it back to the Appeal Court in Edinburgh.

In December 2001, Joe and T.C. were once again released on bail pending an appeal. This time everyone is hopeful. Jim has settled into the city way of life with his family and friends and prays for Joe and T.C.'s conviction to be quashed.

Joe is a grandfather and seems to be happy. Like me, he has vowed to help others who have suffered like him.

And as for Ma, well, I still hear her sing as she cooks for us.

Johnny Steele,
May 2002